To Travis Williams
My best wishes for success
in your project. I hope
you enjoy my account of
military flying in WA II and
in Vietnam. Regards.

Michael J. Novosel, M.O.H.

DUSTOFF

DUSTOFF

The Memoir of an Army Aviator

Michael J. Novosel

PRESIDIO

Published by Presidio Press Inc.
505 B San Marin Drive, Suite 300
Novato, CA 94945-1340

Library of Congress Cataloging-in-Publication Data

Novosel, Michael J.
Dustoff : the memoir of an Army aviator / Michael J. Novosel.
  p.   cm.
ISBN 0-89141-698-6
1. Novosel, Michael J. 2. United States. Army—Aviation Biography. 3. Bomber pilots—United States Biography. 4. World War, 1939–1945 Personal narratives, American. 5. Helicopter pilots—United States Biography. 6. Vietnamese Conflict, 1961–1975 Personal narratives, American. I Title.
UG626.2.N68N68   1999
359'.0092—dc21
[B]   99-35143
                                               CIP

All photos are from the author's collection unless otherwise noted.

Printed in the United States of America

To my dear departed wife; to my son, Michael, who served with me as my copilot on numerous combat missions in Vietnam; to my daughters, Patty and Jeanee; and to my youngest son, John. And with unbounded love and admiration for all the dustoffers who gave their lives so others might live.

Contents

Foreword

Army Air Forces pilots of World War II were routinely called "eagles." This is the story of Mike Novosel—the last eagle—who, upon retirement in 1984, was still on active-duty flight status. It is a narrative of an impressive military career that began before Pearl Harbor, covered forty-four years, and is highlighted by the awarding of the Medal of Honor.

The story begins on the eve of Pearl Harbor and centers on a young soldier, Mike Novosel, who went through the aviation cadet program, then moved on to be an air corps instructor pilot and upgraded to faster, heavier, and more technically advanced airplanes. He tested planes ranging from P-39 pursuits to B-24 bombers. He flew the gigantic B-29 Superfortress on raids over the Japanese Empire and above the ceremonies on the USS *Missouri* when Japan surrendered.

The drawdown of forces after the war had a devastating effect on operations. Novosel was appointed the 9th Bomb Group operations officer and later took command of the 99th Bomb Squadron. Novosel and a cadre of dedicated officers kept the 9th Bomb Group flying. It is the only group in the 313th Bomb Wing that was combat ready. After more than two years, he returned home and was assigned to Eglin Air Force Base as a B-29 test pilot. It proved to be interesting, hard-flying work and was often dangerous; a number of his friends were killed.

Novosel was selected to attend the Air Tactical School, but within a week of graduation his career hopes were dashed by notification that he was on the reduction-in-force (RIF) list. After an unceremonious release from the service, he found success in civilian life.

But this warrior's love of country and the military was not stilled. He continued flying with the Air Force Reserves and rose to the rank of lieutenant colonel.

The assassination of John F. Kennedy had a profound impact on Novosel, who remembered the president's inaugural words, ". . . ask what you can do for your country," Vietnam was heating up, so he volunteered for active duty with the air force, but he was told that he had too much rank. However, the army accepted him as a warrant officer pilot. He served two tours in Vietnam as a dustoff pilot evacuating wounded from the heat of battle. During the second tour he was joined by his son, a newly graduated army aviator. In a span of seven days, while flying with separate crews, this father and son took turns rescuing each other after their helicopters were brought down by enemy fire.

In his two years in Vietnam, Mike Novosel flew 2,543 missions extracted 5,589 wounded, and logged 2,038 hours of combat flying. During this time, he flew the "impossible mission," for which he was awarded the Medal of Honor. He was forty-eight years old when President Richard M. Nixon presented him with the medal.

W.E.B. Griffin

Preface

This is an unusual war story. It is about the people who fought in World War II, Korea, and Vietnam; how they related to one another as they shared fear and tears mixed with humor and courage to form an invincible bond of comradery.

The story begins its journey in 1941 when I enlisted in the army air corps and winds its way through cadet training, advanced transition training in B-24s, and the ultimate weapon of World War II, the B-29.

As I traveled the journey I got to know many people. We shared our triumphs and celebrated together. We also shared our setbacks and comforted and helped one another. At times, when I thought I was on top of the world, I would find myself cut down and discarded. I would face my self pity. But there were the others, traveling the road with me, and together we would find a new niche.

After three wars in our century, our nation faced another, this time in Vietnam. In the midst of a gloomy atmosphere spawned by the assassination of President John F. Kennedy I felt that I must get involved. I wanted to help; and in an irrational act I volunteered my services again. But this time it was with a different group of people. I joined the army and found myself flying with soldiers. It was an entirely new life; soldiers had a different way of doing things. But I found that they had the same bounds of comradery that existed in the army air force and, as I later learned, in the other branches of the services.

I volunteered for the army's aviation program to teach young folks to fly. But the army didn't see it that way and I ended up in Vietnam flying medical evacuation—dustoff—missions. It turned out to be the most dangerous flying in Vietnam.

Circumstances dictated that I fly two tours in Vietnam, the second also for dustoff. This time my son joined me as a dustoff pilot. We sometimes flew together and in one unusual twist of fate came to each others' rescue when our helicopters went down.

The dustoff story tells of sacrifice and reflects the strong bonds of comradery that exists among warriors. It is my great honor to be one of them.

The dialogue in this story has been recreated to the best of my recollection. It is intended to reflect the many emotions spawned among people who find themselves embroiled in war. It is my story about people of whom I am so proud.

Acknowledgments

Thanks to my dear friend Richard K. Tierney for the many hours of invaluable assistance and direction in writing this manuscript.

All photos, maps, and representations were computer rendered and digitally enhanced by my son, John, and Novosoft of Enterprise, Alabama.

1 A World of Turmoil

The 1940 graduating class of Etna High School was sent into a deeply troubled world where economies were shattered and nations struggled to climb out of the economic morass confronting them. Ancient animosities resurfaced and Europe, for the second time in the century, was embroiled in war.

Our nation still suffered the effects of the Great Depression, triggered by the crash of 1929. Many were unemployed, living on the dole, or getting assistance from friends or relatives. The minimum wage, if one could get it, was twenty-five cents an hour.

I lived in Etna, a small mill town in western Pennsylvania, and was a member of the 1940 graduating class. The future did not look encouraging, and jobs were scarce. I found one at the Wildwood Country Club as an assistant to the club pro, but it lasted only until October, when the course closed for the winter. Without employable skills or experience, I was unable to get another job.

The war in Europe continued to heat up, and most Americans felt we soon would be in it. Congress passed a draft law and, along with the efforts of President Franklin D. Roosevelt, was hurriedly bolstering our armed forces. Our military forces were advertising the benefits of their training programs, and their pitches sounded attractive.

I decided to enlist. On February 7, 1941, ten months to the day before the Japanese attacked Pearl Harbor, I joined the U.S. Army Air Corps.

My early days in the air corps were enjoyable, although I suffered a setback in my plans. I wanted to be an airplane mechanic and fly.

But the army had other plans, and I was sent to a school for administration specialists.

I made several new friends, among them Bill Ridley, from Oklahoma; Curvin Miller and Bill Reinsel, from Pennsylvania; and Felix Caplan, from New Jersey. After finishing the school, we were assigned to Sheppard Field in Texas.

Because of my position as chief payroll clerk, I acquired a complete set of army regulations. I discovered one dealing with the aviation cadet program and read and reread it until I knew everything about it. I met all requirements except height, which was five feet four inches. My service record listed me as five feet three and three-quarter inches. Curvin Miller measured me and said I'd grown an eighth of an inch since I'd enlisted. I had to grow a little more.

Ridley said he was going to apply for flight training and that I should also, even though I was a tad too short. "They might let you slide through," he said. We applied.

Our barracks mates knew about our plans and decided to help me "grow." Together they had an enormous amount of talent, initiative, and intelligence. They gave us moral support and a lot of help in other ways. Bill Reinsel, who was assigned to the dispensary, fed me a steady dose of vitamin A. He said it was necessary for good vision.

Miller said he read a magazine article claiming that the body was tallest in the morning right after waking. He said I should remain in bed as long as possible on the morning of my flight physical to maximize my height.

Ridley and I were scheduled for our flight physicals at 7:30 A.M. Miller suggested I shower before going to bed. That way I could remain in a horizontal position longer before reporting for the examination. I showered and hit the sack early.

The next morning Miller, who had organized a crew, made certain that I remained horizontal until I had to leave for the dispensary. While I lay in bed, they slipped me into my fatigues, put on my shoes and socks, and slid me onto a long, narrow board. Four of my mates carried me as I lay stretched out on the board.

I thought they were going to carry me all the way to the dispensary. If they did, surely some officer would see what amounted to a detail of soldiers carrying a stiff. He'd halt the parade and demand an explanation. Officers are funny that way.

The worst scenario would be a military policeman coming upon the scene. Surely he'd march us all to the stockade without asking for an explanation. Military policemen are funny that way too. But I was not aware how efficient my barracks mates were, or how much planning, cooperation, and coordination they were capable of. Felix Caplan, who worked in the motor pool, had conned the motor sergeant out of a three-quarter-ton truck. He'd parked in front of our barracks and was waiting for a load—me on my board.

Miller's crew laid one end of the board on the bed of the truck, shoved the board forward until the tailgate would close, and drove to the dispensary. There they eased me and the board off the truck and proceeded to the physical examination section.

From the moment I was placed on the board, and even as I was unloaded and carried into the dispensary, I voiced my objections to the unceremonious proceedings. I feared we'd be discovered and called before the first sergeant or, even worse, the captain. We'd be court-martialed for sure. My complaints were ignored; my board bearers assured me that everything was all right and they would be gone as soon as my height had been measured.

As we entered the physical examination section, we were met by Bill Reinsel, who did not seem at all surprised to see me lying on the board carried by my barracks mates. Reinsel led the group into a room, where I was placed on the scales; I was vertical for the first time in hours. Reinsel told the attendant to measure my height first. "What do you get?" Reinsel asked anxiously. The medic doing the measuring said, "Five feet three and seven-eighths inches."

There erupted an immediate chattering of disbelief followed almost in unison with profanity and regrets over having done all that work "for nothing." Reinsel pleaded with the medic to change the measurement to five feet four inches. "Who will know?"

The medic was unmoved. He said he wasn't about to make a false entry on an official document. The measurement would stand. There was nothing else to do except go on with the rest of the examination. At least I would know if I were otherwise qualified. I thanked the gang for helping. I could see that Miller was as disappointed as I. He was so sure that the information he had gleaned from the magazine article was a valid basis for his plan to make me "grow." Besides, he had done a lot of work that didn't get the results he wanted. The gang departed with their board.

Bill Ridley arrived for his appointment just as I was being measured. He heard the result and saw the disappointment on my face. "You can always try later when you grow some," he said. "You're only eighteen; you've got more growing to do."

I passed the rest of the exam with flying colors, as did Ridley. But just as we were about to return to the squadron orderly room, Ridley and I were told to see the flight surgeon. His was the last stop, and he was the ultimate pass-fail authority.

Ridley was sent in to see the doctor first. I began to get impatient, because I had a lot of work waiting for me. When Ridley finally came out, he had a big grin on his face. He didn't have to tell me that he'd passed. Then I was called into the office.

The doctor was sitting at a small table looking over the results of my examination. I don't know what doctors mean when they make funny humming sounds as they look over information vital to a person's interest.

I nervously watched him scanning the examination results. I expected him to find that I was a tad too short and tell me to come back when I grew up. After what seemed an eternity, he looked at me. "According to this exam, you're short of the minimum height requirement by an eighth of an inch."

I blurted right out, "I think the medic who measured me made a mistake. I was measured by my friends in the barracks and they found me to be exactly five feet four." Of course that wasn't true, but I was desperate and would have said anything to salvage the situation. The flight surgeon had me stand; he looked me over and told me to turn around.

"How old are you, son?" he asked in a rather soft and relaxed manner.

"Eighteen," I replied.

"Will you promise me you'll grow another eighth of an inch?" he asked.

I came right back with a definite and cheery, "Yes, sir."

I saw him make the appropriate correction on the physical record. I was officially five feet four inches tall. He told me that everything else was in order and that the record of the examination would be forwarded to the proper authorities.

The last thing he said was, "Don't forget to grow some more." With that, I gave him a snappy salute and was out of there.

On September 3, I celebrated my nineteenth birthday. It seemed like ages since I had taken my flight physical; I wondered what had happened to my cadet application. Finally, in mid-October, Ridley and I received word that we'd been accepted for flight training and orders would follow. When November passed without orders for flight school, I voiced my concern to Ridley about the delay. He reassured me we'd soon get them. Neither of us knew how accurate his prognosis was.

I was returning to the base on a Sunday morning when a convertible drove by with its radio blaring the news that the Japanese had bombed Pearl Harbor. The next day, President Roosevelt addressed Congress, and we were officially at war. Not long after, Ridley and I received our orders transferring us to Kelly Field in Texas—and flight school.

2 Kelly Field, Texas: Early 1942

People accepted into the aviation cadet program were assigned to a cadet processing center. They would spend about six weeks there, get their shots, be issued uniforms, and attend preflight training. Then they would go to flight school.

When I received my new uniform, it was evident that cadets were expected to present a sharp military appearance. The people issuing clothing made every effort to make our uniforms fit well—quite different from my days as a recruit, when a specialist looked at me and said, "This is about your size; it should fit well enough," then threw the item over the counter in my general direction. This time, as a cadet, I was measured first, given a uniform to try on, and was inspected for proper fit.

A few days before completing preflight at Kelly, I saw my first Army Air Forces pilot. He was inspecting cadets in formation and looked sharp in his "pinks and greens," the term for the army officer's uniform. He was a captain of medium height and ramrod-straight posture. I watched him proceed down the line of cadets. At first I didn't notice, but then I was shocked to see that he had only one arm. The empty sleeve was folded under neatly and pinned so that it did not hang loosely at his side. Normally this officer would have been medically discharged. He couldn't fly airplanes, but he could help young cadets get started in their flying careers. Most importantly, he was proof that aviation had its dangerous side. The captain was my first lesson in aviation safety. I learned that in a moment of distraction or inattention to his duties, he inadvertently stepped into the path of a spinning propeller and his arm was severed at the shoulder. I never learned the captain's name, but I never forgot his lesson.

When I entered the cadet flight program, I did not know that its images and recollections would last a lifetime. It was almost a year of new experiences, challenges, occasional setbacks, and finally success. I was part of a special breed—young men who were fierce competitors, highly motivated, and intelligent and did not believe in failure. It was a most satisfying period.

Preflight was over; I was going to learn to fly. I started on an adventure that would be my life.

There were three phases to flight training: primary, basic, and advanced. Each phase was conducted at a separate base using succeedingly more advanced and more complicated airplanes. The primary trainer was an open-cockpit, bare-bones airplane with fixed landing gear. The basic trainer had an enclosed cockpit, radio, and fixed landing gear. The advanced trainer had an enclosed cockpit, radio, and retractable landing gear and was equipped with machine guns and bombs.

Primary, after the student soloed, was designed to teach the fledgling seat-of-the-pants flying. This phase culled the cadets and eliminated the unsatisfactory performers.

The program was fast paced. Cadets had to reach a predetermined level of proficiency on schedule. The process was draconian. The cadets were given evaluation checks by civilian and military pilots, and those who didn't measure up were recommended for elimination. There was no reconsideration of this action. Washout rates in excess of 50 percent were not uncommon. Most of those eliminated from pilot training elected to remain in the aviation cadet program and went on to navigator or bombardier training.

When the cadet finished primary, he had sixty hours of flying time and was able to perform every acrobatic maneuver known to man. I managed to learn on schedule and meet all levels of proficiency, but the pressure was great and unrelenting.

Airplane engines did not always perform as they were meant to. I had a mechanical problem one day, and my inexperience didn't help. I was on my way to the practice area when I was confronted with an in-flight emergency.

I was not aware of it at the time, but a spark plug from one of the cylinders had let go. The airplane nose section started to vibrate, but I didn't know why. Because I was flying solo, I had to resolve the problem myself. The engine was delivering power, so I decided to return to Jones Field to have the plane checked by maintenance.

As I flew, the vibrations became more intense and worked back along the fuselage until they reached my cockpit area. I was afraid that the engine might blow up or catch fire, because the problem originated there. I sorted out my options: I could continue to Jones Field, make an emergency landing in some farmer's field, or (if things really became uncontrollable) bail out.

I decided against the emergency landing, because I might hit an obstacle and crash where there wouldn't be anyone to help. Because the engine wasn't on fire, I decided not to jump but instead continued on my way. When I got to Jones Field and entered traffic, the vibrations were so violent that I was afraid of structural failure and loss of control. Because of my inexperience, I believed the situation to be so critical that I made all banks and turns extremely shallow. This resulted in a wider and more extended traffic pattern.

Not surprisingly, during my turn onto the final approach I violated the airspace of the opposite traffic pattern and forced a pilot there to take evasive action to avoid a collision. The pilot in that plane was Lieutenant Marshall, one of the military check pilots. He landed behind me, and as I taxied toward the parking area he came alongside, waved wildly, and motioned me to cut the engine.

I did as ordered. The lieutenant was fuming, saying that some "Dumb John" of a cadet had tried to kill him. That Dumb John, of course, was me. I cut the engine and got out of the aircraft. I expected the worst. I knew I was in for a real old-fashioned ass-chewing from the main military check pilot. I was certain he'd eliminate me from the program. As he came toward me, I snapped to rigid attention and awaited my fate.

"Mister, what the hell did you think you were doing? You damned near caused a collision on the base leg. Who's your instructor?" Lieutenant Marshall had removed his helmet and was thrashing the air with it.

All I managed to say rather timidly was, "I'm sorry, Lieutenant. I was having a hard time trying to control my plane."

"What do you mean?" he fired back. "Did your instructor release you for solo without teaching you how to make turns?"

I replied as well and as politely as I could. "Sir, I had an emergency. The engine was not running right. The airplane was shaking all over and I was scared."

"We'll see," the lieutenant replied. "You better be right about that engine. Get the crank. I want the engine started so I can see how it runs."

As he climbed into the cockpit, I protested. "You don't want to start that engine, Lieutenant. It might blow up."

"Start cranking." The lieutenant was not about to take advice from some Dumb-John cadet.

I cranked the starter, and the engine fired immediately. I never saw anyone look as startled as the lieutenant. The plane shook violently back and forth and up and down at the same time. If the lieutenant had had false teeth, they'd have popped right out of his mouth.

Lieutenant Marshall cut the engine as fast as he could. He looked at me as he got out of the craft, and to my relief gave me a big smile. "Mister, you did all right. You did fine bringing that plane back to base the way that engine was acting up. Forget what I said earlier."

It appeared I had made a favorable impression. As things turned out, my final check ride was with Lieutenant Marshall, who passed me with an excellent grade.

When a cadet reached basic training, the pressure of learning on schedule eased, because most of the flying honed skills learned in primary. New subjects were introduced, such as instruments and formation flying; if a cadet was eliminated, it was probably because of them.

The same was true of advanced training. No member of my class was eliminated in advanced, although one cadet was killed during a night flight. Flying was still dangerous in 1942; my class had four fatalities during training.

I finished my cadet training at Lake Charles, Louisiana. The graduation ceremony was a memorable event. There were diplomas, our commissioning as second lieutenants, and the presentation of pilot wings. A major general was the featured speaker. I have no idea who he was, what he represented, or what he said. I was too excited

over making it through flight training to care. We were told the day
we entered the cadet program that it was the most demanding course
of instruction conceived by man and that most would not make it.
But I had. It was the fulfillment of all my boyhood dreams, and I
could not have been happier.

I was anxious to join the fighting; I knew I could be the next ace
if only given the chance. I was looking forward to an assignment with
a pursuit squadron, because all my training was directed toward that
end. But it didn't happen. I was assigned to Laredo Army Air Field
as an instructor.

Two of my friends were on the same set of orders: Fred Nelson,
from Denver; and John Molinaro, from Cincinnati. There never was
a more dejected trio of army pilots.

3 Laredo, Texas

When Fred Nelson, John Molinaro, and I arrived at Laredo Army Air Field, the installation was still under construction. There weren't any runways, and all operations were conducted on the parking ramp.

Living conditions at Laredo were austere. Fred, John, and I were lucky enough to be assigned to one of the just-completed officers' quarters. We had individual although spartanly equipped rooms, each with an unpainted clothes closet, a table and chair, and a small metal bed. Lighting was furnished by a single, glaring electric bulb hanging from one of the rafters. A latrine and shower were located in the central section of the building.

Laredo, a typical Texas border town on the Rio Grande, offered little in the way of social activity. Fortunately, its sister city—Nuevo Laredo, across the river in Mexico—was alive with all manner of commercial activity. There were several nightclubs and plenty of bars and restaurants.

Artisans in precious stones, jewelry, silver, and leather plied their trades in several shops. Those working in leather were especially skilled, and their prices were reasonable. I had one of the shoemakers custom-make all my shoes and flight boots.

The pilots' favorite watering hole and restaurant was the Cadillac Bar, located a block off the main drag. Most evenings after flying we'd assemble there around a massive round table. We formed an informal organization called the Boots and Riding Crop Club. All that was required to partake of the club's benefits was presence at the round table and the ante of a two-dollar bill. Anybody at the table could order as many as desired of any drink. When the money was gone, everybody anted up another two-dollar bill. So it went into the night.

The Cadillac was noted for its drinks, especially rum and coke (Cuba Libre) and its Ramos Gin Fizz. The wood bar, the longest I'd ever seen, appeared to be constructed of hand-carved oak and gave the appearance of great strength and weight. It would have served well as a backdrop for a Hollywood western.

Our duty day began at 6:00 A.M. Even as hard as we worked, there were no complaints. For the most part, we were all young and wanted all the flight time we could get. My assignment at Laredo Army Air Field was the best thing that had ever happened to me; it turned out to be my maturing period as an Army Air Forces pilot. I gained excellent flight experience and logged plenty of flight time.

The director of flight training at Laredo was Maj. Gordon L. Paulson. His deputy was Capt. Cliff Hammond. My work must have been satisfactory, because in the summer of 1943 I was promoted; I became a twenty-year-old first lieutenant who could not legally buy a drink or vote.

The base's mission was constantly changed as the technical character of the training was elevated. In one year we progressed from the AT-6, AT-11, and AT-18 to the B-26.

The AT-18 was a training version of the Lockheed Hudson bomber, an aircraft used extensively by the British Royal Air Force. It had conventional landing gear (it was a tail dragger), which presented control problems on landing. The aircraft had a tendency to ground loop, which often damaged a wing and ruptured the fuel tank. There was always the danger of fire. Hence this aircraft, which was built at Lockheed's Burbank plant, was forever labeled the Burbank Bonfire.

My checkout in the bird is worth noting. The AT-18 had only one set of controls, so my instructor sat on a box next to me as I did the stick and rudder work. He was 1st Lt. Tommy Vaughn, a six-foot Texas Aggie. I was still trying to reach five feet four.

I put a four-inch-thick cushion behind me to help me reach the controls. I had to stretch to get complete control travel, and that worried Tommy, especially during landing. I could tell by his antsy movements that he desperately wanted to assist with the controls. Each time I landed the craft, Tommy cautioned me, "Now watch it, Mike, watch it. Don't ground loop, don't ground loop." After an hour of fidgeting and cautioning me not to ground loop, Tommy couldn't take it any longer. "That's enough, Mike," he said. "You're checked out."

So with one hour of dual instruction behind me, I was a full-fledged Lockheed Hudson bomber pilot. I flew my first mission in the AT-18 the next day and everything went just fine. By the time I'd flown two missions and was completing my third of the day, my take-offs and landings were uneventful. I kept Tommy's admonitions about the ground loops uppermost in my mind.

After flying all day, I was cleared to land on the southwest runway. Tommy's warning loomed in my mind as I landed; surprisingly it was a real "greaser," a smooth landing with no bouncing. As I taxied to the ramp, I saw an AT-18 landing. When I looked again, I saw a cloud of dust as the aircraft ground looped. It was my instructor, Tommy Vaughn. He was greatly embarrassed by the incident.

In the fall we were given the mission of training gunners and B-24 copilots. I received orders for temporary duty at Smyrna Army Air Field in Tennessee to undergo transition training in the B-24 Liberator bomber.

When I signed in at base headquarters at Smyrna, there were a dozen or so pilots who were also to attend transition training. One smart-ass captain asked me if I hadn't made a mistake being there. He badgered me about my size: "The B-24 is a man's airplane. Why don't you go find a nice little P-39 school? That's more your style."

"Go suck a lemon," I told him. "It might improve your disposition."

I was aware of my size and the problems it might create, but I didn't need his insensitive remarks. I was aware of the physical characteristics that the school recommended for B-24 transition training: five feet eight inches tall, at least 160 pounds, and a minimum of 1,500 hours of flight experience. At least I met the flying time requirements.

We met the director of flight training, Captain Frecker, a no-nonsense professional. He outlined the course objective, gave a cursory description of the curriculum, and outlined what he expected of us. He cautioned us about the dangers of too much nightlife in nearby Nashville; we were at Smyrna to learn. He said that even the weather would not deter us from training. When the weather threatened to delay or interfere with the schedule, we'd simply fly off to other locations where instruction could continue.

After the briefing, Frecker asked me where I'd been stationed. I told him, "Laredo Army Air Field."

"What kind of equipment did you fly at Laredo?" he asked.

"The Lockheed AT-18, the Hudson," I replied, "and I was about to get my checkout in the Martin B-26 when I was ordered to report here."

"The Baltimore Whore," he commented.

I could see that he was familiar with the reputation of the B-26, which was manufactured in Baltimore. The hottest bomber in the army, it had an extremely short wingspan, which gave the wags the opportunity to describe the B-26 as having "no visible means of support." Others said it had the gliding characteristics of a flatiron.

I liked the bird, although it did have a rather steep glide angle on final approach, and it landed hot. Its transition training record at MacDill Army Air Field, on Tampa Bay, was far from satisfactory. The detractors of the plane had a field day when an accident occurred. "One a day in Tampa Bay," was their refrain.

Captain Frecker took more than a casual interest in me. I was not certain why until he asked, "How tall are you, Lieutenant?"

I answered in a firm voice, "Five feet eight inches, sir." I knew that although the legal limit for aviation cadets is five feet four inches, the desirable attribute of a B-24 pilot was five feet eight inches because the B-24 has a big cockpit.

"And how much do you weigh?"

"One hundred and sixty pounds, sir," I replied in an equally positive tone of voice.

Frecker hesitated for a moment. "You're the smallest five-foot-eight-inch, one-hundred-sixty-pound pilot I've ever known. No matter, we'll soon find out if you measure up."

That ended the conversation, and we bid each other good day. I knew I'd be seeing much more of Captain Frecker.

My instructor was 1st Lt. J. P. Stevens, taller than I but no six-footer.

He introduced me and his two other students to the B-24 Liberator bomber.

Because the B-24's cockpit was huge, I couldn't effectively reach the controls even with the rudder pedals adjusted all the way toward me and the seat adjusted full forward. I needed help, so I went to the supply section and signed for two cushions, each four inches thick. That did the trick. With both cushions behind me, I got full, effective travel of the rudder pedals and could see over the instrument panel. I was ready for flight.

For my first time at the B-24's controls, Stevens sat in the copilot's seat. We started the engines. After all the items on the checklist were covered, Lieutenant Stevens said, "You've got the airplane. Move it out."

That was the first occasion when I had control of four throttles at the same time. I was pleased at how easily the big ship taxied. I proceeded to the run-up position, performed the engine magneto and power checks, and after clearance from the tower took the runway.

Stevens just sat in his seat and reminded me, "It's all yours. Let's go." He was giving me the opportunity to do it all, to make this first takeoff. He would not interfere unless safety of flight was compromised.

I advanced the throttles to the full open position, and the aircraft accelerated down the runway. The nose came up easily, and after a short run the plane flew itself off the runway. The small amount of back pressure on the control column to take off surprised me, especially because I'd heard that the control forces on the B-24 were extremely heavy. I would learn that indeed they were, especially when simulating engine failure.

Emergency procedure training seemed to consume most of the training time. Simulated engine failure during takeoff was a daily occurrence. As the aircraft gathered speed but before the rudders became effective, the instructor would cut an outboard engine. I was expected to continue the takeoff but maintain directional control by retarding the throttle of the other outboard engine until the airspeed increased and rudder control became effective. Then the retarded throttle was brought back on line and the takeoff continued on three engines.

Opposite rudder pressure was required to counteract asymmetrical thrust caused by the inoperative engine. As soon as the aircraft lifted off, the instructor would cut the other engine on the same side. Immediate, full opposite rudder was required to counter the severe yawing effect produced by two engines at takeoff power on one side of the aircraft while the other two engines were inoperative. The order for "gear up" had to be given immediately to reduce drag and increase airspeed for better rudder control. Then the flaps were "milked up" to further reduce drag and get more speed. Rudder forces were extremely heavy, but I had one advantage due to my size: When I applied full rudder, my leg would be fully extended and my knee was in a locked position.

If the pilot needed assistance to hold the rudder, he called for help from his copilot. Although tall and short pilots could jam full rudder whenever required, it was the short ones who did so with a straight leg and the knee locked. Tall, long-legged pilots couldn't straighten their legs, so their knees remained flexed. The big gorillas, their legs and knees quivering from the strain, often had to ask for assistance.

When scheduled for my final check ride, I was not surprised to learn that it was with Frecker. I knew he wanted to see how I handled emergency situations, especially engine failures, and that gave me an edge. I was prepared for the worst he could lay on me.

Frecker put me through everything I expected, plus. The ride lasted two hours, most of the time flying on two engines. Toward the end of the ride, I was nearly exhausted and asked him to help with the rudder. "I can't," he replied. "I've just been killed. Crew members are killed in combat, you know. You'll have to hold it yourself."

I immediately called the flight engineer. "Remove this dead meat from the copilot's seat and give me some help with the rudder."

Frecker looked at me, gave me a big grin, and shoved hard on the rudder. Then he slowly brought the two inoperative engines on line. "You're okay, shorty," he said. "That should be enough for today. Let me make the landing. I don't get a chance to land these birds often."

I knew I'd been tested and was confident that the check ride was satisfactory. Frecker said that I'd done well and the grade slip would be sent to my instructor. I felt great.

Six pilots had final check rides that day and all passed. We celebrated at the club and after dinner relaxed and had a few drinks. The base commander came by and chatted with us. When we told him we'd passed our check rides that afternoon, he congratulated us and wished us success in our new assignments. That was the only time I saw Col. Stanley M. Umstead, a test pilot of considerable reputation. In the mid-1930s, he flew and tested the army's largest bomber, the B-19.

The next day I met with Stevens in the briefing room. He said that Frecker gave me an excellent grade and wrote, "Lieutenant Novosel, in spite of his short stature, is an above average B-24 aircraft commander."

When I returned to Laredo as an instructor, it was greatly changed. The ramp had dozens of B-24 and B-26 bombers along with P-39, P-40, and P-63 pursuit planes. What surprised me most was the presence of Women Army Service Pilots (WASPs). There were about a dozen, and they were flying the Martin B-26, the aircraft with the worst reputation in the Army Air Forces. They towed aerial targets at which student gunners fired live .50-caliber ammunition. It looked as if the traditional roles of males and females had undergone a traumatic reversal. The women were given the most dangerous jobs.

The pursuit planes were used in a different phase of aerial gunnery training. The pilots simulated enemy gun runs on the bombers while the students "fired" at the attackers with 16mm motion picture cameras. An unusual reel showed an attacking P-40 covered by the gunner's reticle. The film revealed a puff of smoke that came from the plane's engine. The smoke was followed by flames that rapidly increased in size and intensity. The P-40's canopy was seen to open, and the pilot bailed out while the aircraft, engulfed in flames, went out of control and crashed. It was an incredible bit of timing. The P-40's engine malfunctioned and caught fire as the pilot made his simulated gun run. At that instant, the student gunner fired at the pursuit ship and "shot" him out of the sky with his gun camera. The P-40 pilot got out of his stricken craft in the nick of time. The hair on the nape of his neck was singed by flames as he bailed out.

The director of supply and maintenance at Laredo, Lt. Col. Tommy T. Todd (T3), needed a flight test engineering pilot and recruited me for the job. The position dictated that I be checked out in all aircraft assigned to Laredo. Once I tested a P-39 in the morning, a B-24 in the afternoon, and a B-26 just before nightfall.

In the autumn of 1944, an accident killed the two ranking test pilots. A reorganization followed, and I was appointed the officer in charge (OIC) of the flight test engineering division. A short time later I was promoted to captain.

A new bomber, the B-29, made its operational debut. I talked to T3 about the new plane and said I'd like to fly it some day. He said to forget any thought of leaving my position; everything was operating smoothly and there would be no changes. He said he wasn't going through another reshuffling of his test division. Meanwhile, Laredo continued to grind out gunners, and I went about my routine.

I'd occasionally run into my friend Major Riley, the base adjutant, at the club. He said the base continued to receive monthly levies for volunteers for the B-29 program. I told him I was still interested, but my work prevented me from volunteering. He nodded. "Let me know when things change," he said. "I'm sure I can get you into the program."

I should have been satisfied with my assignment; it was the best flying job at Laredo. But I was a twenty-two-year-old Army Air Forces pilot with three years of wartime service and had yet to be in combat. That fact weighed heavily on me.

There were rumors that the student load might be reduced because the air war over Germany was going well. We were not losing as many aircrews as in the past. The base commander was summoned to a conference at Army Air Forces headquarters in Washington, and T3 had been on temporary duty (TDY) elsewhere. I met with T3 in his office when he returned and updated him on the test division. He was satisfied and said he'd be leaving again for a meeting at training command. I asked if the meetings that he and the base commander were attending meant that changes were coming to Laredo.

"I'm not sure, but it wouldn't surprise me if it did," he replied. "See you in a few days."

The day after his departure, I learned that the base received a levy for two pilots for B-29 training. I called Major Riley and said I wanted to be given one of the slots.

"Does Colonel Todd know you're volunteering for the program?" he asked.

"Of course. You don't think I'd call without him knowing all about it, do you?"

"Okay, Mike. I'll put your name down. You'll get orders soon."

In two days I was gone. I don't know what T3 said when he returned, but I hoped he had a good sense of humor and wouldn't give me a bad efficiency report.

I found out later that he didn't. He gave me a good report.

4 The B-29 Superfortress

The Army Air Forces pilot accepted into the B-29 program had to be a top-notch military aviator. To qualify for training as a B-29 aircraft commander, he had to have a minimum of five hundred hours in a four-engine bomber, either the B-17 or the B-24, and at least fifteen hundred hours of flying time. I easily met those qualifications; I had more than two thousand hours, including eight hundred as a B-24 test pilot. I felt honored to be selected. The B-29 was the top of the line—technologically the most advanced aircraft of World War II.

Compared to the B-24, which had a 110-foot wingspan, four 1,200-horsepower engines, and weighed more than 30 tons, the B-29 was a monster. It had a wingspan of 141 feet, 3 inches, and four 2,200-horsepower engines driving four-bladed propellers each 16 feet, 7 inches in diameter. It weighed more than 71 tons.

There were other refinements unique to the B-29. The crew compartments were pressurized, eliminating the need for constant use of oxygen at altitude. The defensive armament was contained in turrets remotely controlled by a sophisticated electronic system that allowed for transfer between selected gunnery stations. All stations had computing sights that were easy to operate and (properly used) produced excellent results. The B-29, with a maximum bomb load of ten tons, was capable of extremely long-range operations, making it ideally suited for the air offensive against Japan.

I was assigned to Maxwell Army Air Field at Montgomery, Alabama, for transition training. There I met my copilot and flight engineer. Unlike B-24 transition, where instruction was on an individual basis, B-29 training focused on the flight crew to develop team-work. My copilot, a recent flight school graduate qualified in the B-24, was Lt. Robert Oakley, from White Plains, New York. The flight engineer, Lt. Robert Peirent, also fresh out of flight school, was from Lowell, Massachusetts. We flew together and attended ground school classes as a unit.

As usual, training began with an orientation session. I was flab-bergasted when the director of flight training was introduced. It was my old nemesis, Frecker, who I knew as the director of flight training at Smyrna. He'd been promoted to major. He looked us over and eyed me. "*Captain* Novosel. Glad to see you again. Are you still five feet eight and one hundred sixty pounds?"

I came right back at him. "Since I saw you last, *Major*, I haven't changed a bit."

Major Frecker told the group that we were acquaintances, then proceeded with his presentation.

Our instructor was Maj. Mike McCoy, a B-24 veteran of the air offensive over Germany. At Smyrna our instructors had been first lieutenants, as were most of the students, but at Maxwell the instructors and students were captains and majors. There had to have been a law stating that as military technology advanced, so did the officer corps.

During training, McCoy sat in the copilot's seat and gave me control of the aircraft. Engine starting procedures were unique. Only the flight engineer had the controls, dials, and switches for that. I observed the starting procedure from the aircraft commander's seat. It was strange watching Peirent start those huge Wright Cyclones.

After Peirent completed the engine starts and McCoy and I finished the before-taxi checklist, we were ready to move out. McCoy motioned with his left hand, indicating that I had the airplane. I advanced the throttles, and the ship rolled forward smoothly. It was easier to taxi than the B-24 and responded well to power and brake applications in turns. I felt comfortable with the B-29.

The instructor assumed all communications duties, which allowed me to devote my attention to the airplane. I taxied to the run-up position, where Peirent made the magneto and power checks, and we were ready to go. I checked runway alignment with the nose of the aircraft, applied power, and released the brakes. We picked up speed rapidly and the nose came up easily. I used the slightest amount of back pressure on the control column as the plane lifted off.

The B-29 flew as fast in a climb as the P-40 pursuit did in straight and level flight. McCoy and I performed normal turns, timed turns, steep turns, and even stalls in steep turns. The B-29's stability while stalled in a sixty-degree bank was impressive.

After McCoy checked me out, Oakley took his position in the copilot's seat. We were on our own. Occasionally McCoy came along, but only to monitor our progress.

At the end of the course, we received our only flight check. Evidently Frecker had had enough of me, because he sent someone else to give the check ride. I managed to do the right things at the right times and passed. After that, I was off to combat crew training.

Oakley, Peirent, and I were assigned to Kirtland Field at Albuquerque, New Mexico. The rest of our crew joined us there. My job was to polish an assortment of strangers into a tightly knit, highly efficient, and professional crew ready for combat.

I had outstanding and well-educated people assigned to me. My radar operator–navigator was Capt. Nathan Weiner, a New Yorker and graduate of City College of New York; the navigator was 1st Lt. John Newman, a former electrical engineer with General Electric; the bombardier was Lt. Sam Rosh, from Chicago; our radio operator was Sgt. Meredith Ackley, from Boise, Idaho; central fire control was Sgt. Leo Fischer, from St. Louis, Missouri; scanners were Sgt. Boniface (Bunny) Kolbo, from St. Paul, Minnesota, and Sgt. Raymond Baczynski, of Hamtramck, Michigan; and the tail gunner was Sgt. Earl Holliday, from Pine Bluff, Arkansas. With the assignment of the eight crewmen, we were a complete combat crew. We faced a rigorous and intensive training schedule for the next two months.

We knew we had a good crew, but we were surprised to be selected "Crew of the Class." The award featured a three-day trip to Hollywood for fun and relaxation and included a day at a movie studio to observe some of the stars in action. We were given a B-17 (I had not checked out in the bird) for the trip. I talked it over with Bob Oakley, who said he had never been in a B-17 but was eager to go. We were afraid to tell the operations folks of our dilemma, because they might cancel the flight.

I went to the airplane and looked it over. I knew I could start the engines but wasn't familiar with its fuel management. About then the ship's crew chief came up, greeted me, and said he was raring to go. He said he'd been crewing the aircraft for more than a year. I asked about the plane's latest inspection, maintenance record, and fuel consumption. His answers convinced me he was thoroughly familiar with his plane, so I decided to go. I told Oakley and cautioned him not to say a thing to anyone about our earlier conversation. He gave me a sly grin. "Do you think I'm crazy? What they don't know, they don't have to know."

I rounded up the crew, and we got aboard the B-17. After looking over the cockpit area, the instruments, and the controls, I started the engines. The R-1820 Wrights of the B-17 were not complicated. I'd had the same basic engines on other planes, so I was familiar with their operation. There wasn't much to flying the B-17; it was not the fastest thing in the air, which allowed plenty of time to make a decision. It was heavy on the controls but not more difficult to handle than a B-24.

Takeoff was uneventful, and we were off for Los Angeles. Everything went well except for one important phase—the landing. Our destination was Mines Field, which did not have runways of any great length. I set up an approach as I would a B-24 but forgot that the B-17 landed more like a little Piper Cub.

As I came over the end of the runway and reduced power, I noticed I was a little hot. I cut the power completely but was still too fast, and I floated half the length of the runway before touchdown. I hit the brakes. There wasn't much runway left, and we were rushing rapidly toward the cyclone fence bordering the airfield. I stomped and pumped the brakes, and the B-17's tail was high up from my heavy braking. Finally I got the aircraft to stop a few yards from the fence, its tail still in the air. Then suddenly it slammed to the ground.

I knew I'd broken something in the rear and visualized a blown tail-wheel tire, maybe a collapsed strut, or, far worse, a buckled fuselage. But luck was with me. Miraculously the big bird was okay. I taxied to the ramp, shaking from the close call, and shut down the engines. We made it, not gracefully or legally, but we made it.

We were in Los Angeles for a good time, so we headed into town. There were nightclubs, good restaurants, and good-looking women. We had three fun-filled days before an uneventful flight back to Albuquerque. Not long after, we were on our way to the Pacific.

We arrived at Tinian, in the Mariana Islands, in early July 1945 and were assigned to the 58th Bomb Wing. We ended up in the 462d Bomb Group, known as the Hellbirds. Its motto was "With Malice Toward Some."

I was given an aerial orientation and checked out. My first flight to the Japanese Empire was a night mission, a fire bombing raid flown at seven thousand feet. There was little opposition, no enemy fighters, and negligible antiaircraft fire.

Major Allen Rowlett, the operations officer, scheduled a training mission because he was not satisfied with the way the squadron looked in formation. We formed up quickly after takeoff, and I took my position on his right wing, being careful to keep the same spacing as the other pilots. Rowlett came over the radio: "Tighten up this formation. You're all too loose." I obeyed, holding the same spacing as the others. The formation looked much tighter and better.

All "new guys" in a combat outfit were looked upon with suspicion. After all, they were fresh from the training command and were not thought to be as capable or aggressive as the old-timers. Giving the new guy an occasional jab was customary, and Major Rowlett was not one to flaunt tradition. His next radio transmission was directed at me: "Let's tighten it up, Novosel. You're in combat now."

I knew what Rowlett was doing and didn't appreciate it one bit. My spacing in formation was the same as the others. I decided to give it right back to him, and then some. I replied with one word, "Roger"; then I moved in on him and placed my wing tip inside his inboard engine. My left wing was directly behind his right wing. He was in the left seat and couldn't see me, but his copilot glanced in my direction, then immediately turned his head to tell Rowlett how close I was. Sergeant Kolbo reported that three of Rowlett's crewmen were crowded around the right scanner's position anxiously staring at my wing tip, which was jammed right in their faces. There must have been a lot of chatter back and forth in Rowlett's ship, yet he never said a word. I visualized his crewmen's agitated rear ends puckered up and tweaking their seat cushions. I continued to hold my position for at least five minutes, then eased off a bit. But I stayed closer to him than the other ships in the formation. Rowlett never again told me to "tighten it up."

In the next two weeks, our squadron flew two more missions to the Japanese Empire without losses. Morale was high, and enemy opposition was almost nonexistent. We felt that the war couldn't go on much longer. It was the first week of August 1945.

Everyone on Tinian was aware of the 509th Composite Group. But the 509th was a mystery to us, and it generated a considerable amount of discussion.

The mystery and the guessing disappeared on August 6, 1945, with the official announcement of the first use of the atomic bomb. Colonel Tibbets flew the *Enola Gay* as bombardier Tom Ferebee released the bomb that destroyed Hiroshima. We received the initial reports with mixed emotions. If they were true and we could drop atomic bombs on other targets, the war was certain to be over. The report of one bomb's equivalence to twenty thousand tons of conventional explosives was difficult to believe. Our normal bomb load was seven tons, and we knew what those seven tons could do. To think that one bomb could have such power was incomprehensible.

It wasn't long before all speculation about the bomb was put to rest. On August 9, another atomic bomb was dropped, this time on Nagasaki. The reports of devastation and deaths of thousands of people were repetitions of earlier statements regarding Hiroshima. The Japanese accepted Allied terms of unconditional surrender on August 14. The last of the Axis powers surrendered; only the formal ceremonies remained.

Meanwhile, there was concern for the thousands of prisoners of war (POWs) held by the Japanese. From late August past mid-September, about nine hundred missions were flown, delivering food, medicine, and clothing to sustain the POWs. We flew the missions at a thousand feet; the low altitude assured us of accurate drops.

Relations with the media were excellent during the war. The reporters were a nuisance, but the combatants knew that the press had to do its job covering the war. Cooperating with the media was never in doubt.

Some reporters were gullible and could be sold incredulous yarns. They'd take them hook, line, and sinker. I heard of one wild story that allegedly made the papers back home. After completing a combat mission, a pilot found a small, half-starved, mangy-looking pup on the hardstand. The pilot, a practical joker, smeared oil from one of the dirty engine nacelles all over the pup. The haggard creature was a truly pathetic sight. Then the pilot, to dramatize the situation, used his cigarette lighter to singe the pup's oil-soaked hairs. He was careful not to harm the creature. Satisfied that he had created the desired effect, the pilot left the area with the pup cradled in his arms. Reporters were always hanging around looking for good human interest stories, and the scrawny pup was a natural. One reporter took the bait: "Where did you find that dirty little mutt?"

The pilot proceeded to unwind this story. He said his aircraft was at five thousand feet in the last half of a stream of B-29s fire-bombing Tokyo one night. Updrafts from the extensive fires and exploding bombs rocked their ship back and forth, and occasional heavy blasts seemed to lift them hundreds of feet. They continued the bomb run as the sky glowed red from the inferno raging below. The bombardier reported, "Bombs away," as an unusually strong blast from one of the heavier bombs hit their B-29 with such force that the crewmen feared the ship was damaged. One of the crew reported that the ship might have been hit by an antiaircraft shell.

The aircraft commander maneuvered away from the fiery scene and had his crew inspect the ship. Because the blast hit the craft while the bomb bay doors were open, he also ordered an inspection of the bomb bays. The bombardier checked the rear bay and found nothing amiss; the pilot inspected the forward bay, which also was okay. As the pilot was about to return to his position, he thought he heard a noise like a yelp from an animal. He looked around and heard another yelp. Then he saw a small pup cowering from fright and wedged into a corner of the bomb bay. He retrieved the animal and surmised it had been blown into the air by the violent explosion and by good fortune landed in the airplane's bomb bay.

"Yep," the pilot told the wide-eyed reporter, "it had to be that last strong blast. It sent this here small puppy flying through the air right into our bomb bay. What do you think of that?"

The reporter sat entranced with mouth agape. The pilot was a master storyteller. He never smiled or let on that such an incident was impossible.

The pilot insisted that his name not be mentioned in the news release. He didn't want his family to "worry about him," and the story might generate anxiety about his activities in combat. If his family knew that during combat missions he had to fly through maelstroms such as he had just described, they would be upset. It was agreed that the reporter would not mention the pilot's name, but he did want a close-up of the bedraggled pup in his arms. He promised that the story would be in the next day's shipment of news for the home front. The arrangement pleased everybody. The reporter got his story, and the aircrewmen had their laughs.

After my session with the newsman, I saw Major Rowlett. He said the group was scheduled for an important mission in two days and the squadron would be involved.

"Can you tell me if my crew will be on the mission?" I asked.

"Your crew will be included. We'll need eleven flight crews."

The squadron was to furnish an eleven-ship formation that would be part of the covering force for surrender ceremonies on board the USS *Missouri*. The Twentieth Air Force would form a gigantic air armada and fly over the battleship, squadron after squadron, in a continuous stream.

The briefing at group operations covered all the essential elements, from the objective to intelligence on enemy forces, dispositions, and capabilities. Operations added the rendezvous areas and locations of rescue aircraft, submarines, and surface vessels in case of emergency. Capping it all was the safety message.

The group operations officer reminded us that the Soviet Union was still off-limits to all aircrews. We were also cautioned not to land at any of the airfields in Japan because of the uncertain welcome that the crew might receive. In the event of an emergency, we were to proceed to Iwo Jima, about 650 miles south of Tokyo. We received a time hack from the group navigator and set our watches, and the briefing was over.

We departed for the flight line. It was still dark when we arrived at our hardstand, where rations were being loaded onto our ship. We joked about the rations being balanced meals. Three boxes of rations were placed in the forward pressurized crew compartment and were balanced by three boxes in the rear crew compartment.

I called for the customary inspection, and the crew lined up in front of the ship. I checked their parachute harnesses, Mae West life vests, and dog tags (metal identification badges), then ordered everyone aboard the aircraft.

After all stations reported ready, I gave the order to start engines. I moved out on schedule, took my position in line, and proceeded to the runway for takeoff.

Departures were scheduled thirty seconds apart. Oakley checked the time. On his signal I advanced the throttles and reached their forward stops just as he called out "takeoff." I released the brakes, and we were on our way.

After we reached cruise altitude, John Newman gave me the heading. Nathan Weiner was picking up radar returns of the volcanic islands on the route to Iwo. Newman asked Weiner for an "estimate" to Sarigan, one of the islands. This never failed to anger Weiner, who would tell Newman that radar produced an exact measurement of distance, not an estimate. "For your information," said Weiner, "Sarigan is *exactly* nine and a half slant range miles from our position."

Newman came right back with, "That's about the same estimate I had." I could not see Weiner back at his station, but I knew he was fuming.

It was about midmorning when we passed Iwo, and from all indications it would be a beautiful day. There were a few clouds, mostly fair-weather cumulus, and the ocean had only an occasional whitecap.

When we were ten minutes from the rendezvous site, Sam Rosh, Oakley, and I were all intent on picking up the lead aircraft. It wasn't long before somebody spotted it circling to the left. There were three B-29s ahead of us maneuvering to get into formation. Rowlett was in a shallow turn, which made it easy to form up.

I got into position and others joined to complete the formation, then Major Rowlett maneuvered the squadron behind the group leader. The signal to move out was received, and we were on our way to Tokyo Bay.

"Let's tighten up this formation," Rowlett ordered. "Show those clowns down there what a good formation of B-29s looks like. I can see the *Missouri* up ahead." We closed it up, and I knew we looked good. There were 462 B-29s in the air armada.

All through the surrender proceedings, the B-29s kept up their steady, monotonous drone over the great battleship. When MacArthur closed the ceremonies, our part in the ritual was over. Somewhere south of Tokyo Bay the formations broke up and we headed for home. I made a slight deviation from the flight plan to do something I'd wanted to do for a long time. I headed for Mount Fujiyama.

At twelve thousand feet plus, Fujiyama was the highest mountain in Japan, sacred to some. I had seen pictures of it and learned in school of its significance in Japanese history and culture. I'd seen it while flying previous missions to the empire and decided that one day I would fly directly over it. This was my opportunity.

When I neared the mountain, I was in a climb to cruising altitude but still below its crest. I was less than half a mile from the mountain when I was at its altitude; then, while still climbing, I flew directly over it. I put the aircraft into a sixty-degree bank and had one of my crew take a picture looking down into the huge crater. After this joyride, I continued the climb and turned on course.

An interesting anecdote concerning the return to Tinian and navigator John Newman is worth relating. John was intelligent and well educated, dedicated to his specialty, and a tireless crewman who possessed an abundance of self-confidence. The return to Tinian was an outstanding example of his unswerving belief in himself and his conclusions. John gave me the heading, and I set it with the autopilot.

We cruised somewhere in the middle of the 462 B-29s; the sky ahead and to our rear was dotted with aircraft. But not for long, because the Twentieth Air Force started to drift to our left. Puzzled, I asked John to confirm the heading. He said we were on course, that our heading was correct.

About half an hour later, we were alone. The other B-29s were barely visible off to our left. I called John from his navigator's station and showed him the disappearing Twentieth Air Force. He didn't hesitate a second. "They're off course," he said and retreated back to his sanctum sanctorum.

While John was immersed in his charts and tables, I tuned in the beacon at Iwo Jima and saw the radio compass needle deflect to the left. Using the autopilot, I nudged the nose of our B-29 to line up with the needle. John apparently didn't notice the slow heading change. So far, so good, I thought. He was either dozing or into his books.

Eventually the Twentieth came back into view. When we passed over Iwo, John came forward, looked out to the left, and said, "See, I told you we were on course."

"Yep, right on course," I said. "Somehow the Twentieth Air Force came back to join us." Before he returned to his station, John gave me the new heading for Tinian.

As we flew toward the base, I reflected on the significance of the long day's activities. We had participated in and witnessed one of history's greatest events. But I must admit that while we flew over the surrender ceremony, I was primarily concerned with keeping a good, tight position in formation. A person has to live with the priorities of the moment.

My ruminations drifted back to my enlistment in the army air corps and the subsequent attack on Pearl Harbor. I recalled the many weeks and months spent as an aviation cadet with its strict discipline and the brutally difficult days of flight training.

I had been an air corps pilot since the first year of the war and somehow managed to emerge unscathed. I wondered if the world would ever see another war of such magnitude, one where almost every part of the globe witnessed horrendous fighting that resulted in casualties by the thousands. Would another war be as destructive?

My thoughts turned to the future and what it held for me. It was then I realized that the next day would be my twenty-third birthday. During what ordinarily are the most formative and best years of a person's life, I experienced only war and preparation for war. What was in store for me? What would I do now that the conflict was over? I decided to stop worrying about the future. There would be time enough to make plans later. We'd been airborne for more than sixteen hours. I trimmed the aircraft for a shallow descent.

Saipan came into view, then the smaller island of Tinian. Still descending, I called for the landing checklist. Bob Peirent furnished me with the computed landing weight and approach airspeed. Oakley lowered the landing gear upon my command and reported, "Gear down and locked."

I turned on the final approach, lined up with the runway, checked the airspeed, called for flaps, rounded out, reduced power, brought the nose up slightly, and made a smooth touchdown. I parked on the hardstand and cut the engines. The entry I made in the aircraft log was "17 hours, 10 minutes flying time; 1 landing."

World War II was over.

5 Tinian, Clark Field, Okinawa: 1945–47

The war wasn't over more than a few days when the men of the 58th Bomb Wing were told they would be going home. In short order the leadership of the group and squadrons departed for the States and were replaced by lower-ranking officers. I assumed the same happened at wing level. Departures were determined by the number of points garnered for missions and time overseas.

It was apparent that the policies and procedures for returning home did not include me or my crew. We were so new to the outfit that we didn't have enough points to transfer to another island. That was Bob Oakley's appraisal of the situation.

After the "surrender mission," I made a few test flights of aircraft being returned to the States and flew one more mission—a supply drop to the POWs still in the empire.

The 462d Bomb Group was leaving, and something had to be done about those who stayed behind. Eventually we were transferred to the 313th Bomb Wing at North Field, where we were assigned to the 5th Bombardment Squadron of the 9th Bomb Group. There we discovered the same traumatic drawdown of personnel. The major difference was that the 58th was returning to the States and we were staying at Tinian.

Upon reporting to the group, I was introduced to Col. Dave Wade. As the group commander, he had an entire Quonset hut to himself. To get acquainted with the newcomers from the 58th, Colonel Wade invited all officers to a soiree at his quarters. The bash was a resounding success; there were not many sober heads the next morning. After that, we called his Quonset "Duffy's Tavern," a name borrowed from a popular radio program, and Wade was affectionately known as Duffy.

The colonel was not given to long discussions when difficulties were presented to him. He gave his subordinates free rein to pursue their missions and solve their own problems. But he was always accessible and listened attentively.

I went to the colonel for assistance with a matter I considered crucial. He showed great interest, and when I finished he leaned back in his chair and looked up at the ceiling for a minute. Then he leaned forward, put his hands together on his desk, and said, "Mike, you've listed your problems with great care. I think you know your priorities and where they must be directed. Any advice I give would be superfluous and could be wrong. You're doing a fine job. Continue what you're doing. Is there anything else I should know?"

What could I say? There was never a dull moment working for Duffy.

Wade's method of meting out duty assignments was typical of successful military commanders. When they found officers who got things done, they gave them the important jobs. The best commanders surrounded themselves with as many can-do people as they could find. These officers became their cliques, their fair-haired boys, and the major duty assignments were loaded onto their shoulders. Operating in this manner, commanders knew that their missions would be met on time and in a superior manner.

It was my privilege to work for Dave Wade. In October 1945, my first full month with the organization, I was made the group operations officer and held the positions of group instrument instructor and flight standardization instructor.

Wade intended to maintain a full operational capability even though the unit was understrength and working around the clock. The 9th flew more than the other three groups of the 313th combined and was the only one that was combat ready. During the typhoon season, only the 9th was able to launch reconnaissance missions. I flew two.

October spawned a particularly strong typhoon south of the Marianas. It sideswiped Guam, came over Tinian and Saipan, and continued northwest to strike Okinawa, which it devastated. I flew my first reconnaissance of this storm when it was between Guam and Tinian. I penetrated the typhoon at an altitude of five hundred feet under the direction of the ship's radar and flew through the eye of the storm to determine its exact position. The eye was a classic type—absolutely clear and void of rain.

I flew a second recon of the same typhoon as it neared Okinawa. The storm had grown in size and intensified greatly. Flying through such a violent storm left me exhausted, because it had to be done manually. The C-1 autopilot could not be engaged because of safety considerations.

One of the training flights was typical of the demands made on the aircrews of the 9th. It was a night flight of squadron strength from Tinian to Eniwetok and back. The flight was subjected to steady rain, and the visibility was poor. I could tell by the radio chatter among the aircraft commanders that there was an uneasiness about the length of the flight and the weather. But the mission went as planned, and all aircraft returned to base without major mechanical difficulties. Wade was elated with the afteraction report.

Later that month when I was flying with a pilot who was being upgraded to aircraft commander, I ran into a bizarre chain of events involving the navy. I was flying over Tinian demonstrating the maneuverability of the B-29. We were at about nine thousand feet and had just completed a chandelle (a maximum-performance 180-degree climbing turn) when I noticed a burst of flak about five hundred yards off my nose. At the same time, the tail gunner reported flak about five hundred yards aft of our aircraft.

The war was over—Japan had surrendered weeks earlier—but some clowns were firing at us. I did a steep turn and looked down. I saw an aircraft carrier below and automatically assumed it was the source of the flak. In my excited state I didn't notice the escort ships nearby. More than likely the escorts were responsible.

I decided to take corrective action and did a wingover. I was diving to a lower altitude when I saw another burst of flak about five hundred yards off my nose; the tail gunner again reported flak to his rear. The navy had me bracketed, and it was too close to suit me. The war was over and they knew it. They were just showing off.

I continued diving and turned away from the carrier, but I was fit to be tied and wanted to get even. The navy had no right to use my aircraft for target practice. At a thousand feet I leveled off, reversed course, and headed for the carrier. I entered its traffic pattern, lowered the landing gear on the downwind, turned on base leg, and lowered half flaps. When I turned on the final approach, I lowered full flaps and ordered the bomb bay doors opened. I wanted the jokers to see the size of the bay and the massive load of destruction it could drop on them. It was payback time.

I really wanted to bounce my landing gear on the ship's deck, but its island was too near so I broke to the left. As I turned away, I clearly saw the ship's landing signal officer (LSO) violently giving me a series of wave-offs. He evidently thought I was actually trying to land. In the instant before wave-off, I saw the ship's identification, CV-31. It was the USS *Bon Homme Richard,* better known as the Bonnie Dick.

I sure wish the carrier hadn't had an island. I could have left a deep impression on the deck.

A major reshuffling of people occurred, and in early January I was given command of the 99th Bombardment Squadron and its seven hundred officers and men. I was twenty-three years old at the time but a senior captain in the group. I was relieved of duties as group operations officer.

On my first day as commanding officer (CO) of the 99th, the first sergeant gave me the keys to a jeep that came with the job of squadron commander. I told him to give the keys to the driver. He said there was no driver, that the jeep was mine and I would do the driving. "The other squadron commanders had their jeeps and did their own driving," he volunteered. I asked if he knew who delivered the jeep and he said he did.

"Is the vehicle operating satisfactorily? Are you satisfied with it?" I asked.

"Sir, the jeep has recently been through a major inspection and it's in tip-top shape."

I decided that a demonstration of its operation was in order. "Let's go for a ride," I suggested. "You drive while I observe. Here's the keys." I tossed them to him.

"If you say so, sir. But I don't see why we're going. The jeep's in perfect shape."

We got on board and were off for a demonstration ride. I told the sergeant to head for an old, abandoned Japanese airstrip. When we arrived, I told him to proceed to the far end because I wanted to discuss a problem. I had to tell him the truth: I didn't know how to drive. I never learned or even tried to operate an automobile. Here I was, a B-29 aircraft commander, a squadron commander at that. I'd flown five different trainers, three pursuits, four transports, and four bombers. But I couldn't drive a simple automobile. I was embarrassed.

I decided on the direct approach. "Sergeant, I've never learned to drive."

"You've got to be shittin' me, sir."

I told him that when I turned eighteen and enlisted in the air corps, I didn't have time to learn.

"Before we return to the squadron area, you're going to teach me the fine art of operating this vehicle. We will not return until I can be seen driving up to our orderly room in my jeep. Do you read me, Sergeant?"

"I understand, sir, but I don't know if I can do it in such a short time. Let's get someone from the motor pool to do it."

"Sergeant, no one else is to know of my inability to drive. You are the only one with that information, which I consider to be privileged. If after our return to the squadron area I detect any snickering or unusual activity behind my back, it will be evident that my secret has been compromised and I'll sure as hell know who let the cat out of the bag. Sergeant, if that were to happen, your ass would be grass and I would be the lawn mower. Do I make my position clear?"

"Don't worry, sir. Your secret is safe with me."

"Let's get to work. Teach me how to make this machine go."

The sergeeant showed me the coordination necessary to operate the jeep: the use of the clutch, the accelerator, and the gearshift. Everything worked like a charm while he was driving, but every time I tried, the vehicle jerked and stalled. I couldn't make the clutch, accelerator, and gears work together. It was frustrating for me as well as the sergeant.

After about an hour of lurching all over the airstrip, I finally got the hang of it. I'd get the jeep moving (without stalling), and he'd have me race to the end of the strip, shift, turn around, and head back to the other end. He cautioned me about making sharp turns; the jeep had a nasty habit of rolling over if turned too abruptly.

At long last, we were both satisfied that I had conquered the jeep and agreed I could drive back to the squadron. He muttered something about his neck bothering him from all the whiplashing I had caused. I told him to keep such remarks to himself and to watch what he said once back at the office. I drove back to the base and the matter was forgotten, I think. At the orderly room I noticed the sergeant rubbing the back of his neck. I wondered if it was really sore or if he was just putting me on.

Things were going well. I was the commander of the 99th Bombardment Squadron and liked my job as group instrument instructor and flight standardization instructor, and drove my jeep.

What happened next shouldn't have surprised me. The military doesn't like things going too well for too long. Our units were performing like clockwork when the wing received orders to relocate to Clark Field in the Philippines.

I was responsible for moving seventeen B-29s and all support equipment plus seven hundred officers and men. The planes were flown to Clark, but I stayed behind with the rear detachment. The squadron's heavy equipment would be transferred on board a liberty ship. I supervised the loading and complied with the final chapter of my departure orders—the destruction by fire of all privies. After the inevitable "last call," we poured gallons and gallons of gasoline and diesel oil into the privies, applied the torches, and cheered when the flames shot up and consumed the structures. We stayed until the flames were extinguished, took one last look at the empty Quonset huts, and departed for the dock area. It would be my first journey by sea.

Dave Wade was determined that the 9th would remain the leading group of the 313th Bomb Wing. We were still losing people who rotated home but were pleasantly surprised when a dozen new officers reported for duty. They had just finished B-29 transition training in the States. Most were graduates of West Point, class of '44. One was Capt. Bill Steger, a product of the three-year accelerated wartime course at "The Point." I made him my adjutant.

Bill and I occasionally got to Manila. On one trip we didn't pay attention to the time and started back late. I was in danger of violating the curfew and was moving right along. All went well until I passed through Angeles, where the military police (MPs) gave me a ticket.

The speeding ticket required an answer from the unit commander (myself) about the action taken against the driver (me). I didn't waste time with administrative details. I punished the driver by taking away his driving privileges for a month. I complied with the stiff sentence to the letter. Bill Steger drove me on my rounds.

My duties increased when I was made a member of the Thirteenth Air Force general court. I'd often be in session all morning and sometimes the whole day. After six months I was appointed the court's law member, a position akin to that of a judge. I made rulings on procedures, legal matters, and admissibility of evidence.

Soon it was evident that my views on confessions and their admissibility were more restrictive than what the Thirteenth Air Force preferred. This triggered a visit from the command legal officer. He complimented me for my excellent work as law member, then engaged me in a general discussion on rules of evidence. We had a good exchange of views, not a one-sided affair as one would suspect. Still, he was a colonel and a lawyer and I was merely a twenty-four-year-old captain and a pilot. It was clear that the command wanted a more relaxed position on confessions.

I reminded the command "legal eagle" that none of my decisions as law member had been reversed and that a tainted confession wouldn't be grounds for reversal of a conviction in my court. I felt that the accused didn't know their rights and were ignorant of the damaging effect of confessions that went unchallenged. The colonel indicated that the command's views were basically in line with mine but that my concerns about the reviewing authority reversing findings were unwarranted. I thanked him for the intercommunication and said the command's views would be taken under advisement. I continued with my duties and balanced the command's position with

my interpretation of the law. The command must have been satisfied with my performance, because I remained the law member of
the general court as long as I stayed at Clark Field.

In February 1947 we received orders to fly some B-29s to the States.
The ones selected were the oldest, the "war wearies." I was told I'd
fly one back; it would be my first trip to the mainland in more than
eighteen months. We were to deliver the planes to Pyote, Texas, after stops for maintenance and fuel at Guam, Kwajalein, and Oahu.

First Lieutenant Charles C. Bailey, nicknamed Sycamore, was my
copilot. He was the squadron maintenance officer, an individual of
utmost professional competence.

The selected aircraft were to rendezvous at Guam and be given a
thorough inspection before making the flight to Texas. On the flight
to Guam we discovered that our aircraft used excessive oil in two engines. They had to be replaced before proceeding farther—a job that
took ten days.

The flight to Kwajalein was uneventful. We arrived in time for dinner and had beef stew. The last time I had passed through, almost
two years earlier, I had beef stew. I wondered if they still had the same
cook; the stew looked familiar.

The next day we took off for Hawaii. It was a long flight to our
destination, Barbers Point Naval Air Station, a few miles west of Honolulu. After landing I told the tower we'd refuel the next day. We'd
flown twelve and a half hours and needed rest.

The sun was high when we got up, and it was noon before we arrived at base operations for the requested refueling. When the
navy's fuel truck arrived, I figured they must have thought we were
a navy aircraft, some small puddle jumper. Their little tanker could
never slacken the thirst of my big bird, especially after our long flight.
I sent the driver back to his section with directions to return with a
real tanker.

Mission orders required us to fill all the main tanks plus the auxiliary tanks in the bomb bays. After taking on fuel, we had almost
seven thousand gallons aboard—enough to keep us airborne for a
whole day. We put a gigantic dent in the navy's aviation gas supply
that day.

We had five days before heading for the mainland, so we went into Honolulu. We had a wonderful time wining and dining. The flight to the States was next.

We departed on schedule. We leveled off at twenty thousand feet and settled in for a long flight to the metropolis of Pyote. When everything was set up for cruising, Bailey switched on the radio compass and tuned in a commercial station in Los Angeles; the needle came around to indicate station bearing off the nose of the aircraft. I told him to make certain he had Los Angeles, California, tuned in and not Angeles in the Philippines. He just nodded and grinned, but Bailey always had a big grin on his face.

We flew through the night, and finally the far sky developed a dim glow with a thin streak of light outlining the horizon. It was the sign of a new day dawning. We were treated to a beautiful sunrise as the city of Los Angeles came into view. It was my first sight of the United States mainland in almost two years—too long as far as I was concerned. I envied the people down there in tidy, little homes and neat surroundings. We'd occupy their world for about a week but then would go back to our dismal routine.

We were back in a special world where beer came in tall brown glass bottles, icy cold—not in rusty, old tin cans. We could choose a special brand instead of the beer du jour. And the steaks were specially cut from aged beef, not some prefabricated piece of meat frozen in a mammoth cardboard box.

Below was a world where fresh vegetables didn't have to be washed in a solution of Clorox to prevent an intestinal disorder rumored to be "government issue." Why else was the stomach affliction known as the GIs? Yes, we were back where caraway seeds in bread were really caraway seeds, not a protein supplement, where eggs came in shells instead of posing as fake yellow powder, where the odors were from the effects of civilization, not privies.

I could have daydreamed forever about the world below, but I had things to do and position reports to make. I came back to reality and made my report to Los Angeles radio, then continued eastbound toward Phoenix on airway Green 5. Our flight plan took us along Green 5 through El Paso to the Wink radio range, then south to Pyote.

After passing the Salt Flat radio range, I contacted the radio station at Wink and advised the operator of our intention to land at Pyote. Wink is in a desolate part of Texas. I supposed the radio operator there got lonely, because he wanted to talk with us. But I had other priorities and broke off the conversation by telling him I was switching over to the Pyote tower frequency.

I cranked in 272 kilocycles, contacted the tower, and let the operator know we were inbound for landing. Bailey was flying the B-29 while I handled communication. He made a nice landing and after looking around said, "Where the hell are we?"

There were few people about, and only a few structures dotted the area. We taxied behind a truck to our parking spot, which was surrounded by hundreds of B-29s. After gathering our gear, we jumped into the truck, which took us to a building near the tower. I handed the aircraft's papers to a lone civilian at a counter. Our mission was complete.

The flight from Barbers Point to Pyote had taken sixteen hours and fifteen minutes. We needed a good meal, so we went to the finest restaurant in Pyote. The name of that four-star establishment, I seem to recall, was Pyote Joe's. We ordered steaks and french fries.

We asked for beer while waiting for our food and were pleasantly surprised to see tall, slim brown bottles dripping wet from icy condensation. My dreams had become reality. We ordered another round. No product of the brewer's art ever satisfied a thirst like that wonderful beer we had at Joe's. Then the steaks arrived. Pyote Joe had really outdone himself. The steaks set before us covered huge platters and were as tasty as they could be.

After traveling for two days, we arrived in San Francisco. For five glorious days we lived high on the hog. Then it was over. We had danced long enough; now it was time to pay the band. We reported to Fairfield-Suisun and boarded a C-54 for the flight to Clark.

The return to the Philippines was a shocker. After being away for only six weeks, I found the place in turmoil. Colonel Wade called me into his office, and what he said was not entirely to my liking. He was being transferred to Guam to take command of the 19th Bomb Group. I was going to the 22d Bomb Group on Okinawa.

Wade read the disappointment on my face and made me an offer. "Mike, you'll be going back stateside in a short while, probably
to an assignment you may not like or want. I'd be happy to have you
join me on Guam. I know I can get your assignment to Okinawa
changed. I promise that you won't be sorry if you choose to come
along. It would of course mean that you'd have to extend your overseas tour to take the assignment."

I thanked him for his faith in me and my work, but I hesitated to
accept his offer. An extension could add two more years to my tour,
and that was out of the question. I planned to leave as soon as possible and get married when I returned to the States.

I could see that Wade was disappointed, and I wished with all my
heart I could give him an affirmative reply. But I knew he understood. I'd soon celebrate my twenty-fifth birthday. He had his family with him and I had yet to start one. To delay my plans another
two years was not possible. Dave Wade had given me command of
the 99th Bombardment Squadron when I was only twenty-three years
old. That was almost two years before.

We reminisced about the things we'd done on Tinian and Clark
and the good times we'd had together. It wasn't easy for friends to
part. We made our stammering good-byes as men do who have
known each other, worked together, and admired each other. There
was no doubt he was destined for star rank.

It was years before I saw Dave Wade again; I visited him at his home
after he retired. He had received his stars, three of them.

I arrived at the 22d Bomb Group and was given limited duties
while awaiting orders for my transfer. In late October 1947, the orders arrived and I went home.

6 The Best of Times, the Worst of Times

I had been gone more than two years when I finally returned to Etna, Pennsylvania, my hometown. I knew that things would not be the same. I had last seen my family in April 1945, when everyone appeared to be doing well. A few months later I received a letter from my sister, Ann, informing me that our father had cancer. When I returned from a mission in August, I received news of his passing; a cablegram had been placed on my bunk. I was not surprised by the message but was shocked that the cable was seven days old. My father's burial had taken place days before.

My world had changed, and the process was not mine to control. The home and family I had known since infancy were gone. My mother was living with my sister and her husband. My younger brother, Frank, a P-51 pilot, had accepted his discharge in Fairbanks, Alaska, at war's end and was in business there.

I arrived at my sister's home late at night. Everyone was up waiting for me. We celebrated my homecoming by just sitting around talking, eating, and drinking. Being home after so long was just what I needed. It was my reassurance that everything was still all right with the world.

Most important after coming home was seeing the woman I was going to marry. I phoned Ethel; she'd expected me to call and didn't sound surprised when I said, "We're going out for dinner, take in a few clubs, and talk."

Ethel and I had met during our first days at school. She lived across the street from me with her parents, five brothers, and a sister. As children we played together. As teenagers we went to the movies, football games, dances, and other activities.

It was interesting how Ethel and I managed to get together for our first prom. She conned me into taking her, although she never admitted it. We were walking home from school when she asked if I was going to the prom. I hadn't given the matter much thought. Ethel said Warren Reynolds had asked her to go but she hadn't answered him yet. She knew I didn't get along with Warren. Ethel didn't look surprised when I said, "Why don't you go with me?"

"Okay," she said without hesitation.

Over dinner that night we talked about that first prom and had a good laugh, but we both knew what was really on our minds. Just as quickly as Ethel had said "okay" to the prom, she said yes to my proposal. We were married a month later. We left on an extended honeymoon and traveled down the East Coast to Florida before we arrived at Eglin Air Force Base.

The land around Eglin offered much in an aesthetic sense. There was the Gulf of Mexico, with its beautiful beaches and snow-white sand, reputed to be the whitest in the world. The area was interlaced with numerous bayous that branched off the large bay south of the military complex. The extensive beaches were dominated by huge sand dunes deposited and sculpted by countless hurricanes. There was usually a strong breeze that blew the sand along the beach. At night it looked like snow and even drifted as snow does.

Ethel and I fell in love with the area and made plans to build a home when we found a suitable site. Our plans took off when we met Lloyd Gibson, a local landowner who had a home on Cinco Bayou. We were shown a proposed site there with a beautiful view. By chance a brisk breeze was coming off the bayou. It was refreshing on a hot summer day. It was late afternoon as we surveyed the area and discussed building options. The sun was low on the horizon and soon would set behind the tall pines on the far shore. Ethel commented about the scene; the sunset was indescribably beautiful. We agreed to the terms proposed by Lloyd. We were finally going to have our own home.

My assignment at Eglin Air Force Base was with the Very Heavy Test Squadron. The operations officer was Capt. John Linebaugh, who introduced me to Capt. Les Urquhart, Capt. Joe Cotton, Lieutenants Coggins and Laightly, and a man I'll call Hewey. I don't want to embarrass him by using his real name.

The squadron had B-29s and B-50s, and a B-36 was due to arrive. In addition to test duties, we flew demonstrations about once a month. They were designed to show visiting dignitaries, usually influential members of Congress and leaders of the business community, the capabilities of the air force.

Interservice rivalries were a continuing feature of the quest for defense dollars, and the air force recognized the importance of good public relations. Considerable resources were expended to ensure successful, eye-popping firepower demonstrations. All types of aircraft were involved—jets, fighters, and bombers. My firepower mission was to drop 196 hundred-pound bombs on a simulated tank column.

After each demonstration, low-level passes were made in front of the stands to give spectators and the news media photo opportunities. One of these resulted in a tragic accident when F-84s made simulated gun runs on a formation of B-29s. One F-84, piloted by Major Johnson, encountered the bombers' prop wash. The F-84's wings collapsed, and it crashed in a gigantic explosion and fireball in front of the stands. A few years later, Johnson Hall was named in honor of the major.

Test flying was not the safest job, and Eglin's mission was operational testing. One test examined the interception of bombers by radar-directed fighters. The missions were flown at night regardless of weather. The fighter was an F-84 equipped with an advanced radar acquisition and firing system. I flew my share of the missions and never finished before midnight.

It was midwinter in north Florida—low gray clouds, steady rain, and bone-chilling cold but not freezing temperatures. It had been raining since sunup, and the prognosis for that night was not good. John Linebaugh called me into his office to say he had a problem. "Hewey's scheduled to fly tonight's intercept, and I'm afraid to send him up in weather as stinking as this. It will be raining all night, and the ceiling could be near minimums around midnight. I've flown with him in weather and he's weak. I think he's afraid. You'd do me and the outfit a favor if you'd take this mission."

"Damnit, John, that's not right. I've never asked anyone to cover for me. What the hell's he doing in a test outfit if he doesn't know how to fly?" Ethel was expecting me home and now I'd have to call her and say I had to work late. "Why me?" I asked.

"You're the only one who hasn't flown today."

That was true, but I'd worked all day on details of the previous day's test flights.

John knew I was unhappy about the situation and gave me what was probably his most effective argument for the switch. "Mike, Hewey's excitable in tight situations. He could wipe out a whole crew. You've got to take the flight. That's all there is to it."

"Whatever you say, John." I called Ethel, who was not happy about the situation.

It was still raining, cold, and windy, and the ceiling was reported as four hundred feet variable. It was pitch-dark taking off over the Gulf, and I was immediately on the gauges. All four engines operated with an overly rich mixture, which caused them to torch. The flaming exhausts (two on each engine) lit up the area around the plane in an eerie glow as we climbed through rain and clouds into the blackness of the night.

I wondered how the F-84 pilot felt with the weather being so poor. As an afterthought I wondered if he too had replaced another pilot. I was not in a good mood but knew I shouldn't have such thoughts. We climbed to twenty thousand feet, then received radar vectors to a position over the Gulf where we orbited until instructed to proceed toward Eglin. That's all there was to it. I could have done as well when I was a cadet. What was so difficult?

We listened to the chatter on the test frequency. The F-84 pilot was given vectors to intercept us. He was directed to a position about a mile off our tail. He interpreted his radar to close in for the kill. The B-29 exterior lights were off, so the intercept, if accomplished, would be entirely the work of the fighter's radar system. The F-84 automatically locked on the target when within range.

We went through the drill a couple of times, then the F-84 returned to Eglin to refuel. The test continued when he returned, and we worked until 1:00 A.M. It was a good night's work, one of the best in the test program.

We received radar vectors to the base, made a ground-controlled approach (GCA), and landed. The ceiling had dropped to three hundred feet—no challenge for a pilot flying an aircraft as stable as a B-29. It was well after two in the morning when I got home. I was bushed and decided that my next duty day would start when I felt like getting up. I had a nightcap before going to bed and wondered how Hewey enjoyed his night off.

By early 1949, Ethel and I had settled down nicely in our new home on Cinco Bayou. Not many families had built there, but more and more people were arriving. I bought a sailboat and built a dock. After much backbreaking labor, such as clearing brush and palmetto, Ethel and I had a respectable lawn. We put in a circular driveway and a concrete parking pad for the car. In March we found out that Ethel was pregnant. We began the usual preparations that expectant parents always seem to overdo.

The services were always fair game for the budget crunchers, so it was not surprising that Eglin's operating funds were hit. The cutbacks affected benefits taken for granted by military people, such as medical care. Eglin could barely take care of its active-duty people, so dependent care was available only in emergencies. Thus we had to rely on civilian doctors in Fort Walton (there were two) for Ethel's prenatal care and delivery of the baby. There wasn't a hospital in Fort Walton, so Eglin made its delivery room available to local doctors caring for military dependents. But I, not the air force, paid the doctor. The situation caused us financial problems, but we managed. In those days we took such things in stride.

By midsummer, Ethel's condition showed. September brought unexpected news: I was selected to attend the Air Tactical School at Tyndall Air Force Base at Panama City, Florida, so Ethel and I found an apartment and moved there. I would be on temporary duty and return to Eglin after graduation.

Ethel continued to see her doctor in Fort Walton. In October he prescribed iron pills for her, because tests indicated a slight anemic condition. He cautioned Ethel to be alert to any abnormal occurrence and, although the baby was not due until late November, not to be surprised if she went into labor earlier. She was to get in touch with me immediately and I was to drop whatever I was doing and bring her to the hospital.

It happened on November 17. Ethel called me at school to say she was having contractions. I hurried home and we threw her prepacked things in the car and were off to the hospital at Eglin. The doctor checked Ethel and said it wasn't time. He kept her, sent me home, and said, "Call me in the morning."

The next day nothing had changed. I went to class but called every hour during the breaks. I could tell by the responses that my calls were expected but not with enthusiasm. I returned to Eglin after class.

I was a typical first-time expectant father, bothering everybody and being a general nuisance. A hospital staff member said it would probably be a long night and it might be wise to get some dinner. That was good advice. At least it got me out of the way.

I returned and tried to take a nap but woke up every few minutes. It was well past midnight when a nurse approached me. "It's a boy. Everyone's all right and doing fine."

It was 3:00 A.M. on November 19, 1949. Later I saw my son, then Ethel. She was still groggy and didn't make much sense when she talked. But I remember quite clearly her saying, "He's a beautiful baby." Then I fell asleep.

Five days later I took Ethel and Michael Joseph Jr. home. I was amazed how a young mother knew just what to do. Ethel settled down to her motherly duties while I continued my classes and looked forward to graduation in a few weeks. Our future looked promising.

Ethel and I were relaxing one evening after dinner when the manager of the apartment complex knocked on our door. He said there was a phone call for me at his office. I wondered who would call me at such a late hour.

"How's everything going at the Air Tactical School?" It was Les Urquhart, from the squadron.

"Everything's all right. I'm ready to graduate in a few days. We get our class standings tomorrow, and I'm supposed to be in the upper 10 percent. Ethel and the baby are fine. What's new at the squadron?"

Les stammered and stuttered as if he didn't know what to say. I didn't know what to think but could tell he was troubled. He finally found the nerve to do what he had been ordered to do. "Mike, I've got to let you know that you've been selected for the next RIF [reduction in force]. I'm sorry as all hell to have to tell you this."

The news took the wind right out of my sails. It was as if someone had hit me in the pit of the stomach in an unguarded moment and left me breathless. "I don't believe it. What kind of joke is this?"

"It's no joke, Mike. I wish it were."

It began to sink in. I was about to be sacked. Unceremoniously sacked. All of us at the Air Tactical School knew of an impending reduction in force, but I never dreamed it would hit me. I had survived too many RIFs. As if trying to find some error, I asked Les, "Does the squadron commander know about me being selected?"

"Mike, he's the one who selected you. He also selected Lieutenant Laightly. The levy came down to the command, and they put the onus on the squadrons. Just about every unit at Eglin was affected. It's the largest RIF in years. It was ordered by Secretary of Defense Johnson in order to help balance the budget."

I could not understand how my commander had chosen me. It would have been easier to accept if air force headquarters had made the selection. My commander thought so little of me that he didn't bother to investigate my standing in the class, didn't consider that my wife had just given birth to our first child, and had a subordinate use a phone to tell me of the end of my military career.

I groped for an answer to resolve my state of mind. "Is the colonel aware of the fact that my wife had a baby just three weeks ago?" I shouted. I was angry, and Les was the only one at whom I could vent my spleen. "And why the hell are *you* giving me the bad news? Why didn't *he* have the courtesy to tell me personally what he did and why? That cowardly bastard."

I thought of the time I had commanded a squadron more than three times the size of his. I never had anyone take care of my unpleasant duties. I always met my responsibilities head-on, pleasant or not.

Les tried to give me a hint about Lieutenant Colonel Dreckopf's actions. "Mike, I think your being away at school may have been the reason you were selected. The squadron was meeting its obligations while you were gone, and, as illogical as it sounds, the CO used that fact as his rationale for picking you. His reason for selecting Laightly was that he had not qualified as an aircraft commander. I don't know if the CO felt he could pick you and not have to face you when it was time to give you the bad news. I agree that he should be talking to you about this, not me."

I knew that what Les said was probably true. He'd been privy to conversations in the commander's office. After all, he was the squadron adjutant. "Les, you tell Colonel Dreckopf that I'm mad as hell and I consider it an act of outright cowardice to use the telephone to inform a young officer of the end of his career. Furthermore, delegating such a mission to one of his underlings is the most craven act I can recall in all my years of service."

The way I saw it, Dreckopf should have talked to me as one officer to another. He owed me that. I'd seen RIFs where the selections were made by air force headquarters. Even so, commanders made efforts to personally inform affected officers of the news, especially to express their dismay and disbelief about the selections.

Les interrupted my thoughts. "Mike, what do you want me to tell the colonel? Are you going to stay to finish the course, or are you coming back to Eglin as soon as you can? You only have sixty days left on duty. You might not want to waste time with a school that will do you no good now."

"Look, Les, I was sent here to attend the Air Tactical School, and by God I'm staying here to finish it and graduate. My personal sense of responsibility guides me in that direction. You can tell Dreckopf that I'll see him when I return, if he can find the backbone to face me." With that I slammed down the receiver. Later I was sorry I didn't give Les a chance to say something. In my moment of anger, I ignored the fact that we were friends. He was given a repugnant task and had no choice but to obey his commander's orders.

I took a deep breath and tried to sort out what had happened and why. It was all so confusing; nothing seemed to make sense. When I commanded the 99th Bomb Squadron, my group commander, Colonel Wade, gave me an efficiency rating of superior, then the highest possible. I considered all the arguments indicating that my selection for discharge was a mistake. It took a while, but I realized that it was an exercise in futility. My head was spinning as I walked back to our apartment trying to decide what to do next. I had to tell Ethel what happened; it wouldn't be right to make up a story. Lying would only lead to more lying in an attempt to keep the unpleasant news from her. Sooner or later I'd have to face the truth. In sixty days I'd have to tell her I was being kicked out of the air force. I had never lied to Ethel, and I was not going to lie to her now. In that moment of great personal trauma, I felt sorrow beyond measure and utmost compassion for my wife and child. I wondered what the future held for them.

"Who was on the phone?" Ethel asked as I entered our apartment. "Who wanted you at this late hour?"

"It was Les Urquhart."

"You two had a lot to talk about. You've been gone over half an hour," she said.

"Les had some important news, and none of it was good." I almost choked on my words. "I'm on the next RIF list. Les said I'll be a civilian in sixty days. You sure picked a bummer for a husband and father for your kid."

I saw the shocked look on Ethel's face. Her eyes became watery, and in an instant the tears flowed as she sobbed into her cupped hands. "You poor man. It's not fair, it's not fair. You've worked so hard."

It was obvious we were concerned for each other more than for ourselves.

"Who else is getting out, or are you the only one?" she asked, looking at me through her tears.

I told her that Laightly was on the list, and she commented that we two were the newest members of the squadron.

"How could they have picked you? Don't they realize that we just had a baby? You've worked so hard for the squadron and at the school. You're way up in the class standing. Doesn't that mean anything? You've taken flights and missions for the other pilots. I don't remember anybody taking flights for you. What are we going to do? What's going to happen to little Mike?"

Ethel continued sobbing. I was angry because I couldn't do anything to allay her fears. I didn't have ready answers.

"Don't worry," I said. "I'll think of something. It will do us no good to panic. The best thing we can do now is get a good night's sleep and have clear heads in the morning. I've got a few more days of school, then we can go home. I'm sure things will look better back on the bayou."

We went to bed. Little Mike was asleep, but there was the mid-morning bottle to look forward to. Try as we might, we couldn't rest. We both got up for the morning feeding. Ethel smiled for the first time since learning I was to be kicked out of the air force. She was at peace with the world as she looked at her son, so snug in her loving arms. I knew then that everything would be okay.

I reported for class the next day as usual and received my class standing. I was forty-ninth out of 750. That put me in the top 7 percent. I suppose that was my reward for taking the course seriously, but it meant nothing as far as my career was concerned. Strange, but I recalled the words of the school commandant when he spoke to the class on the first day. "You have been selected for attendance at this course of instruction because of your record. Your past performance shows that you have the potential for duties and assignments of greater responsibility. You are the future leaders of the air force."

I wondered what he'd say if I told him I'd be kicked out in less than sixty days? Such thoughts were not doing me any good and didn't offer a solution. It was as if I felt sorry for myself, which I definitely was not. Mad as hell, yes, but not sorry.

The squadron finally sent me written notice of my selection for the RIF and informed me that my separation from the service was scheduled for February 11, 1950. Dreckopf signed the letter with no additional comment. I really didn't expect anything more of him. It was the usual form letter with the usual trite phrases, handed out to thousands of young officers, many of whom were simply at the wrong place at the wrong time. The phrase that really hurt was, "Your being selected for discharge is no reflection on the past performance of your duties." Then why were we selected? Nobody ever came up with a satisfactory answer to that question.

Ethel and I and little Mike returned to our home on the bayou the day after graduation. We were busy with housekeeping chores and converting the spare room into a suitable nursery.

I had a meeting with Linebaugh, who said he was shocked by my selection for the RIF. He told me I wasn't going to be scheduled to fly. I could have been vindictive by asking if he was sure he didn't need me to cover one of his pilots when the weather turned sour, but I dropped the matter.

I didn't have to worry about social obligations at Eglin. Ethel and I didn't receive any invitations to the parties and activities that usually took place during the holidays. Not a soul from our test squadron visited us, and we didn't receive any Christmas cards or congratulations on the birth of our son. It seemed as if we were no better than lepers as far as the Eglin community was concerned. Until now I had no idea of the far-reaching effects of the RIF.

It was not the best of times for our small family. Although Ethel regained her strength and recovered from the effects of childbirth, the continuous worry about the RIF and developing a source of income had a debilitating impact on us. Little Mike, on the other hand, did well and was oblivious to the trials and tribulations of his parents.

At times such as we experienced, it helped to get a new frame of reference, to get away from it all. A visit to our families seemed to offer the medicine we so desperately needed. Ethel and I looked forward to the visit, and I wanted to see an old friend, a mentor who had befriended me when I was a young, impressionable sixteen-year-old. Tom Trimble Jr. was like another father to me.

The trip to Pennsylvania took two days. We didn't tell either family about the RIF but did say we were going to leave the air force. They wondered what our plans were and thought it highly unusual that we'd leave the service so soon after the birth of our son. We told them I wanted to go into business in Florida.

I made an appointment with Tom to have lunch with Ethel and me. We had not seen him since our wedding two years earlier. I explained what had happened and told him of my limited options. I said I'd probably go into business in Fort Walton, because our home was there. I asked what he thought and if he had any suggestions.

He asked if we had money set aside and I told him we had enough to meet our expenses for at least six months. He said he could put me to work with his construction business but would rather see me work out my problem.

"Mike, be your own boss. I know you have the ability to succeed in the business world. Just don't do anything foolish. Don't go for the fast buck; be steady and reliable and, above all, honest." He continued, "I've known you over ten years. I know your family; they brought you up right. I know you have what it takes. You've married a beautiful woman and you have a son. Don't think the world gave you a raw deal. Instead turn it around and look at your situation as an opportunity to explore new horizons, to meet new challenges, to prove to yourself that you're a far better man than the circumstances indicate."

I thanked Tom for his advice. The lunch was a pleasant experience for Ethel; it was her first chance to get to know Tom. She thanked him for the beautiful Swedish glassware that he and his wife, Henrietta, had sent as a wedding present. I told Tom that Ethel wouldn't let me use the glasses, that they were kept in a cabinet in our dining room. He laughed and said I shouldn't expect Ethel to set aside that restriction.

We spent ten days with our families and had a marvelous time. It was our first chance in months to get out by ourselves. The change of pace did wonders for us, and for the first time I felt at ease about my upcoming discharge.

It was bright, clear, and cold as we left for the warmer weather of Florida. We were tired when we got home, but little Mike had been an excellent traveler. He slept most of the trip.

I had just a few days of active duty remaining when I found a good location on the main street of Fort Walton to open a restaurant. I had an extensive background in the business; I'd been a mess officer and twice managed officers' clubs. I would be the owner and manager of the business. I secured a lease and was ready for work as soon as I left the air force.

Laightly and I were called for a meeting with Lieutenant Colonel Dreckopf in early February 1950, a few days before our discharge. During the weeks prior to separation, we hadn't had one word of explanation from him, not one offer of assistance in preparation for civilian life, and not one word of encouragement. What Dreckopf would say at this stage was a mystery.

This meeting should have been a one-on-one situation. In my case it should have dealt with the personal trauma of rejection by the service I'd been a member of for more than nine years. The meeting was almost two months late. If higher headquarters had not decreed that it take place, Dreckopf would probably have found a way to be unavailable. I wasn't looking forward to the meeting. I'd long ago lost my desire for a confrontation with him.

As Laightly and I entered Dreckopf's office, we were not offered seats, although chairs were available. We just stood before his desk like a couple of ne'er-do-wells about to be reprimanded. He didn't acknowledge us by name. I saw no need for a salute, although it was customary. He stuttered and stammered as he rambled on while complying with the dictates of higher command. He finally stated that budgetary constraints were responsible for the air force's decision for drastic personnel cuts, and we were the victims of that decision. He also said if we wished or were in financial straits we could enlist with the rank of master sergeant. This was the only assistance offered since we'd been told of our RIF. He didn't even advise us of the opportunity of joining the Air Reserve or the Air National Guard. Neither Laightly nor I said a word. We were not asked any questions or offered an opportunity to make any statements. Dreckopf told us where to report for discharge, then stood and said, "That's it." He'd done his duty. We left his office, having uttered not a word.

After the meeting, I told Laightly about my decision to go into the restaurant business in Fort Walton. He said he wasn't able to do anything like that. He and his wife were going to move in with his parents until he could find a job. He was totally lost and demoralized. He was not alone; the RIF had long-lasting effects on many families.

I reported to the discharge point on February 11, 1950, my last day on active duty. Laightly joined me a few minutes later. We were in a long, dimly lit room with a row of desks for administrative personnel. I went down that long row, signed papers at a couple of stations, and handed in my military identification card. There was little or no conversation or military courtesy. It seemed that even the enlisted people were briefed about our situation and apparently saw no need to render honors to a couple of rejects.

I found it hard to believe that the air force had no transition program to smooth our way to civilian life. There was no provision for hardship cases, illness, or emergencies. I thanked God we were all well. I didn't receive severance or terminal leave pay after more than nine years of service, which included all of World War II, from the day of the Pearl Harbor attack to the Japanese surrender.

I received a check for eleven days' pay. At the last desk a specialist had me sign my Certificate of Service, WDAGO Form 53-98. The air force used blank army forms; I was not even discharged with an air force document. The specialist slid a manila envelope across the desk and said, "That's yours too." It was all over. I was a full-fledged civilian.

What a difference between coming in and going out, I thought. When I was graduated from flight school, a major general welcomed me aboard and gave me my wings. Now, as I was leaving the air force, an unnamed specialist handed me a discharge and shoved a manila envelope across the desk in my general direction. Oh well. Sic transit gloria mundi. How soon they forget. I went home to Ethel and little Mike.

This was a new beginning for us, so Ethel and I had a small celebration. That evening we barbecued some steaks and had a bottle of wine, which we didn't have a problem draining. After dinner we made a couple of phone calls to let our families know that I was out of the air force and keep them up to date about our situation. All they seemed interested in was the doings of little Mike.

The next day I was hard at work at the restaurant. It opened on schedule and did far better than I ever dreamed. In the early weeks and months of operation, I devoted many hours every day, seven days a week, to making certain that the business prospered. It did. I expanded into other business ventures in Fort Walton, with similar success.

Four months after I left the air force, war broke out in Korea. I was not called back to active duty because I was not in a reserve unit. I also suspect there was resistance to bringing back individuals so recently labeled as rejects.

Ethel and I were extremely happy with the way things were going. She was pregnant again and on November 25, 1951, gave birth to a beautiful girl, Patricia Ellen.

The Korean War continued with little change. I wanted to make my contribution to the war effort, so I applied for active duty. I was assigned to Maxwell Air Force Base, and attended the Air Command

and Staff School. My business enterprises were handled by a capable manager.

Ethel and the two children had a good time in Montgomery. Little Mike was three years old and Patty was one and walking; they kept their mother busy. But we still had time for a full social life and entertained frequently.

The Air Command and Staff School at Maxwell was on a much higher level than the Air Tactical School at Tyndall. I studied hard, but there was stiff competition among the officers in the class. I didn't do as well as at the Air Tactical School but managed to graduate in the middle of the class.

The war in Korea reached a stalemate. The front fluctuated, with neither side gaining an advantage. It was like a heavyweight boxing match in which both fighters were almost out of wind; they possessed knockout punches but couldn't deliver the blow. Eventually an armistice was arranged and I left active duty. We returned to our home on the bayou, where I resumed my business activities.

Ethel and I had become reacquainted with a normal lifestyle while at Maxwell, where I worked a typical five-day week and had weekends off. My businesses at Fort Walton Beach were successful and I enjoyed the benefits of a good income, but I was losing touch with my growing family. Some days I didn't see them except when they were asleep. Business problems frequently required my personal attention and I'd be gone for hours. I got tired of the rat race and sold my businesses.

The area was growing and I had no difficulty finding employment; I became the manager of a private club. A third child, Jean Marie, was added to our growing family on March 24, 1954.

I had a reserve assignment at Eglin Air Force Base with the Directorate of Plans and Programs and was promoted to lieutenant colonel in 1955. I had been RIFed as a captain in 1950 and promoted to lieutenant colonel five years later. It didn't make sense.

The short stint in the air force and my reserve assignment at Eglin got me back to flying, and I realized how much I missed it. I should have been satisfied but kept alert for a flying job.

My opportunity arrived when I answered a call from a friend with Southern Airways. The company was in need of pilots for their schools, and I was promised a position with the airline when its projected expansion materialized. In the meantime, I took a job at Bainbridge Air Base in Georgia as a flight instructor in the T-37, the "Tweetie Bird." Some called it the Converter, because it converted JP-4 into noise. I stayed there until the contract with the air force expired, then I was sent to instruct helicopter pilots for the army at Fort Wolters in Texas. I went to the airline from there and was assigned to the Southern Airways Atlanta base.

We settled into a beautiful home in a good neighborhood, and the children were enrolled in a private school. We were pleasantly surprised when Ethel again became pregnant. In due time we were blessed with a fourth child, John Mark, born at Piedmont General Hospital on March 22, 1963. He was a welcomed addition to the family.

I maintained my affiliation with the Air Reserve and was aware of the trouble in Southeast Asia. Our presence in Vietnam was growing, but the anticipated results were not forthcoming. The communist insurgency there was gaining ground whereas the government of South Vietnam seemed to be floundering. President Diem and his brother were killed by their own military in Saigon, and the news surprised no one.

But the assassination of President Kennedy in Dallas was a heart-wrenching catastrophe. It seemed that assassination was the accepted method of removing people whose philosophical, ideological, and political beliefs conflicted with those who had different agendas.

I was shocked by the senseless killing of the president. Watching the funeral procession, I saw his small son salute the caisson as the cortege passed. The president's son and mine shared the same name and were the same age. The scene had a profound, lasting effect on me. I decided to accept the president's challenge and do something for my country.

I told the director of reserve activities at Eglin that I wanted a tour of active duty. My aviation experience would be of great value in training new pilots. I reminded him of my qualifications in reciprocating engines, jets, and helicopters and of my extensive training background.

The director said that he appreciated my work with the Air Force Reserve and my request for active duty was laudable, but acceptance was doubtful. The air force was top heavy with field-grade officers, and as a senior lieutenant colonel I would exacerbate an already serious staffing problem. I accepted the explanation but was taken aback when he added, "I should think an individual of your age would be ready to settle down and not be looking for action. You could be sent to Vietnam if you were on duty."

I was only forty-one years old; I wasn't ready for a rocking chair. I told Ethel about the discussion with the director. She felt that he had made sense. "Don't you think you're a little old for that kind of duty?" she asked. It really hit me.

I was "deadheading" on a company flight to Eglin for a weekend drill when the captain, an army reservist, told me that his service was seeking volunteers for three-year tours. I told him that the air force wasn't enthusiastic about my effort to go on active duty. Half jokingly he said, "Why don't you volunteer for duty with the army?"

I learned that the army had a special program to recruit pilots trained and rated by the other services. I got an application form for active duty with army aviation and showed it to Ethel. "You're serious about this, aren't you?" she said.

I thought the matter over. There would be a reduction in pay, something I didn't mention to Ethel. A problem was giving up my Air Force Reserve lieutenant colonel's position for an army chief warrant officer slot. Then there was Southern Airways, which I'd have to inform. I wondered what Everett Martin, Southern's vice president for personnel, would say.

I realized I was thinking as if the army had already accepted my application. What was I doing, and why? I suppose everyone has moments of irrationality, and I was having mine. I mailed my application to the army the next day. I felt relieved. I did what I thought was proper, and my future was now in the hands of others.

It was early summer 1964 when I returned from a flight to Charlotte, North Carolina. Ethel greeted me and said I had a big, fat letter from the army. It had been six months since I'd sent in my application for active duty. It looked as though I finally had an answer. I was almost afraid to open it. Suppose the army wanted me on its team?

What have I gotten myself into? I thought as I opened the envelope. There was a cover letter informing me of my acceptance into the army aviation program and some names and phone numbers to call if I needed assistance or explanation of the contents. The envelope also contained several copies of orders to report for active duty with the 6th Special Forces Group, a Green Beret unit at Fort Bragg, North Carolina. I showed the letter and a copy of my orders to Ethel.

"I was afraid it would come to this," she said. "What are you going to tell the people at Southern? I'll bet they'll be surprised and not at all happy."

I had time to think about the situation. I'd heard about the Green Berets and their reputation. By some accounts they were an unsavory lot, involved in all types of clandestine operations. I knew them as favorites of the late President Kennedy. If they were admired by him, I would be more than happy to be part of their organization. But I did not understand why the army thought I could be an asset to such an outfit.

I called Southern the next day. "Everett, I've received orders calling me to active duty with the army within the month," I said bluntly.

There was a considerable silence. "You're not joking, are you, Mike? We're not at war; there's no national emergency. Why the hell should they want you?"

I stretched the facts. "They asked me to accept an active-duty tour about six months ago and I agreed. Hell, Everett, I had completely forgotten about it."

He said he didn't have a replacement for me and I should call the army and ask for a delay until fall. I said it wasn't proper for me to make the call, but if he wanted a delay he should arrange it. I gave him the names and phone numbers.

I made my scheduled flights the next day and got home late in the evening. Ethel said that Everett Martin had called: The army granted the delay. It gave me time to prepare for a sensible transition to military life, an entirely new life—one with the army.

When the new orders arrived, I was given a reporting date of September 2, 1964. My plans were to fly off my line of time in August, then leave for Fort Bragg. If all went as scheduled, I'd be able to complete flying for Southern by the last week of the month.

All was going as planned when the aviation assignments officer at the Department of the Army called. He voiced his concern about my aeronautical rating; it had been given me by the Army Air Forces, which ceased to exist when the air force was created. He said it would be best to be officially rated as an army aviator by one of the army's aviation schools. He told me to go to Fort Wolters in Texas to get an army aviator rating before reporting to Fort Bragg. That was the extent of his instructions. Unaware of all the ramifications of the call, I didn't ask for more detailed instructions or an amendment to my orders. I didn't even bother to get the officer's name or phone number.

It was an idiotic situation. I was to go to Fort Wolters and ask to be given an army aeronautical rating. I did not have documentation for such a request. The only thing I had was orders placing me on active duty at Fort Bragg. What a bucket of worms.

I finished flying with Southern on August 25 just about as planned. I had plenty of time and decided to leave for Wolters in a couple of days. I said my good-byes to my friends and fellow pilots, who all knew I was leaving for the army. The last two pilots I saw as I left Southern operations were Terry Knight and Bill Chagares. Their parting words to me were, "Be careful the Viet Cong don't get you in Vietnam."

7 You're in the Army Now

When I arrived at Fort Wolters on August 27, 1964, I was told that all transient quarters were taken. I went into Mineral Wells and got a room at the Holiday Inn. It was late afternoon, so I decided to wait until morning to sign in at Wolters.

Mineral Wells was not noted for its flourishing nightlife, so I went to the officers' club. I had a fine dinner, then went to the bar, which was packed, but I didn't see anyone I knew. Most of the officers were young and, I assumed, students going through flight training. There was the inevitable bevy of beautiful young women found at all service flying schools. I knew from years of experience that some would get lucky and their relationships would lead to marriage, whereas others would be disappointed when the men of their dreams completed training, never to be seen or heard from again. Not to worry, though; a new flight class would soon arrive with possibilities for new relationships.

I felt ill at ease. I was old enough to be the father of most people in the place. I had to change my attitude; I had to swim with the tide.

The next day I went to Wolters to sign in and find someone who could grant me an army aviator's rating. I had no idea who that might be or what I'd have to do. The Department of the Army hadn't given me the name of anyone to contact or an office to report to. The only orders I had were those assigning me to active duty at Fort Bragg. I concluded that my situation was absolutely insane.

I knew where flight operations was, but much had changed since I'd last seen the installation. I was troubled because I didn't see any familiar faces. I went into operations and was greeted by a civilian seated at a desk. There weren't any military people around, so I un-loaded the problem on him. His methods may not have been army, but he took charge and handled the situation in an expeditious man-ner. He didn't challenge me or ask for identification, even though I was dressed casually in a short-sleeved shirt, slacks, and loafers. I didn't have military identification, dog tags, a uniform, or anything in the way of flight gear.

I told him that the Department of the Army had sent me to get a rating as an army aviator. I handed him a copy of my orders assign-ing me to Special Forces at Fort Bragg and told him that's where I would be headed as soon as I got the aeronautical rating. He asked if I knew how to fly the H-23 helicopter; I told him I had instructed in it for a few months. He asked me where I had my flight gear; I said I didn't have any.

"Well, if we're to give you a rating as an army aviator, we've got to give you a check ride," he said. "Come with me." We went into a room that contained a row of lockers. He checked a few and found a flight suit he said should fit. It was at least a size too large, but it had to do. I tried a helmet; it was about the right size. He changed into his flight clothes, got his helmet and gloves, and took me to the flight line.

We made a quick preflight of an H-23. That done, he entered our names in the aircraft logbook and asked if I was ready to fly. I an-swered in the affirmative.

He had me start the engine and make the engine run-up and the magneto checks, then told me to pick the helicopter up to a hover. He handled the radio transmissions as I proceeded to the takeoff po-sition. Although I had not flown a helicopter for some time, I was surprised how well it went. The check pilot gave me a heading to one of the stage fields in the Wolters complex. After telling me to enter the traffic pattern, he had me demonstrate a normal approach and landing.

I made an approach that he should have liked, but he said, "Around here we make those a little steeper. Now make a maximum performance takeoff and a steep approach." I made the max take-off and he didn't comment, but I knew that the maneuver was satis-factory. I continued in the traffic pattern and, remembering his com-ment about my normal approach, made what I thought was a steep approach that he would like. He commented, "Around here we don't make them quite that steep. Let's take off and get out of here."

I made a normal takeoff and left the traffic pattern. We soon were flying over a paved road when he cut the throttle. He wanted to see my forced landing procedure, so I autorotated straight ahead and landed on the road. He said, "Okay, I've got it," and he flew us back to the heliport at Wolters. The entire episode lasted a mere half hour. That check ride was the basis for the people at Fort Wolters to designate me a bona fide army aviator. My old air force associates would have been aghast at such footloose procedures. We hadn't even filed a flight plan.

I knew then that flying for the army was going to be a new experience. I'd have to set aside all the strictures and regulations so common in the air force. I thought of my early days in the Army Air Forces of World War II and realized that I was returning to military flying such as I knew as a young second lieutenant.

The check pilot took me to an office that was the administrative center of the installation. A copy of the orders calling me to active duty and an oral statement from the check pilot were the only evidence in support of my becoming an army aviator. As I handed a copy of my orders to the clerk, someone behind me called out rather loudly, "Mike Novosel. What the hell are you doing here at Fort Wolters?"

I turned and saw Dexter Nash, one of the division chiefs at Fort Wolters and an old friend. He said he was glad to see me but was incredulous at my being here to become an army warrant officer aviator. He knew I was a lieutenant colonel in the Air Force Reserve. He asked if I'd given up my commission in the air force.

I replied that I hoped not. In fact I hadn't notified anyone at my reserve headquarters of my actions. I knew that in due time the air force would know that I was in the army. "When my tour of duty with the army is over, I hope to resume my affiliation with the Air Force Reserve," I said.

Dexter didn't think I'd embarked on an intelligent course of action. His choice of words were somewhat more earthy. I stated that he was probably correct but the deed was done; there was no turning back.

Dexter invited me into his office, where we had coffee and engaged in the usual small talk of pilots who hadn't seen each other in a while. I told him it was important for me to be on my way as soon as the matter of the aeronautical rating was resolved. Dexter said I'd have my rating in the morning and there was just one more thing to do. He had his secretary prepare a "Certificate of Training," which he presented to me. It was a document certifying that I had attended a special "Q" course (qualification course). I was somewhat amused in that I had amassed a grand total of thirty minutes' flying time. Dexter told me that the certificate was the only one of its kind. We had a big laugh when the mock graduation ceremony was over.

Then Dexter said he'd see me at the club if I'd be there that evening; he'd try to round up a few of our other acquaintances.

What a day. I was a casually dressed civilian, without military identification, without TDY orders, requesting and receiving an aeronautical rating from the army. No one had asked to see my flight physical (I didn't have a copy, and the one that existed was probably out of date). I felt good about the day and looked forward to duty at Fort Bragg.

I went to the officers' club and saw two old friends waiting for me—J. J. Greenhalgh and Jim Guthrie. When Dexter arrived with another old friend, Jack Rowan, he told everyone I'd volunteered for active duty with the army. Their comments were generally in line with Dexter's assessment of the situation. I said that the decision—right or wrong, good or bad—was mine and it was final. The subject was dropped and we concentrated on having a good time.

The rest of the evening was spent drinking, telling stories, and enjoying one another's company. We broke up the session when informed that the bar and club were closing. I didn't know if I'd ever see any of the men again. In the morning I picked up the orders designating me an army aviator; they were dated September 1, 1964. Two days later I celebrated my forty-second birthday and reported for duty at Fort Bragg.

I'd never been to Bragg. After a few stops to ask for directions, I was at a two-story wood building (circa World War II), where I reported to Special Forces. My first contact with Special Forces aviation was Lt. Col. Marquis D. Hilbert. I gave him copies of my orders assigning me to Bragg and designating me an army aviator. He seemed confused. If I were in his position, I'd have been confused too. He saw a forty-two-year-old reporting for duty with the army's elite Special Forces, dressed in a short-sleeved shirt, slacks, and a pair of casual loafers. I told him I had just arrived from Fort Wolters, where I received my aeronautical rating. He asked if I had attended the rotary-wing aviator course. I replied no but told him about the thirty-minute check ride and how I overcompensated the steep approach after being too shallow on the normal approach. He laughed and said he knew the experience.

He asked if I had any identification; I replied that I had only my driver's license and an airline employee card. He asked about my uniform. When I said I didn't have one, he threw up his arms. "You mean to tell me that you were at an army installation, flew army aircraft, were not in uniform, had no military ID, and were awarded army aeronautical orders, and no one bothered to ask for identification?"

"That's right."

"You mean to tell me all that occurred without someone checking with higher authority?" Hilbert continued.

"Well, I did show orders assigning me to Fort Bragg and that seemed to satisfy them. That plus the explanation that I was there at the direction of DA [Department of the Army]."

Colonel Hilbert thought for a moment. "I can't believe that things could be so loose. Hell, you could have been an enemy agent."

I nodded in agreement. "I was surprised myself that it wasn't more difficult, but you've got to remember that no one challenged my presence at Fort Bragg either. Everyone was more than helpful directing me to your office."

We settled down to a general discussion of flying and my background in aviation. The colonel was a likeable person, always seemed to have a smile on his face, and had an enormous sense of humor. He said he was glad to have me on board even though I was out of uniform. He added that although the army was short of aviators, Special Forces had some of the most experienced found in any service, and my experience in many types of aircraft would augment that reputation.

"You're being assigned to the 6th Aviation Company, commanded by Captain Leroy Hoeffler. I'm sure you'll fit right in. They can use someone with your background. First they'll have to outfit you with uniforms. We can't have you wearing a green beret with those casual clothes. I'll call Hoeffler and tell him you're coming."

It was too late in the afternoon to report to the company, so Colonel Hilbert suggested I go to billeting for temporary quarters and report to Hoeffler in the morning. After a long day of traveling, the suggestion was welcome.

I was at the company orderly room bright and early, still in civilian clothes. I asked for Captain Hoeffler but had to wait a short while until he arrived. I could imagine the thoughts of the people in the orderly room. They had a forty-two-year-old civilian sitting there waiting to see the commanding officer. That I was one of their new army aviators was probably the last thought that could have come to mind. When Hoeffler arrived, I introduced myself: "I'm Mike Novosel. Colonel Hilbert directed me to report to you."

Leroy Hoeffler was in his late thirties, a few inches taller than I, and slightly overweight. I thought he was a little old to be a captain. Evidently the army had personnel staffing problems similar to those of the air force. Hoeffler shook my hand and asked me to step into his office. I took a seat across from his desk.

The captain, who had been told that I had considerable aviation experience, asked if I'd flown any army aircraft. I said that the aircraft I'd flown in World War II had "US ARMY" on the wings, so, yes, I'd flown army aircraft. Hoeffler looked surprised. "Marquis didn't say you flew in World War II. He just said you'd flown with the air force."

I added that I was a B-29 aircraft commander in the war, was on active duty when the air force was established, and served during the Korean conflict.

When Hoeffler heard that the only army aircraft I had flown lately was the H-23, he said I'd be qualified in the CH-34. He finally turned to the occasion's more important issues: uniforms, identification card, dog tags, and processing through finance. Captain Hoeffler assigned Warrant Officer Meeks, a recent flight school graduate, to help me. He had a week to transform me from a civilian into an army aviator of the elite Special Forces.

Meeks had a number of years of prior army enlisted service and knew his way around Fort Bragg, the army, and its bureaucracy. He knew the right sergeant to see in each office, and I had my identification card, dog tags, and finance records before lunch. The first item he had me purchase was a pair of boots, then he had me outfitted with a flight helmet and flight suits. At least I could present myself at the company's ready room and on the flight line. I also purchased a class A uniform, shirts, socks, underwear, and fatigue uniforms. I was issued a couple of Special Forces jungle fatigues, jungle boots, and my green beret. Meeks did his job well. He made a proper Green Beret trooper out of a sloppily dressed civilian. I was ready to go to work.

I was no sooner fitted out with uniforms and flight gear than I was told that the unit was scheduled for its monthly ten-mile night march. Hoeffler said I should attempt the march but not to worry because a military ambulance always brought up the rear. Because it was my first experience on such an exercise, he'd understand if I dropped out.

Dress for the march was jungle fatigues and boots. We'd carry our backpacks but wouldn't be armed. Captain Hoeffler would lead, followed by the first sergeant with the enlisted men. The officers would bring up the rear.

Before we left, there was the usual good-natured bantering. These troops had done this with regularity and knew just what to expect. It was not a big deal to them, but I didn't know how it would turn out for me even though I was confident I could go ten miles. I was in better physical condition than the average civilian my age. After all, I played golf regularly and carried my clubs. The pace didn't seem too fast. Meeks marched alongside me and asked how I was doing. I said I felt fine.

We were fortunate that the night was cool. Early September in North Carolina can be uncomfortable, even at night. I wasn't aware of the passage of time and was surprised to hear the order to halt. The first sergeant yelled, "Take five." Everyone found a spot to stretch out by the side of the road. I tried to look as though I knew what was going on and did likewise. In truth I didn't expect the rest period, but there turned out to be one every hour. I took a sip of water from my canteen. Meeks cautioned me to take it easy, because we still had

a long way to go. At the same time, Leroy Hoeffler came huffing and
puffing from his position up front to check on me. I told him I had
no difficulty keeping up. I wasn't even breathing hard, although I
noticed that Leroy's jungle fatigues showed evidence of perspiration.
I attributed that to his hurrying all the way from his lead position to
see how his "civilian" was doing. As the march continued, I got used
to the pace and was surprised that my jungle boots didn't bother me.
I was afraid they might cause a blister.

As we passed some 82d Airborne troops, one of them yelled, "Hey,
Sneaky Petes, you better not stay out too late." I was aware of the so-
briquet, but this was the first time I'd heard the term. I asked Meeks
if we were called "Sneaky Petes" by all the troops. He replied that
soldiers at Bragg usually called us that because of the nature of our
missions.

Our conversation was interrupted by the order to halt. This time
I immediately found a grassy spot and sat down. I had another
sip of water and took off my jungle boots to straighten my socks. I
was lacing my boots when Hoeffler came running back and asked
if everything was all right. I said, "Fine." Actually I was beginning
to feel the effects of the exercise, but I'd made up my mind to finish no matter what. Leroy was perspiring profusely, and his fatigues
showed it. This was the second rest period in two hours, but he
hadn't taken any breaks because he was concerned about me. We
still had another hour to march. I knew I'd finish, but Leroy was
another matter. I wished he would look after himself and forget
about me.

When Fort Bragg's lights came into view, I knew that my first night
march would soon be under my belt. The straps of my backpack aggravated my sides and I was tired, but I was going to make it. I noticed that no one had used the ambulance. Rightly or wrongly, I believed it was there solely for my benefit.

The column finally came to a halt at the company orderly room.
Captain Hoeffler reminded the officers that they'd get together at
the annex. Meeks said that the 6th Group had an officers' club annex in the area, and it was traditional to end the evening there after a night march.

Meeks and three others bunched the tables into a large square
and the officers took seats around it. Pitchers of beer and bowls of

pretzels and popcorn were brought in. This was the first time I'd witnessed an army outfit relaxing. There was no attempt at formality, just pleasant conversation in a relaxed atmosphere after a night's strenuous activity. We lounged around, letting the soreness in our muscles ease. Hoeffler was drinking Coke instead of beer. He was a member of the Church of Latter Day Saints.

Hoeffler introduced me to the company. There were officers I had not met, and this was an appropriate time to get to know them. He mentioned my experience with the air force and my airline background and congratulated me on completing the ten-mile march. We continued with the beer and pretzels for about an hour, then broke up the session. We had the rest of the weekend off, so I planned to go house hunting.

I knew that my ability to find suitable quarters was not my strongest asset. I also knew that a wife and four children should have a house with at least four bedrooms and two baths. My problem was I couldn't find anything close enough to town to please Ethel. I finally found a place at the edge of town. It had only three bedrooms but did have two baths. Hoeffler gave me a week off to move my family and said to let him know if I needed more time.

The move was made on schedule, and after getting settled the children were enrolled in the Fayetteville public school system. Ethel was not pleased to find that the house didn't have city water and sewage. She said as soon as we found better housing we'd move. I told her we had to sign a year's lease to get the place and housing was in short supply. She reminded me that we could afford something better and would hold me to my promise that her standard of living was not to be affected by my military pursuits. I saw that there would be changes made but didn't know when or how. I had to admit that with a little more effort I could have found a better place.

It was the middle of September. I had left home on August 27, was rated an army aviator on September 1, reported to Fort Bragg on September 3, learned to wear army uniforms in a week, completed a ten-mile night march, and moved my family to Fayetteville and enrolled the children in school. With all that behind me, I was scheduled for a checkout in the CH-34 helicopter. Things moved fast in Special Forces.

My instructor was CWO Charlie Quann, a highly regarded aviator who had just returned from a tour of duty in Vietnam. He showed me the walk-around inspection of the CH-34 and told me to climb up into the pilot's seat. This was my first experience with the bird, but I could see the hand-holds and used them as I climbed up the side of the ship. I took hold of a fixture I thought was there to assist me into the aircraft. Much to my embarrassment, I pulled the pilot's side window out of its position. Charlie laughed. "Now you know what that's for. Don't worry, I'll put it back in place."

We spent the better part of an afternoon in the chopper. This was the first time I'd flown a helicopter with wheels. I learned to taxi, made running takeoffs like a fixed-winged airplane, and tried some autorotative landings. Charlie's instruction was hands on, fast paced, and thorough. I was checked out in the chopper within the week.

Special Forces units were mission oriented. Many operations took place at night, and weather was treated as just one more obstacle to overcome. During one mission the rain was so intense that forward visibility was measured in feet. Yet we pressed on to deliver a team to its destination. We had to hover along roads and read signs to check directions and determine our exact location.

The aviator shortage that plagued the army was made worse by the increasing commitment in Vietnam. The army was also in the midst of its experiment with the airmobility concept. General Hamilton H. Howze, who was in charge, was instrumental in the activation of the 11th Air Assault Division (Test) at Fort Benning for this purpose.

When the 6th Aviation Company was tasked to support the experiment, four of us army aviators found ourselves on temporary duty at Fort Jackson in South Carolina. We arrived there without maintenance support and relied on Fort Jackson's facilities for requisition of parts and equipment. We added four CH-34s to the growing experimental fleet. I'm sure the folks at Fort Jackson were sorely pressed by the burden of so many additional aircraft under their jurisdiction.

My crew chief was SSgt. Ray Owens, a veteran of almost ten years with army aviation. He and the other crew chiefs worked as a team whenever one of the birds required extra maintenance, and in that spirit of cooperative effort they kept the four helicopters flying. We didn't miss a mission due to maintenance.

Our isolated situation limited communication with our families. Once when I was able to call home, Ethel said she was having difficulty with the heating system. I told her to call the company commander and ask him to put pressure on the real estate people managing the residence. I was certain he could straighten things out. Having apparently settled that matter, I told Ethel we'd be home soon.

When we landed at Simmons Army Air Field, we were met by Maj. Charles P. Frinks, who had replaced Captain Hoeffler as commander. Frinks told me that Ethel had called him, that he had sent Mrs. Frinks to assist her, and that the problem with the house was corrected. The solution was that the wives found a more suitable place for us to live, and our family was moved into new quarters the same day.

I couldn't believe what I'd heard. Things really did move fast in the army. I thanked the major for all the help.

Our new home was in a pleasant residential area within walking distance of a huge shopping complex. Ethel was pleased as punch about it and let me know that it took less than two hours to find it. I was being admonished in a most pleasant manner for my poor performance as a house hunter. I deserved every bit of it.

When I saw Major Frinks on the flight line the next day, I told him that Ethel loved the new house, thanked him again for all his help, and asked him to convey our appreciation to his wife for all her help. He said he would. "You know, Mike, I would have expected the same from you if our roles had been reversed."

I liked the way Frinks got things done. Then he let me in on the latest development. The unit was getting UH-1 Huey helicopters to replace the CH-34s. The new aircraft would arrive over a two-week period beginning in a week. "For your information," he said, "you're the only one in the company who hasn't flown the UH-1. You'll be checked out as soon as possible. Then I want you checked out in the U-10 Helio Courier."

"Roger on the checkouts, Major. But you forgot to tell me to get my qualification in the Caribou [CV-2]."

"I haven't forgotten. In due time you'll be in that bird too." Again I found that things moved fast in the army, especially in Special Forces.

The UH-1s arrived—the latest model, the UH-1B. I was to get ten hours of instruction, which was required to qualify in the bird.

The UH-1B was quite stable for a helicopter and easy to fly. The most difficult part of the checkout was the insistence of the instructor that I hover the Huey the length of the airfield runway with the hydraulics off. The UH-1's control pressures with the hydraulics inoperative were heavy—far greater than flying the B-24 with two engines out on one side. When the system was shut off or failed, the controls relied entirely on muscle power. Often the required force was so great that it was all that two pilots could do to move the controls. I managed to pass the test and hovered the length of the runway to the instructor's satisfaction. The rest of the Huey transition training was a piece of cake.

I acquired most of my operational experience in the Huey in support of the group's mission. There were night insertions of troops into clearings so small we had to make vertical descents and takeoffs. We flew formation assaults into landing zones where we touched down, then skidded a few feet as the troops jumped off (they had ten seconds). Supply drops were flown at all hours. As usual, weather was an obstacle to overcome, not a deterrent to the mission. All in all, I acquired confidence in flying the Huey.

After the company received its UH-1s, we were ordered to deliver four surplus CH-34s to San Francisco for transfer to the Vietnamese Air Force (VNAF). At the time, the CH-34s were the mainstay of the VNAF helicopter fleet. I was selected to make the flight with Capt. Ron Perry, Capt. Leroy Hoeffler, and Chief Warrant Officer Taylor. There were two crewmen per aircraft—one aviator and one crew chief. Perry, who was in charge, decided that the flight would be in loose formation. In that way we could keep an eye on one another and be in position to render assistance if anyone developed mechanical difficulties.

We made it to New Orleans the first day, flying low level, never higher than a thousand feet. We landed at Lakefront Airport and spent the night at a nearby motel. We were too tired to take in the nightlife of the Crescent City.

The next day we flew to Fort Stockton in Texas. The legally dry town was in a sparsely populated desert area of west Texas where oil was the main industry. We stayed at the Palm Motel, which entitled us to membership in the Palm Club. There we enjoyed an excellent meal and after dinner retired to the lounge, where we spent a good part of the evening. There was nothing dry about the Palm Club or, for that matter, Fort Stockton. This wet-dry dichotomy, prevalent throughout the South and Southwest, was a mystery to me. I wondered why the religious factions that seemed to control local politics could never control local bootlegging.

After a late start the next morning, we made a short day of it by stopping at Fort Bliss in El Paso, Texas. That night we crossed the Rio Grande to Juarez to sample the nightlife in Mexico. Leroy said he'd never been to a border city and was anxious to see what it was like. We gave him a quick course in dealing with the locals, especially the *chiquitas* who frequented the local drinking establishments and whom he was bound to meet. We warned him that as soon as he took a seat at the bar, one of the local beauties would sidle up against him, flick her eyelashes, and in an enticing manner ask, "You buy me drink, señor?" We told Leroy to give her the brush-off with a definitive, "Get lost, babe." If he acted in a less assertive manner, he'd be picking up the tab for exotic drinks that were far above the regular tariff. He said he understood.

We thought that such a simple set of instructions could be followed easily. Yet Leroy failed to respond as directed. He assumed his religious rules and restrictions did not apply in Mexico. The double shot of bourbon he had ordered with his Coke undoubtedly clouded his mind and diminished his ability to follow the advice given him.

Leroy was sipping his spiked drink at the bar when one of the señoritas came up to him, took his right arm, and placed it around her body where his hand could not help but nestle against her breast.

"You have big drink, is okay?" she asked. Leroy said it was fine.

"Let me see, give me taste," she said. She took a sip and said, "Is good."

Leroy did not object. Admittedly, the scenario didn't follow word for word what he'd been told. But he should have seen that he was being outflanked and disarmed.

Nestling ever closer to Leroy, whispering in his ear, she said, "Buy me drink?"

This was more than Leroy could stand. "Give the lady a bourbon and Coke," he told the bartender.

The bartender poured a shot of bourbon, placed a small glass of Coke on the side, and asked Leroy for an amount three times what he'd paid for his own drink. Leroy objected, but the bartender stated that the "lady" drank only her special brand and the price was correct. While Leroy and the bartender argued, the "lady" downed the shot of bourbon and poured another from the bottle that had been left on the bar—more by design than oversight. The bartender took notice of the second drink and charged Leroy for that too. Leroy was getting hot under the collar. He shouted loudly that he was not going to be shafted like that.

It was evident that the situation was about to get out of hand. There we were, American army aviators, Special Forces troops at that, in a foreign country, about to be involved in an altercation with one of its citizens. This was a no-win situation. We could all wind up in a Mexican jail if the bartender decided to call the *policia*.

Leroy yelled that he would not pay for the second drink. The bartender, in an equally assertive voice, shouted that Leroy was responsible for his lady friend's drinks. Leroy bellowed at the top of his voice, "She's not my lady friend, she's some damned—"

That was all Leroy was able to say before Ron Perry's hand was over his mouth. "Give the man his damn money, Leroy. We're getting the hell out of here before we're thrown in jail. The local cop is probably the bartender's uncle or some other relative and the babe is probably related to both of them."

Leroy grudgingly paid up. Disaster was averted and we were out of there. Even if only Leroy had been jailed, we all would have been stuck in El Paso trying to negotiate his release with the Mexican authorities. It would have been expensive, and there would have been the embarrassing afteraction report to headquarters. We left the bar immediately, walked along the Avenida de Benito Juarez toward the bridge, and crossed to El Paso. Then we took a cab to our motel. We were lucky to escape the clutches of the Mexican justice system. We were scheduled for a long flight the next day, so we all turned in.

The next day's weather was perfect—cool, clear, and no wind—and we planned to arrive at Las Vegas by nightfall. We low-leveled most of the way. In earlier years when I'd flown all over the country for the army and the air force, we usually flew at altitude, often at thirty thousand feet. It was quite different to see the country from three hundred feet and lower. I observed desert areas close up and saw that they contained all sorts of life and vegetation. It was a different view from up high, where all detail was lost and the terrain took on an obscure, sometimes formless, light brown sandy texture.

I flew my CH-34 as low as possible over Hoover Dam. The electrical generating apparatus was in full view, and the high-tension cables were right below me. I realized it was not the safest place to be if my engine failed. I'd end up a crispy critter, but I just had to see the dam up close.

The Grand Canyon was an awesome sight—vast yet empty—when viewed at such close range. Lake Mead, the part of the Colorado River impounded by Hoover Dam, stretched for miles between sheer stone cliffs. The same scene from thirty thousand feet loses its majesty and dynamic characteristics. It is reduced to a thin, flat ribbon of water in a sea of nondescript brownness.

We arrived in Las Vegas early enough to find lodging. Ron Perry sent a remain overnight (RON) message to Fort Bragg flight operations with the additional information that Chief Warrant Officer Taylor's helicopter needed maintenance that might cause an additional day or two delay. The people at Fort Bragg no doubt thought it strange that the maintenance difficulty occurred when we reached Las Vegas.

That night we visited the casinos and tried our luck at the blackjack tables. There was plenty of booze and excellent food at giveaway prices. We knew there was little chance of winning, but the expectation was always there. Eventually we made our "donations" to the establishments that were designed to separate individuals from their money.

Two days and two nights were sufficient to diminish our enthusiasm for the games and the glare and glitter of the strip. I was ready to proceed with the mission and get going with the last leg of the trip. Besides, we were running out of money and might not have enough to get back to Fort Bragg. It was time to leave.

The trip to San Francisco didn't take long, and we delivered the helicopters. We agreed that it had been an enjoyable excursion. We'd flown across the country, low-leveled almost the entire distance, and had a ball. The next day we boarded an airliner for Fayetteville. It was time to return to the family and relax.

We arrived at Fort Bragg late Wednesday afternoon, and Major Frinks gave us the rest of the week off. It was a welcome rest and as long a period with my family as I'd had since coming on duty with the Green Berets. Ethel and I went shopping with the children; they seemed to need new clothes all the time. We dined out a couple of nights but only after we took the children to their favorite places for hamburgers, french fries, and soft drinks. They were growing up. Mike Jr. was fifteen, Patty was thirteen, Jean was eleven, and John was two. Mike Jr. was preparing to get his driver's license as soon as he turned sixteen. I wouldn't be the only driver in the house much longer.

A few weeks after our West Coast escapade, the company received a special tasking in support of an upcoming National Aeronautics and Space Administration (NASA) manned space mission. Captain George Dorsey and I got the job; our crew chief was SSgt. Ray Owens.

We were to go to Khormaksar Airfield, a Royal Air Force (RAF) base in the Aden Protectorate, which was located in the southwestern part of the Arabian peninsula and was still a part of the British Empire. The mission would be a joint one with the air force, which would transport us, our Huey, and a Special Forces A Team. This would be a perfect time to see just how well the two services cooperated. The Special Forces team was commanded by Capt. Doyle E. Smith, a tall, powerfully built officer from Georgia. His twelve enlisted team members presented the same appearance of strength and competence. The air force was to fly us in a C-130 from nearby Pope Air Force Base and remain with us until the mission was completed. Dorsey, Owens, and I were responsible for preparing the Huey for shipment. That meant removing the head (main rotor system) so the Huey would fit into the transport.

I learned we were going to Aden in support of the Gemini GT-5 space mission. In the event of an emergency landing by the spacecraft in our operational area, Dorsey and I would transport the Special Forces team to secure the impact site and lend assistance to the downed astronauts. The Aden area was selected as one of the staging locations because it was in the orbital path of the Gemini capsule.

While loading our Huey, I met the C-130 aircraft commander, a captain and command pilot with more than eighteen years of service under his belt. He was one of many excellent air force officers not promoted due to overstaffing of field-grade officers. Unless things got better, he would most likely retire after twenty years of service as a captain.

We left early the next morning and flew to Nova Scotia, then England, then made overnight stops in Spain and Libya. We finally arrived at Khormaksar Airfield and boarded buses for the Red Sea Hotel, an RAF billet in Aden. What I saw was most unexpected. The buses had heavy metal screens over the windows to protect against grenade attacks, and there were sandbag barriers at entrances to many of the buildings. It appeared that the Brits had an insurrection on their hands and no one had thought to tell us.

An air force major who was assigned as our escort and liaison officer was responsible for our billeting arrangements with the RAF. We all wore Special Forces combat gear (jungle boots, uniforms, and green berets) and had M16 rifles. The major was visibly alarmed with what he considered to be our aggressive appearance. He cautioned us to be careful with our weapons and to keep a low profile with them because of the revolutionary elements in the Aden Protectorate; the British governor general had been assassinated two days before.

The major was a typical administrative type assigned to rear-area support roles. Such officers don't often see enemy activity but are prone to embellish and exaggerate any contact. They are not used to being in contact with heavily armed, camouflaged, sweaty, grimy combat troops. To put it bluntly, "our major" was dealing with men who had an unwarranted reputation for love of combat, and they scared the hell out of him.

This was the opportunity that one of our troopers was looking for. Staff Sergeant Rafael Zamarripa had a huge dried salami wrapped in brown butcher paper. He produced a long-bladed knife from an ankle case, made a number of quick cuts to the salami, and offered each of us a piece of "smoked rattlesnake meat." As he was doling it out, one of the men yelled at Rafael, "Damnit, Zamarripa, why didn't you tell me that there snake hadn't been skinned? It's as tough as shoe leather."

Zamarripa cut off a big piece and offered it to the major, who wouldn't even look at it. He seemed to be turning green at the gills as he said, "I've already eaten, thank you."

When we arrived at the Red Sea Hotel, we noticed that the entrance was heavily sandbagged and guarded by a couple of Tommies (British soldiers), each equipped with an automatic rifle. Other troops were in the immediate area, all armed with similar weapons.

The construction of the hotel was typically Arabic. The walls were at least three feet thick and the windows were small. The heat was oppressive: The temperature remained around 110 degrees or higher except after sundown, when it dropped to about 90 degrees. It was still daylight and well above a hundred degrees when we entered the hotel. It was somewhat cooler inside but still uncomfortably warm; the lobby was not air-conditioned. We spent our first night sleeping on cots in a huge room cooled by large fans. We were informed that better accommodations were on hand for us the next day.

I didn't sleep well, and neither did the rest of the troops. We arose with the sun, but the temperature was already in the high nineties. We had a breakfast of scrambled eggs, toast, sausage, and coffee— similar to an American morning meal except that the bangers (sausages) were not as spicy as ours.

After breakfast, I and Dorsey, Owens, and the entire C-130 crew went to Khormaksar Airfield. We unloaded the UH-1, reassembled and remounted the main rotor on the helicopter, and prepared it for flight. We received generous assistance from the British maintenance people, who made their heavy-lift equipment available. The C-130 flight engineer and crew pitched in to help.

We worked all day in the sun with the temperature on the ramp approaching 120 degrees, but we followed the British custom of taking ten-minute breaks. Their people also worked in the open, but after fifty minutes they went into an air-conditioned canteen and had a cold beer. They relaxed, drank their beer, smoked, and chatted until their rest period was over. We copied their system but didn't accept the beer; we opted for soft drinks. There was wisdom to their method; after all, the Brits had been in Aden for decades and had learned to live and work in uncomfortable conditions. The system worked well for us, too, even with our slight modification.

Our job wasn't completed at the end of the day; we'd have it done the next morning. As we rode the bus back to the Red Sea Hotel, we saw that the Brits had tightened security; a lot more troops were patrolling the road. I wondered if the increased security was for our benefit.

As promised, we got air-conditioned rooms, which assured us of a good night's rest. After cleaning up, we went to the officers' mess. I was startled to learn that this RAF base on the edge of the desert offered a menu with five entrees, including one of seafood. I selected roast beef, which was delicious.

After dinner we repaired to the bar, where I sampled the British version of gin and tonic. The main difference between the American and the British versions is the amount of ice. The Brits use much less, which allows for more tonic and enhances the flavor. American bartenders fill the glass with ice, pour in the gin, then add tonic in the space remaining. The result is super-cold gin and minimum tonic—a drink sufficiently cold to dull the senses but without the unique flavor. I learned to appreciate the British version.

Dorsey and I spent about three hours talking with our Royal Air Force hosts, who were superb conversationalists. We spent an enjoyable evening with them and hated to leave such good company. But the next day would be a busy one.

I arose refreshed, had breakfast with Dorsey and Owens, and departed for the airfield. We worked for about an hour getting the Huey ready for flight. "We must have done our work correctly," said Dorsey. "I don't see any parts left over."

We agreed I'd start the engine while Dorsey and Owens observed from both sides of the helicopter. In that way they could detect anything not right and signal me to cut the power. The engine started without difficulty. All instruments indicated normal operation. I motioned my two associates into the ship. They got on board and, after hooking up to the intercom, said that everything appeared to be operating normally. I ran up to full throttle and hovered the helicopter around the ramp.

There was plenty of room, so we hovered back and forth and maneuvered in all directions. We were trying out the helicopter and hoping nothing flew off. After about half an hour, we agreed that the craft was reassembled properly. I made a normal takeoff and climbed to five hundred feet. We flew around for an hour, then decided we'd seen enough and landed. We were satisfied that the helicopter was okay.

When we returned to the hotel it was still early afternoon, so Dorsey and I decided to take in the sights of downtown Aden. We ignored the liaison officer's warning of "revolutionary elements" and decided that, dressed in our civilian attire, we would not be bothered.

After window shopping and browsing, Dorsey and I found an establishment that we took to be a restaurant. Upon entry we discovered that the clientele were drinking, not dining. Yet the majority of the patrons were Arabs, devotees of Islam, who were supposed to shun alcoholic beverages.

Because we were not bound by any antialcoholic dogma, and we were hot and thirsty, we did the natural thing and ordered a couple of beers. We relaxed and enjoyed the leisure period, slowly sipping the wonderful brew.

That evening we dined at the officers' mess and had another enjoyable dinner. We adjourned to the bar, where I had my customary gin and tonic. I stayed for two drinks, then left to hit the hay.

I'd been sleeping soundly when I was awakened by loud noises and shouting. People were running up and down the hallway as I opened the door. "What the hell's going on?" I asked. "Why all the commotion?"

Just then I heard the chatter of a lone machine gun in the distance. "We're under attack," someone yelled. Then there was a strange silence. I found out that it was a hit-and-run raid, probably the same gang that had assassinated the governor general. They threw a couple of grenades at the sandbagged guard post and fired three rocket-propelled grenades at the hotel. There were no casualties. I went back to bed.

The next morning, Dorsey and I checked the battle scars from the previous night's action. The impacts from the grenades were barely visible. There were three small chipped areas in the hotel's wall, hardly worthy of so much noise and effort.

When we arrived at Khormaksar Airfield, the C-130 aircraft commander told us that his plane had been the target of a mortar attack at the time the hotel was under fire. Three mortar rounds were fired, but the only one that exploded hit more than two hundred yards from the aircraft. Our helicopter was parked next to the C-130 and could have been the real target. When I mentioned that to George Dorsey, he said, "The air force could never accept such a theory."

After NASA released us from the Gemini mission, we left for home, stopping at Wheelus Air Base in Tripoli, and at Seville and Madrid, Spain, before crossing the Atlantic to Nova Scotia and finally Pope Air Force Base. At long last we were home.

I finished my first year with the army and Special Forces and also celebrated my forty-third birthday. I seemed to have adjusted well to army life, despite the periods of TDY.

We had been back from Arabia less than a month when the company was alerted for yet another important mission, this time in the Dominican Republic. The people of the island republic had elected a president who was not supported by the country's military leadership and was politically too far to the left to suit the United States. American military forces were sent to correct the political situation. The force was made up of units from the 82d Airborne Division, Special Forces, the air force, and the navy. The 82d brought along its helicopters and medical evacuation unit. The air force provided transport for logistical support and augmented the navy's capability.

Special Forces teams were sent into the interior to act as listening posts and gather intelligence. Two aircraft were deployed by the 6th Aviation Company to support the Green Berets. One was a Caribou flown by Capt. Don Ancelin. The other was a Huey, which I flew with SSgt. Ray Owens, my crew chief.

Our helicopter was painted a special bright red, so we named it El Diablo Rojo, the Red Devil. It had an auxiliary fuel tank to increase its range, which gave me about three and a half hours of flying time. The added time aloft let me cover the entire country from my base at San Isidro Airport, near the capital city of Santo Domingo.

My mission was to supply Green Beret outposts scattered throughout the island. It involved weekly flights to many cities, including San Pedro de Macoris and La Romana, on the southern coast, and La Vega and Santiago, in the interior. Our headquarters maintained radio communication with each outpost. When emergencies arose, affected teams were assisted by our helicopter or the Caribou.

It seemed that we had some sort of emergency every day. More than once we were called in the middle of the night to assist injured people or critically ill children. Our response time for emergencies could not have been quicker. Our tent was about fifty yards from our helicopter, and we were airborne in less than a minute. I remember a mission to evacuate a baby gravely ill from dehydration. Owens and I took off as soon as we received the request for assistance. Other emergencies were generated by stabbings and injuries that occurred during drunken weekend brawls. Rum was a cheap commodity that the poor could buy. They often didn't have enough to eat but somehow found money for rum. Because one of the main agricultural crops was sugarcane, the ready supply of cheap rum was understandable.

One of my favorite supply runs was to La Romana. There were about twenty American families there, all employees of a large sugar plantation. Most were in research to improve the reproductive process of sugarcane and were highly regarded experts in their fields. We were always invited to lunch.

The intervention in the affairs of the island nation interrupted normal trade, so newspapers and magazines couldn't be brought in. Our friends at La Romana asked us to bring all the magazines and newspapers we could so they could keep abreast of the news. A week-old news magazine was eagerly accepted as a rare and precious gift.

In our spare time we organized an informal club at San Isidro. It was called the E-1 through O-9 club, open to all military. Owens knew that C-130s brought all supplies into San Isidro, where they were handled by air force and army personnel and delivered to storage facilities on flatbed trucks.

Our club was surrounded by waist-high weeds that extended up to the aircraft parking area and the road leading to the warehouses. The road passed within feet of the entrance to our club and was deeply rutted. It was inevitable that items carried by the flatbed trucks would occasionally slip off, unnoticed by the driver, as the trucks bumped along. Owens was not surprised to find a case of steaks lying in the weeds when he went to open the club. When that happened he invited a bunch of air force and army supply people to a steakfest. It was a most serendipitous occasion. The club was a huge success.

Special Forces was responsible for gathering, processing, and disseminating intelligence. It was in this command structure that I met an army intelligence officer, a first lieutenant, who was rumored to have worked for the Batista government of Cuba. I met other officers with similarly alleged backgrounds, and the thought of having such people in our officer corps bothered me. My ideas of dedication to democratic principles were rooted in my educational background. How anyone who worked for the Batista regime could share the same views and principles was beyond my comprehension. But there was little value in working up a lather. My political education needed updating; I displayed too much naivete and was behind the times. These officers were strong anticommunists, and that was what mattered.

The lieutenant briefed me about reported sightings of Cuban communists attempting to infiltrate the island. I was to fly him to the town of Samana, in the northeastern part of the country. The mouth of Samana Bay was situated south of the town; the bay stretched to the west. We were to meet a Dominican agent familiar with the area and reconnoiter the bay, where the communist infiltrators were supposed to have landed. The lieutenant was to identify the agent who was supposed to assist with the recon.

I took on a full load of fuel, and we were off to save the Dominican Republic from Cuban invaders. All went as planned; the agent was waiting for us. There was little conversation and there were no introductions. This was their mission; I just followed instructions.

The town of Samana was hardly worth that designation. It was in a sparsely populated part of the island, and the reason it existed was unclear. There were few roads in the area, which was a thick, dense jungle.

We flew over the bay on a recon at about five hundred feet. When directed, or when something suspicious was spotted, I'd drop down to the surface and hover over the area for better observation. We didn't find anything unusual along the entire shore of the bay. The beach on either shore didn't show signs of transients, and there wasn't any evidence of movement by people or equipment. The entire area looked pristine and undisturbed. The dense vegetation and trees came right up to the narrow beaches, and there weren't any roads going inland. There was little to see except for a few primitive hamlets on the bay. It was as I expected; we were chasing phantoms. There were no infiltrators from Cuba or anywhere else. At most there were only rumors, and those had probably been conjured up by the lieutenant or his Dominican friend. Besides, there were more favorable locations on the north coast of the country for infiltrators to come ashore.

I told the "intelligence experts" that my fuel was getting low and we had to leave. They agreed there was nothing more to do, and I headed for Santo Domingo. I was about to drop the Dominican at his original location but was surprised to learn he would be returning to the base with us. I thought that if these clowns really feared communist infiltration, someone would remain and keep the area under observation. I guess I didn't think like a good intelligence officer, or maybe the Dominican was just tired of being in the boondocks and wanted to see some nightlife in the capital.

The more I thought about the mission, the more I was convinced that we had wasted our time. The lieutenant and his sidekick must have known that they wouldn't find anything. It was all a figment of their imaginations, an attempt to justify their positions and enhance their anticommunist credentials. When we returned to the base, the lieutenant and the Dominican left, talking and laughing, saying nothing to me. I was glad to get them out of my hair.

The American base at San Isidro was under the command of the air force, and one night the base commander made his first visit to the club. He introduced himself as Colonel Duncan and asked if I was the pilot of the Huey parked nearby. When I said I was, he told me he'd never flown in a helicopter and asked if he could fly with me. I told him he'd have to be ready to go at a moment's notice if we had an emergency mission. Otherwise, we'd let him know when we were flying to the outposts. I warned him that those missions could last for three to four hours, sometimes longer, and he might be away from his office awhile. He said there would be no problem taking time off.

As it turned out, the colonel went with us on our next mission. As soon as we reached cruising altitude, I gave him the controls. He was surprised at how responsive the controls were, but soon he got the feel of the craft and did well. The mission for the day was to resupply the Special Forces outpost at La Vega, on a high plateau in the central mountain region. The weather was dreary, with low gray skies and intermittent rain. As the day wore on, it turned stormy, with one thunderstorm following another.

As we flew into the interior, I saw two huge rainstorms along our flight path. Because of the pattern of deteriorating weather, I knew that we would encounter additional storms. Colonel Duncan, still at the controls, noted the two squalls and asked if we were going to fly through them. He was uneasy about the situation, so I took the controls and said we'd maneuver around them. I tried to put him at ease by telling him that the helo could handle the weather.

Our flight path skirted both thunderstorms, but we were in heavy rain for about fifteen minutes. I had the windshield washers operating on high speed. At least the rain gave me the opportunity to clear the Plexiglas of all the insect smears we'd picked up. After we passed the storms, the weather cleared momentarily and I could make out La Vega in the distance. Another huge rainstorm hung over the town. I descended until I was low-leveling up the road leading to the Green Beret compound.

We were at a crawl going through more rain. Colonel Duncan didn't say a word; I'm sure he wished he had never made the trip. The rain stopped as abruptly as it had started, and I spotted the outpost a short distance ahead. We arrived without further difficulty and dropped off the supplies without shutting down the engine. I wanted to get airborne before the weather really turned bad and prevented us from leaving. My experience told me that the weather could turn sour in a hurry in the mountains in late afternoon.

It started raining again as we lifted off. I followed the road out of town, and for a while we were in the clear. About five miles ahead was the edge of the plateau where the terrain dropped off to the central plain about two thousand feet below. A line of thunderstorms was situated over the edge of the plateau. Heavy rain poured out of the rolling clouds as the sky rapidly darkened. I headed for a small break in the long line of clouds, hoping to get through before they closed in.

Colonel Duncan saw me turn toward the break. "Are you going to try to get through that hole?" he asked.

"We'll make it in plenty of time," I assured him. Shortly, we flew through the opening just as the clouds closed in behind us. One minute we'd been low-leveling, then suddenly we passed the edge of the plateau and were two thousand feet above the ground. It was an awesome sight.

I began a descent toward the plain. We had encountered strong turbulence and rain when we raced through the break in the clouds, but it soon smoothed out and the rain stopped. I continued the descent until I was low-leveling again. I told Duncan to observe my next maneuver. "Remember the scene on the plateau when we were racing the storm for the opening in the clouds? If the break in the clouds had closed before we made it through, all I'd have to do is reduce power, do a side flare, and set the helicopter on the ground. That's something we couldn't do with a fixed-wing aircraft, but it's duck soup with a chopper."

It was dark when we got back to San Isidro, so I invited the colonel to the club for drinks. Owens barbecued some New York strip steaks, and we had a pleasant dinner there. Duncan and I enjoyed each other's company. We were about the same age and were both survivors of World War II. After our initial meeting, we often flew together; it was not uncommon for me to be firing up the chopper's engine and see him hightailing it through the weeds to join me.

In the following weeks the political situation cooled considerably. The Special Forces maintained its outposts, and the weekly supply runs continued as before. Owens and I, ever mindful of the excellent food at La Romana, always managed to be there around noon. The community returned to normal; even the mail was coming through.

Charlie Frinks came down to observe his aviation in action and made a few flights with me. I didn't get much mail during my tour of duty in the Dominican Republic, but on this day I received a letter from the Department of the Army, forwarded from Fort Bragg; it had been almost a month since it was mailed. When I opened the letter, I was shocked; it contained orders transferring me to Vietnam with a reporting date that I couldn't possibly meet. I showed the orders to Frinks, who also was surprised. He said he'd inform Warrant Officer Branch of my situation when he returned to Bragg and would send a replacement for me. I had been in the Dominican Republic for about two months.

Frinks departed the next day, and my replacement arrived two days later. I left on the same plane later in the day. When I reported to the company, Frinks told me that the original orders had been canceled by Warrant Officer Branch and new orders with a more appropriate reporting date for Vietnam would be issued. According to the old orders, I was AWOL from that assignment. Talk about a mixup.

When I volunteered for active duty with army aviation, I believed that my considerable experience would be put to use training army aviators. I never thought I'd be sent to Vietnam as a combatant, certainly not at my age.

Well, the new orders from DA straightened out everything. My reporting date in Vietnam was changed to January 25, 1966. At long last I was going to have plenty of time between assignments to make personal and financial arrangements.

Ethel already knew I'd be going to Vietnam thanks to the wives' communication network, which was more efficient than the most sophisticated military equipment. She even knew about the original orders I had received. Ethel could have complained about being stuck with four children, but that was not her way. She was a real trouper and a brave woman; at least she acted bravely around me. Mike Jr. was sixteen years old and driving. He was to be the man of the house, and he'd be available to drive his mother around town so she could shop and tend to other household duties.

My orders allowed me thirty days' leave, so we decided to go to Pennsylvania to stay with Ethel's family, and I'd visit my mother before going overseas. We'd be there for the Christmas holidays. It might be a year before Ethel could see her parents again.

My decision to volunteer for duty with the army was never enthusiastically received by her family, and I didn't expect my leaving for a combat assignment to be viewed in a better light. I was thankful that the subject came up only once while we were there, and that was in a conversation with one of Ethel's brothers. He asked me why I took leave from the airline and left my assignment as a lieutenant colonel in the Air Force Reserve for, as he phrased it, a position as a "lowly warrant officer" with the army. He said he would never have done anything as ridiculous. "You're going to war, leaving your wife and children for a year and maybe even getting killed."

I replied that I was well aware of the risk of my decision and it was entirely my responsibility. He was the type who could never leave home; it was his entire world. I suppose that people like him are needed. But he never could do what I had done and never would. Finally, I told him, "You have no right to ridicule my position as a 'lowly warrant officer.' Hell, you never went beyond private first class when you were in the service." That ended the conversation.

The visits with my mother were subdued. She was seldom enthusiastic about my flying career, but she knew I would never be happy doing anything else. We also knew that our meeting might be our last, if for different reasons. When I left she told me she would pray for me every day.

We stayed with Ethel's parents for about two weeks, then returned to our home in Fayetteville. The children (except for John) returned to school while I made last-minute preparations for my departure.

It was hard to leave my family knowing it would be for a whole year. They were accustomed to my leaving on trips; it had been part of our routine with the airline, and it continued with the Green Berets. It was not unusual for me to be gone for a month or more at a time. But this was different. I don't think that part had fully entered the children's minds, except for Mike Jr. I could tell that he was a little upset about my leaving and having additional responsibilities thrown his way.

My last evening home, Ethel and I stayed up past two in the morning even though we had to be up at six to make it to the airport on time. I had first-class reservations all the way to San Francisco. Friends asked why I was wasting my money when the government would reimburse me only for the regular fare. I told them that any time I departed for a combat assignment, I traveled first class. It could be my last opportunity to do so. Furthermore, I planned to have a fine dinner at one of the better restaurants in the San Francisco area before reporting to Travis Air Force Base. Ethel understood.

Neither of us slept well that night. We faced a situation we had not expected. I was going into combat while others half my age and with limited aviation experience were training aviators. I was not complaining, but I was surprised by it all. I knew that what was happening was the result of my actions. After all, I always prided myself on being the master of my destiny. I was not coerced into becoming an army aviator; I volunteered. When the air force rejected my overtures and hinted that I might be too old, I could have accepted that verdict and left matters alone. Such thoughts raced through my mind as I tossed and turned in a fitful attempt to sleep. I finally gave up trying to sort things out and accepted the situation. If combat was to be my assignment and life for the next year, I'd better be master of that situation.

Ethel and I got up early the next morning and dressed hurriedly. There was not much time for conversation, and there was really little to say. We'd covered all that the night before, repeating our love for each other time and again. Suddenly I realized it was time to leave. Ethel and I embraced. We held each other tightly, neither wanting to let go.

I promised her I'd make it back. She asked, "What if you don't?" Her question surprised me. I hadn't counted on it, but it deserved an answer.

"I know that it can't be guaranteed," I replied quietly, "but I'm coming back. If I don't, then I suppose Arlington would be an appropriate place for an old soldier."

It was time to go. We released each other and I was gone.

8 January 1966: The Flight Over

It was early afternoon on January 28, 1966, when I reported to Travis Air Force Base. The passenger terminal was busy as air force people processed individuals headed overseas. Most of the transients were army troops en route to Vietnam. I presented a copy of my orders to an air force sergeant, who checked the flight manifest, gave me my flight number, and told me I'd leave in a couple of hours. My orders said I was to arrive in Vietnam by January 30. I'd be on schedule.

As I relaxed in one of the chairs in the waiting area, I noticed that most of the people were lower-ranking enlisted men in their teens and early twenties. They wandered about aimlessly, occasionally dropping coins into the numerous vending machines for a soda or candy bar. Some apparently knew one another; most likely they had attended training school together.

They were on their way to a war that none of them had been aware of only a few months before. The possibility that some would not come back may not have entered their minds. A good many were draftees who knew only that their number had come up and it was their duty, their lot, to go and serve. They were repeating the ritual that their fathers, grandfathers, and great-grandfathers had performed in previous wars.

As I looked over the young soldiers, the thought occurred to me that some had made the first flights of their lives getting to San Francisco. If they had been required to make their own airline reservations, they wouldn't have known how. It didn't seem right that soldiers so young and immature in the ways of the world had to leave the security of their homes, friends, and associates to fight a war in a distant land. Then I remembered how I went off to combat twenty-one years earlier. I was twenty-two years old at the time—older than the troopers milling about the terminal—and as a captain I had seen and known a little more about life. Maybe my compassion for the "youngsters" was misdirected or unnecessary, but I couldn't ignore my feelings for them. To me they were young people who harbored secret fears, who were uncertain of their futures, who had no knowledge of their assignments and no idea how they would perform if thrust into combat. These men would be parceled out to various units throughout Vietnam. A few unfortunate ones would be in combat in short order.

Because of the need for a rapid buildup of forces, they were not going overseas as a group or military unit. They were unassigned, which undoubtedly left them in a state of confusion. Military life and effectiveness is based on unit cohesion, which these individuals did not have. Instead they were on their own as they made their way to the other side of the world into a theater of war. Even though most wouldn't see combat or even fire a weapon, their futures were uncertain, and that should be weighing heavily on their minds. They had access to news reports about the fighting in Vietnam; but except for spotty coverage about the lifestyles of the people, there was little information to help prepare them for their assignments.

Soon they'd board huge, four-engine jets to begin the day-and-a-half ordeal of flying to Vietnam. Once there, they'd be assigned to units, where their questions would be answered and their fears allayed or confirmed. The master plan called for them to spend the next year at their new stations. How they perceived this—as an adventure, an imposition, or a bore—was entirely up to them. Whether or not they survived the year and returned home was up to forces beyond their control.

As I thought about the troops, I realized that my situation was similar. I too was alone. I didn't know a soul in the terminal and had travel orders that applied solely to me. How different it had been in World War II, when I passed through the same installation going to combat but wasn't alone. My crew was with me and I knew my assignment: I was an aircraft commander of a B-29 aircrew of six officers and five enlisted men. My copilot and flight engineer were with me for more than six months, and the rest of the crew trained with us for three months. We flew together, lived together, went to night-clubs together, and chased women together. We knew that our job would be dropping bombs on the Japanese Empire. For us there was little uncertainty, no feeling of being lost or alone. Unlike the young soldiers headed for unassigned duty in Vietnam, my crew was a fully trained combat unit capable of performing effectively. When we boarded our aircraft for our overseas destination, we were ready for action and adventure.

There was, however, a marked contrast between the World War II and Vietnam modes of transportation. In World War II, the trip to the Mariana Islands took at least three days and nights aboard a slow, four-engine, propeller-driven aircraft—the Douglas C-54. The flight to Saigon, although more than two thousand miles farther, took a relatively short eighteen hours on a Douglas DC-8, a four-engine jet. We had improved how we went to war.

An army major broke my train of thought as he sat down next to me. "I'm Major Bob French," he said. "It appears we'll be traveling together on the next outbound flight."

"I'm Mike Novosel. I see you're also an army aviator. You going to Saigon?"

"I sure am," he replied.

In the brief conversation we enjoyed before boarding the Trans Air DC-8, I learned that Bob French was looking forward to taking command of a UH-1 company. He commented that I appeared old enough to have served during the Korean War. I told him I had, and he seemed surprised when I added that I flew combat missions in World War II as a B-29 aircraft commander. We traded bits of personal information about our past military assignments. He was somewhat shocked to learn that I'd been back on active duty for less than a year and a half. I did not let him know I had been an Air Force Reserve lieutenant colonel before coming on board with army aviation. That would have been too much for a young army major to assimilate at one sitting.

Bob French was an interesting and engaging person. I knew we would get along during the long flight ahead of us. When the flight was called, we boarded the transport and took adjacent seats. The craft was loaded to capacity. There were at least 175 servicemen on board, a situation that did not put me at ease. In the event of an emergency calling for rapid egress of all passengers, I visualized nothing short of complete chaos. Being a former airline pilot, I was well aware of the general reputation of the many fly-by-night contract carriers doing business with the Department of Defense. Until boarding the flight I'd never heard of Trans Air and was uneasy about the possibility of its aircraft having been discarded by a "legitimate" airline. My imagination ran wild. Where did Trans Air get the flight crew? Were they also discards? Had they been with another company and sacked for nonperformance or disciplined for some violation?

Bob settled into his seat. Seeing me standing and looking around, he asked, "What's going on? See someone you know?"

The question brought me to my senses. I felt silly for letting my imagination get the best of me. I sat down and adjusted and fastened my seat belt. I had a window seat and could see the baggage handlers loading duffel bags and assorted pieces of luggage. Each passenger was authorized to bring 134 pounds of personal effects; it seemed as though each had brought the allowable limit. No doubt we would have a full load on the big bird.

Flight attendants scurried up and down the aisle checking to see that all passengers had their seat belts fastened. The ship's loudspeaker came alive. We were welcomed aboard, then the emergency drill procedures that no one seemed to take seriously were ritually narrated by the flight attendants. We were cautioned to observe the seat belt and no smoking signs at all times and told we'd depart shortly.

I heard the engines "spooling up" as the flight crew prepared for departure, then felt the slight movement of the aircraft as the ship moved slowly forward. I looked out my window and saw the taxiway roll past. At the signal from the cockpit, the flight attendants took their seats and fastened their seat belts. The takeoff run would start any second. I checked to see if the flaps were set for takeoff and from my position saw that they were: Everything was in order. I heard the noise level increase as the engines were advanced to full throttle and felt the brakes being released.

The airplane was probably at its maximum gross weight, because the initial forward movement was excruciatingly slow. But we soon accelerated and raced down the runway. It seemed as if we would never reach flying speed, but I finally felt the gentle liftoff followed by the sound of the landing gear being raised. There was a pause; then I heard the whine of the motor as the flaps slowly retracted. I don't know why I was "flying" the plane; the captain was doing fine.

The aircraft continued its climb to cruise altitude as the course was set for Hawaii. The no smoking and fasten seat belt signs were turned off, and the announcement was made that we could move about the cabin. There was an instantaneous parade of passengers rushing to the lavatories.

Bob and I scanned news magazines and exchanged occasional comments on items that each of us thought interesting. One of the flight attendants served soft drinks and coffee and said that meals would be served shortly. I recalled the World War II C-54 flights when the only food available was at refueling stops. It was usually leftovers.

As we flew on to Hawaii, I thought of the changes that had taken place in air travel. We were crowded like sardines on the big jet but were still more comfortable than in the old C-54s. We were well above 35,000 feet, riding smoothly with no turbulence at a comfortable temperature and being served hot meals. My only complaint was the absence of liquor, which I realized was due to regulations of the Department of Defense. The food was more than I expected. The main course was a small filet mignon, just what I needed to put me into a relaxed mood and enable me to get some shut-eye.

I leaned back, closed my eyes in anticipation of a short nap, and nestled into my seat for comfort. Thoughts of the day's activities floated through my mind for a while, and I couldn't help but think of my family. I wondered what they were doing just then and how they were getting along. I thought of my beautiful wife with our four children on her hands. Young John was only two; the others were old enough to help out. They also were old enough to get into trouble. Ethel had a big load on her shoulders. One thing I was sure of— the children would be well cared for, fed, and clothed. Ethel always bought the best that was available.

My main concern was that an emergency she couldn't handle might come up. Then I recalled how she handled the problems with the old house when I was TDY to the 11th Air Assault Division. She managed to take care of everything. I was worrying needlessly. She didn't know how to drive, but Mike Jr. had the car and his driver's license. If he wasn't available when she needed the car, there were taxies. She never hesitated to call a cab anytime she needed to go someplace. I was sure all was well and I should stop worrying.

I felt somewhat better after thinking things over and dozed off for about an hour. When I awoke I noticed that the cabin lights were subdued; apparently many of the passengers were napping. Bob was up talking to one of the flight attendants at her work station. I noticed he had coffee, so I decided to have a cup. The flight attendant warned me that the coffee was fresh and hot and to be careful. I thanked her and asked about our arrival time in Honolulu. She said we'd be landing in about an hour and all passengers would be off-loaded during refueling. The three of us chatted for a while as I finished my coffee, then I returned to my seat. In a few minutes Bob came back and I jokingly asked how he'd done with the attendant.

"We're going nightclubbing as soon as we get to Honolulu," he said with a laugh. "If there's a lounge in the terminal, I'm going to grab a couple of quick snorts."

"I'll join you. I could use one or two myself."

The flight attendants collected empty glasses and trash in preparation for landing. The usual checks and announcements were made: seat belts fastened, no smoking, and seats in the upright position. I looked forward to disembarking, finding a lounge, and relaxing. Then an announcement was made that we were not to wander around the terminal. We would be restricted to a designated section while refueling was in progress.

"Shit." Bob had said it all.

"I guess they're afraid we might get lost or go AWOL," I added.

We were not a happy lot as we sat in our roped-off area, saying little but imagining a far better diversion. Then, wonderful news: The plane's departure was delayed because of a maintenance problem, and we were allowed to move about the terminal, although we had to be ready to board in one hour sharp. A big cheer emanated from the troops, then a mad dash was made for the main part of the terminal.

Bob and I went to one of the lounges, where we found some of our fellow passengers already holding tall glasses of cold beer. Bob ordered a double scotch on the rocks and I had a gin and tonic. We enjoyed the break and the open space of the terminal. The tunnel of the passenger cabin, the closeness of the seats, the minimum of space for each occupant, and the inability to move about was cruel and unusual punishment. We had a few minutes before we had to return, so we checked the shops. We didn't plan to buy anything; we just enjoyed the diversion. Then we stumbled upon a liquor store.

We knew we couldn't get on board the airplane with a bottle of booze, but as luck would have it the store had miniatures. We each bought four and concealed them in our pockets. We'd have a few drinks later to take the edge off the journey. With the foresight of true veterans, we purchased rum, which went well with the Coke we knew the flight attendants had.

We were soon airborne en route to Kwajalein, in the Marshall Islands, where I had been a few times. The last was during Operation Sunset flying a war-weary B-29 back to the States.

When the attendants made their rounds, Bob and I ordered Cokes. Unobserved, we added the rum and had our Cuba Libres. Later we had an excellent meal and topped it off with another rum and Coke. We were enjoying the flight.

While the plane was refueled at Kwajalein, we stretched our legs and roamed around the terminal for about an hour. There was no quarantine as at Honolulu. After all, where would we, or could we, go on the small atoll?

I thought about my last visit and marveled at the changes that had taken place. The buildings were of relatively recent construction, modern in appearance, and air-conditioned. There were many more buildings than I remembered, and they were much larger. Some were immense structures topped with arrays of antennas of various designs and functions. I didn't know the purpose for the installations, but I could see that the complex was more than a refueling function for the airliners. The Department of Defense had invested heavily in expanding and improving the facility.

We heard the call to board. The next leg of our flight—the longest one—would take us to Clark Air Base in the Philippines. The trip began to take its toll on the passengers; it was boring, confining, and fatiguing. I was exhausted. I tried to sleep but couldn't get into a comfortable position. I'd doze off for a few minutes, then awaken when aches and pains of soft flesh (in competition with aircraft structure) demanded relief. Bob wasn't doing any better. After a couple of curses and uncomplimentary words about the airplane and the flight, he asked me, "Was it this bad in World War II?"

"Worse," I said. But I reminded him that we still had half of our rum ration. "Let's get another Coke and have a drink. It might help."

Bob nodded, went up to the flight attendants' station, and came back with two Cokes and two cups of ice. We sipped our rum and Cokes, which took the edge off our predicament for a while. We'd be served another meal in an hour or so, so we would at least arrive well fed. Tired, but well fed.

I mentioned to Bob that I had flown a B-29 in this same airspace in World War II. I had been based on Tinian and had come through Kwajalein a few times.

"I think you're nuts, volunteering for combat again," he said. "What's the matter, trouble at home?"

Bob's question hit me hard, especially because it was way off the mark. There was no good way to respond, so I simply said, "Maybe I made a mistake when I volunteered for active duty. I never thought I'd be sent into combat, and neither did my wife."

Being on that airplane, going to Vietnam at the ripe old age of forty-three, and leaving a wife with four children was not the most intelligent thing I'd ever done. More than twenty-three years had passed since I was in flight school in the early days of World War II. It was twenty-one years since I flew combat missions in 1945. I was flying to Vietnam at an age when most military folks think about retiring. I was going into combat as an ordinary "peter pilot."

Bob was probably right. It was a crazy situation, and I was caught in the middle of it. On the other hand, there was the challenge of doing something different, something out of the ordinary. It was not my nature to admit that I was not qualified or was unable to perform because of my size or age. I remembered how I overcame the height problem when I applied for flight training. I recalled the answers I gave Frecker about my size when training in the B-24. I not only flew the big bird; I flew it as a test pilot. One thing was certain: All the rationalization I was capable of did not alter my situation one whit. I had to stop reflecting on the past. It didn't produce answers.

I finally responded to Bob's question. "Crazy or not, I'm here because of my own free will. Maybe it wasn't the wisest thing to ask for active duty during a war, but I did. I'll have to live with that, and I'm prepared to see the situation to its conclusion, good or bad. By the way, the wife and I get along famously."

The flight attendants brought an end to the conversation when they arrived with another meal. Whoever was responsible for the food contract with the carrier certainly made sure the passengers were well fed. I knew that airline meals were often called "play food" because of the small portions and miniature utensils. But this time there was more than we could eat and it was better than average. Afterward I leaned back in my seat and dozed off.

I awoke and looked out at the Pacific Ocean far below. The visibility was excellent and there were no clouds in the area. We were so high I couldn't make out any whitecaps on the surface. I scanned the expanse of water but couldn't see any wakes to indicate shipping. I wondered where we were.

At that instant the aircraft's intercom came alive. "This is your captain speaking. For the benefit of the passengers sitting on the right side of the plane, I'm going to bank the ship so you can see the islands of Tinian and Saipan. The *Enola Gay* took off from Tinian to drop the first atomic bomb on Japan."

I'd told Bob about flying off Tinian and operating in the area, and now we were right over the island. The captain banked the aircraft sharply and I saw the islands clearly. While he kept the plane banked steeply for a few seconds, I saw West Field and North Field on Tinian and Isley Field on Saipan. I'd flown many missions from West and North Fields. The captain righted the plane and continued to the Philippines. I'm sure he didn't know that anyone aboard had flown missions during World War II off one of the islands, but I was thankful he had a sense of history and shared it with his passengers.

What a strange set of circumstances. What a coincidence that I occupied a window seat on the right side of the plane. Bob saw that I was elated over the experience and, remembering how he had chided me about going into combat again, apologized for the remark he'd made. I told him to forget it. I was just happy to see my old base again.

My thoughts, which had been about returning to combat, shifted to my B-29 crewmen. I wondered what they were doing. I hadn't seen or heard from any of them since the end of the war. I recalled the good times that Bob Oakley and I had when we were carousing and barhopping. We were especially close as pilot and copilot of a combat crew. Although I had to set aside thoughts of the old days, seeing Tinian rekindled memories of things that occurred twenty-one years ago. Those days were gone, and many of my friends and associates of that period were no longer living.

I nudged Bob. "What do you think of that? Here I am in a jet airliner on my way to the war in Vietnam, and our plane flies right over my old World War II base and I'm able to see it. I'll bet that's never happened before."

"You'll have to admit that for it to happen, you've got to be a damned old fart."

I laughed at Bob's remark. "What do you say to another rum and Coke? It's about time, don't you think? Besides, it shouldn't be long until we land at Clark Air Base."

Bob got a couple of Cokes and ice, then reminded me that this was the last of our rum. I was aware of that bad news. As a joke, I told him that our actions must be in violation of some vague rule or regulation. If the authorities knew we were relaxing with a few drinks, they might remove us from the plane and deprive us of the opportunity to get into combat.

Bob looked at me. "Mike, you know we have to have those high muckety-mucks sitting in their lofty ivory towers making regulations on every subject imaginable. If it were any different, we'd be surrounded by chaos and anarchy."

I smiled as I raised my glass to his. "I'll drink to our chaos and anarchy."

Before long, we landed to refuel at Clark—another base where I'd been stationed. I knew that none of the things that were part of the old Clark would be around. Too many years had passed. What I saw was a completely modern air force installation that could pass for any facility back home. There wasn't anything to remind me of the airfield I knew in 1946 and 1947. Only the heat and humidity were the same.

Refueling didn't take long and we soon were on our way. Next stop: Vietnam and the war. I was tired but didn't try to rest. I suppose I was on edge, in a state of considerable anticipation of what the battle area would have to offer. Bob may have had similar thoughts, because he was not his usual talkative self. I kept my eyes glued to the window trying to make out shipping or other evidence of our naval forces maneuvering about the area. I didn't want to miss an important event.

This was the final leg of our long flight to Saigon. We were told there wouldn't be any more meals. It really didn't matter. I felt that all the food on the flight had the characteristics of the last meal given to the condemned.

As we neared Vietnam, I thought that our government couldn't have gone farther to find a war to fight. If the money spent fighting the war did not bankrupt the country, the price of getting to the war would do it. As I kept looking out my window, I thought I saw an island ahead, or maybe it was the mainland. The distance made the scene hazy and I couldn't make it out. No matter, the captain announced that we would cross the coast of Vietnam in a few minutes and would land at Tan Son Nhut, Saigon's commercial airport. I pressed my head against the window, wanting to see the shoreline as it came into view. We were still quite high when I finally spotted the coast. There wasn't much definition to the scene, but as we slowly descended things became clearer.

We were flying past a heavily wooded area that looked intensely green. Once in a while I thought I could make out individual palm trees. Occasionally I saw a village snuggled into the terrain. There weren't any paved roads, and the narrow dirt lanes coming from the hamlets looked more like trails. These were the only manifestations of communication between villages in the area.

It looked so peaceful and quiet that it made me wonder what kind of war was going on. I noticed one hill with smoke rising from its crest and one of its sides. Suddenly there was a bright orange flash. Flames erupted from the hilltop followed shortly by a second brilliant flash. I finally saw the cause of the smoke and flames: Two A-1Es were bombing and strafing the hill. It was the first combat action of the Vietnam War that I witnessed. It wouldn't be the last.

Bob also wanted to see the action, so I moved out of the way while he took in the scene below. "Wow," he exclaimed. "Those guys mean business. They're really raking over that hillside. Mike, there's a war going on down there."

Like it or not, I was back in combat. It was the third war in my lifetime.

9 Vietnam: 1966

My arrival at Tan Son Nhut airport brought mixed emotions. The scene was not what I expected. There wasn't anything at the airport to indicate that a war was going on. A rainstorm had passed over the area, but it did little to abate the heat and humidity that pressed in on me and caused considerable discomfort.

Men and women, Occidental and Oriental, moved about, some in native dress and others in uniform. I saw several air force people in their blue outfits and army soldiers in fatigues. There were a few Vietnamese soldiers in "no see me" suits strolling about; the local police were easily recognized by their all-white uniforms. Civilians were milling about seemingly unconcerned about the war; they outnumbered the military until our aircraft unloaded.

We were directed to a corner of the terminal, where we took seats in a fenced-off section for a short orientation. We were told that a week ago the Viet Cong (VC) had set off a Claymore mine nearby and killed about a dozen civilians. An army sergeant put the finishing touches to the presentation and welcomed us to Vietnam. After the briefing we boarded buses that would take us to the replacement depot.

Bob French looked at me. "Was this the way it was in the big war, Mike? I can't believe what I'm seeing. All sorts of people walking around a terminal that's supposed to be in the middle of a war zone and no security worthy of the term."

"It does seem weird," I answered. "I don't know what to think myself. Let's be patient; we're new to this war. Things might make more sense later on."

On the way to the depot, I noticed that the heavy metal screening over the windows was similar to the protection on the buses I'd seen in Arabia. We were safe from grenades. But if the Viet Cong wanted to press the issue, we were vulnerable to other mischief.

It was still daylight when we arrived at the replacement depot. I was not surprised to see the bare-bones accommodations—row upon row of cots with minimal spacing between them and no attempt to provide privacy. There were community cold-water showers and latrine facilities for transients.

Bob was surprised but not amused by what he saw. "Damn, is this all we get after a day-and-a-half flight in a tin can packed like sardines? It's hotter than hell with humidity to match and we don't even have a fan."

"Well, it does have the austere aspects of an installation one would expect in a combat theater," I said. "You sort of indicated that you wanted things to look more military and warlike, didn't you?"

"If that's an attempt at humor, Mike, it ain't funny."

"Why don't you take a shower, Bob? It'll cool you off and make you feel better. It might relax us so we can rest better. I'm heading for the showers."

After showering I stretched out on my cot and closed my eyes, anticipating the first real sleep in a couple of days. I was in a semiconscious state when I heard the distant rumble of artillery, the first sound of the war for me. Bob heard it too and almost in a whisper said it wasn't thunder we were hearing. The bombardment continued, but it didn't prevent us from dropping off to sleep.

I slept well until I heard the muffled sounds of people moving about, but I was not ready to get out of bed. I was roused from my soporific state by the blaring of the depot's public address system announcing that breakfast would be served until 0730. According to my watch, it was already 0645. Bob was stirring but didn't attempt to get up. I told him if he wanted breakfast he'd better hurry; the mess hall would close in a short while. When he still didn't move, I assumed he didn't want breakfast.

I headed for the mess hall, but when I saw its condition I opted to forgo breakfast and settle for a couple cups of coffee. The air temperature was already at an uncomfortable level, as was the humidity.

There were huge floor fans about the mess facility, but they didn't offer much relief. It would take time to get acclimated.

When I returned to the replacement depot, Bob was up and about and in a clean uniform. The public address system was constantly announcing the names of people who had assignments and would be moving out. Bob knew where he was going, but his unit representative hadn't arrived. I didn't have any idea where I'd be going. It was about noon when the loudspeakers broke into action again. This time I was summoned to the depot office. Bob wished me luck.

I was greeted by a tall, young first lieutenant. "I'm Lieutenant Sawyer. I'm to take you to the 283d Medical Detachment. It's a dustoff unit. If you'll get your gear, we'll load up the jeep and get you out of this rattrap."

When I returned for my luggage, I told Bob about my assignment. He seemed surprised, almost shocked. He asked if I knew that I'd be flying medical evacuation missions. I admitted that I didn't know a thing about the organization and had never heard of dustoff. I told him I had assisted in the aeromedical evacuation process a few times in the Dominican Republic.

"This is no Dom Rep," he said. "This is Vietnam. There isn't any comparison."

Our conversation was cut short. Bob saw that I was ready to depart. I told him that I'd enjoyed his company and he'd made a long, boring trip bearable. I wished him all the best in his assignment. He shook my hand and said, "Mike, be careful. Dustoff missions aren't the safest in the world. If I were you, I'd look for a change of assignment. Otherwise, see to it that your will is up-to-date."

I assumed he was pulling my leg and making light of the situation. But he was aware of the true nature of dustoff and was deadly serious. That was the last time I saw Maj. Bob French. To this day I don't know what happened to him. Such short acquaintances are not uncommon during war.

Sawyer was waiting for me in the jeep. I threw my things in the back and we were off, headed for Tan Son Nhut. Before long we were inside an ancient wood structure that housed the operational offices of the 283d and the 57th Dustoff Detachment, and I became aware that I was being sized up. I wasn't surprised; after all, I was about twice the age of most of the people there. I sensed that my arrival was not greeted with enthusiasm and learned later that my assignment was viewed with skepticism by some. One of the younger aviators of the 57th made the observation that he was glad he didn't have to check me out on dustoff missions. As it turned out, we never flew together.

Sawyer ushered me into the 283d commander's office and introduced me to Maj. Owen A. Koch. He was slightly taller than I and in his midthirties. He saw I was considerably older than the rest of his aviators but knew that many warrant officer aviators came up through the ranks. He wasn't unduly concerned about my age—that is, until he asked me how long I'd been flying. I answered without hesitation, "Twenty-four years." His jaw dropped. He'd been in the army about fourteen years. He indicated that I must have flown during World War II and asked if I had been an army liaison pilot. I told him I did fly during World War II but had been a bomber pilot, a B-29 aircraft commander. He said he was happy to have someone on board with so much experience and hoped I could share that background for the benefit of the detachment. I said it was my intention to do everything I could toward that end.

Major Koch told Sawyer to show me around the area and introduce me to the aviators of the 283d. Having already met the CO and Sawyer, there were only nine other pilots to meet. I was the twelfth, and that was the total aviator strength of the outfit.

The unit's official designation was the 283d Medical Detachment (Helicopter Ambulance). It had six UH-1D Hueys manned by twelve aviators and enough crewmen to have a medic and crew chief on each helicopter. There were additional administrative and support personnel assigned for the operation of the unit.

The 57th and the 283d Detachments were combined into a provisional company commanded by Maj. Glenn Williams. Because the company was not self-supporting, it was placed under the administrative control of the First Logistical Command, also known as the First Log. The symbol of the First Log was a stubby white arrow set off at an angle and enclosed by a circle. It looked more like an outhouse than an arrow. The troops were quick to note the similarity to a privy and referred to it as the Leaning Shit House.

The First Log Command didn't interfere with the operation of the provisional company or its detachments. About the only intercourse between the command and its units was the submission of recommendations for awards.

Sawyer escorted me around the unit's area and showed me the 57th and 283d flight line, which was on the southwest corner of Tan Son Nhut airport. Everything was out in the open, because the detachments didn't have hangar space. Takeoffs and landings were controlled by the busy Tan Son Nhut tower. It often delayed our operations, which was especially inconvenient when we were dispatched on urgent life-or-death missions.

During our walk through the area, I met Capt. Jim Lombard and WO Charlie Wilson. I was quartered with them in a villa that the Saigon Housing Office had acquired for the 283d. I also met Maj. Chuck Conselman and discovered that he lived in the same villa, which was located on a street not far from the entrance to the airport. I was told that our street was called Claymore Alley, because a number of command-detonated mines had been set off in the area by the Viet Cong. I took such remarks as the usual harassment meted out to all newcomers.

I don't know who coined the term *villa* to describe a house acquired from the local citizenry. In fact, such villas were bare houses owned by Vietnamese who saw opportunities for considerable profit by leasing to the Americans. Our water supply came from a well in the front yard and was pumped into uncovered, internal holding tanks. That made the tanks an ideal breeding ground for mosquitoes, whose population in the immediate area was already sufficient. We didn't know it at the time, but the well was polluted with surface runoff and other debris, including a dead rat. All this was discovered when the pump broke and had to be replaced. We had been taking showers in that water and had even brushed our teeth with it. From then on we brought jerry cans filled with water from the airport for drinking and brushing our teeth, although our showers still used the well water.

It was an unhealthy situation, but we were in far better accommodations than the average combatant. Although our villa was serviced by the local electric company it did not have reliable power, nothing did in Vietnam. The villa's living area was on the second floor, where each of us had the luxury of a private room. We didn't use the cooking area, which was on the first floor, so we converted it into a garage for our jeep.

Claymore Alley was a street dedicated to small businesses. Directly across from the villa was the charcoal merchant, who supplied fuel for hundreds of homes in the area. Off to one side was a Vietnamese establishment that Charlie Wilson and I dubbed the local Howard Johnson's restaurant. When returning from work we often stopped there for Vietnamese tea before going into our villa. The owner and the local gentry took a liking to us and always welcomed us into their midst. We had a good time and enjoyed the company even though we couldn't understand one another. There was a lot of gesturing and sign language, so we managed to convey our thoughts and ideas. The owner often ordered his women to prepare food for Charlie and me. When that happened we knew we'd be there for the rest of the evening. The women made a beautiful salad of fresh vegetables, which they sculpted and shaped into a fancy floral-like display. This was followed by charcoal-broiled chicken or duck, and the tea would give way to high-powered, local "white lightning."

. Charlie and I couldn't let them furnish all the fixings, so we'd bring a bottle of American hooch. We'd also bring candy and cookies for the children, who we assumed belonged to the restaurant owner and his friends. The dining and drinking often lasted past midnight and ended when the booze ran out. We had some good sessions with these people. I'm surprised that neither Charlie nor I got sick from the food. It never met the army's food service standards.

Our time on Claymore Alley went reasonably well until one morning as I was getting ready for work. I heard and felt a violent explosion that shook the floor under my feet. The entire villa trembled, and the windows in my room were blown away. I discovered later that all the windows in the building had shattered. I thought someone had booby-trapped the jeep. Because Jim Lombard usually drove it, I thought he triggered the explosion when he started the engine. I rushed downstairs to check and saw the jeep intact. Jim was in his room when the explosion occurred; he thought it was on my side of the villa and had rushed to my room to help me. All he found was shattered glass strewn about the floor; everything else was intact. Chuck Conselman was in the shower when all hell broke loose. By the time he put on a robe and came out of his room, he saw me running back up the stairs and Lombard coming out of my room.

Jim and I each thought the other had been blown to Kingdom Come. We'd been running back and forth and up and down the villa to help each other. Our concerns were laudable but not necessary. The violent explosion destroyed the building next to ours. The terrorists set off a command-detonated Claymore meant to kill workers boarding an army bus going to Tan Son Nhut. It was fiendishly successful; it killed twenty-two workers and severely damaged the bus and set it on fire. It left little of the building standing and almost made our villa uninhabitable.

It was not a particularly reassuring start for our day. Conselman was furious. "That does it," he pronounced. "We're not staying in the middle of this battle zone another day. I'm going to find safer quarters even if it means sleeping in operations."

Charlie Wilson was not around. He'd pulled night duty and was flying. I imagined how surprised he'd be when he got back and found the area in shambles. There was nothing we could do, and we were expected on duty. Conselman and I got into the jeep with Lombard, who drove us to work. Conselman made a beeline for Glenn Williams's office; he was serious when he said he wouldn't spend another night in the villa.

I had to get the equipment and battle gear required for a combat pilot in Vietnam. The system was rigid. You were not a real-live, honest-to-goodness combat pilot unless you dressed the part. That meant having a black leather belt and holster for a .45-caliber pistol and a bandolier to hold extra rounds. The "brain bucket," or flight helmet, had to be painted olive drab. The paint was not available, so I covered my glaring white helmet with green tape.

Finally there was the drinking shirt. When we were off duty and patronized the officers' club, it was considered gauche not to wear a drinking shirt. Every unit in Vietnam had its identifying patch, and every drinking shirt was embossed with it and the owner's name. I ordered mine from the nearest "Cheap Charlie" shop. Every tailor who catered to the Americans for combat accoutrements was known as Cheap Charlie. I soon was a bona fide, honest-to-goodness, real-live combat pilot, proof of which was my purchase of all the required gear and clothing.

My first mission was with Major Koch and his friend Maj. Jerry Rose. We were to deliver a load of medical supplies to the 25th Medical Battalion at Cu Chi. This was the main base of the 25th Infantry Division, known as Tropic Lightning. Owen Koch had seen that I wasn't doing anything and invited me to come along to observe the area. Cu Chi wasn't far from our base at Tan Son Nhut—usually about a fifteen-minute flight. I was only going along for the ride, so I got aboard with my flight helmet and no other equipment.

Jerry Rose was an army aviator but held a staff position that didn't involve flying. Owen took his position in the aircraft commander's seat, and Jerry sat in the pilot's seat. We took off and I was in the back enjoying the scenery and watching as the terrain passed by. We dropped off the supplies at Cu Chi and took off to return to the base. I was hooked up to the ship's intercom and listened to the jaw-jacking between Jerry and Owen, who was doing the flying.

During the return flight, Owen asked, "What's our position, Jerry?"

"I don't know. You're doing the flying and navigating, aren't you?"

"Hell, Jerry, I thought you were navigating."

They both turned around and looked at me. All I could say was, "Don't look at me. I was only asked to come along for the ride. I thought the two of you knew what you were doing. If you'll let me see the map, maybe I can locate our position."

Jerry handed me his neatly folded, never-before-used map. I located Tan Son Nhut on the chart and found the frequency of its very-high-frequency omni directional radio ranfe (VOR) station. I had Jerry set the VOR receiver on the proper frequency, then center the course deviation indicator (CDI). The number-two needle of the radio magnetic indicator (RMI) pointed about fifty degrees off to our left. I couldn't understand how we managed to be so far off course. The ongoing conversation between Owen and Jerry was no doubt responsible, plus the fact that both thought the other was navigating.

I had Owen turn left until he centered the number-two needle. Then he flew the course until he had the airport in sight. It was an embarrassing situation, but I learned to be better prepared the next time I got on board a helicopter in Vietnam with two majors doing the flying.

My first combat mission in Nam was flown with Capt. Bill Colbert, a Medical Service Corps (MSC) officer. The MSC was responsible for the aeromedical evacuation of combat casualties and helped pioneer the use of the helicopter for such duties. Colonel (later Lieutenant General) Spurgeon Neel and the MSC were instrumental in the development and acquisition of the UH-1 as a medevac helicopter.

Colbert was the aircraft commander; his call sign was Dustoff 38. Each aircraft commander had a call sign, which he used for the duration of his combat tour. We were called into a hot area where troops of the 25th Infantry were making a sweep through an old nursery section of Cu Chi. The growth of shrubs, trees, and other plants covered a considerable part of the terrain where the troops were operating. The nursery complex was laid out in squares and afforded the Viet Cong concealment and also hindered the maneuverability of our troops. Our forces had taken considerable casualties. Even though the battle was still in progress, we were called to evacuate the wounded.

The VC were firing mortars into the area and subjecting it to a steady stream of sniper fire. This made our task difficult, so to present a minimal target we came in fast and low. We flew in and out of the complex twice without being hit. The third time our fast, low approach, coupled with an abrupt flare and landing, rattled one of our soldiers, who accidently fired a burst from his M16 rifle. He got the helicopter, but luckily all hits were in the tail cone. We evacuated eighteen troops, most wounded by mortar fire.

We also brought out a war correspondent who had been hit in the hand. Bob Jones, the Vietnam bureau chief of *The Honolulu Advertiser,* was so grateful that he wrote a complimentary article about his experience. He mentioned our unit, the 283d, and the names of our flight crew. He said he was most appreciative of the fine work of the dustoff crew "for their daring rescue of wounded soldiers while under heavy enemy fire." He also wrote a letter of commendation to the unit commander.

The mission introduced me to the type of flying I'd be doing for the rest of the year. It was not what I expected, yet there was a certain allure to it. I was not inflicting casualties on the enemy but was offering assistance to our wounded and relieving them of the trauma of battle. I saw wounded young men almost every day, heard their cries, and understood their agonies. The first traumatic amputation was a shock, but as time passed the commonality of the wound steeled me to the experience. I saw death so often that saving a life produced an emotional high. I'd be flushed with the triumph of the occasion. At times it was as if I were in a race with death itself. Invariably if the men we found were still alive, the race was decided in our favor. It never occurred to me that the grim reaper who watched my work was at all interested in me. I felt that no matter what, I would not be a casualty of that war. Under the circumstances, that was a most arrogant position to assume. Call it arrogance or foolishness; I never thought I was vulnerable.

Chuck Conselman was true to his word. We didn't spend another night in our rattrap of a villa. With the assistance of Major Williams and some arm twisting, we secured safer and better quarters. Conselman and Lombard got their own rooms, and Charlie Wilson and I shared an extra-large room on the first floor of the Red Bull Inn.

The Red Bull was in a compound directly behind the Third Field Hospital nurses' quarters. There was a guard post at the entrance to the compound, which contained the hospital, the nurses' quarters, and the inn. Charlie and I even had a private bathroom and shower. But unfortunately the electricity was furnished by the local electric company.

The hospital had its own power-generating system. The generators were not far from our room behind a high concrete wall. I told Charlie, who had a friend working for an American engineering company, to get an air conditioner for us. We could mount it in one of our windows, and by hook or crook he could get it connected to the hospital's system. A few of the occupants of the Red Bull Inn had air conditioners, but no part of the inn was tied in with the hospital. Our electricity fluctuated constantly and seemed to be off as often as on.

Within a week Charlie told me he'd be able to get an air conditioner, but it would cost us a gallon of booze. "No sweat, GI. Get your two quarts and I'll match it," I said. I didn't bother going to the exchange; I didn't want to waste time. I borrowed a quart from

Jim Lombard and one from Chuck Conselman and gave them to
Charlie.

I was assigned to field standby with the 1st Infantry Division (The
Big Red One) the next day. I was gone for five days and upon my return saw a huge air conditioner in one of our windows. Our quarters were now comfortably cool.

I took off my jungle fatigues, which were dirty and smelly after five
days in the boondocks. A shower and a change of clothes made all
the difference in the world. I went to the club for some drinks and
decent food. The 1st Division didn't have hot meals when they were
on the move in the field; C rations were more the rule. But that
evening I enjoyed a few drinks and a big steak in the dining hall.

My usual drink in Vietnam was gin and tonic. I didn't take the regular doses of Atabrine to ward off malaria, because it didn't agree
with my constitution. Every time I took the stuff, my gut would be in
rebellion. I knew several people who took the medication regularly,
and they were constantly ill from reactions to it. For better or worse,
I relied on the regular dose of quinine in the tonic to protect me.
My preventive measures proved as effective as the officially decreed
methodology. The disease never brought me down, and I didn't miss
a day of work the entire year. The same couldn't be said of the other
aviators. They had bouts of intestinal ailments, many caused by
Atabrine. There were the usual complaints of diarrhea and dysen-
tery brought on by contaminated food, some bought on the local
market and some served in the military messes. I remained un-
touched by the usual overseas tropical ailments, and I credited my
excellent state of health to good genes and good gin.

Malaria wasn't the only danger. Charlie Wilson was nearly killed
on one mission. He and his crew were on standby with the 25th Infantry Division during a sweep through the Michelin Rubber Plantation, northwest of Cu Chi. They were called to extract a severely
wounded GI from the midst of a firefight. The pickup was successful, but as they departed the battle their Huey was laced by automatic
weapons. Charlie was leaning over the control pedestal to change
the radio frequency when a burst of fire hit his side armor; other
rounds slammed into the ceiling of his Huey. Charlie was hit in the
calf by shrapnel, but he escaped almost certain death because he was

leaning over: The rounds passed over his side armor where his head and shoulders would have been.

When Charlie came into our room that evening, he was still shaken by the experience. Anytime he was upset, his stomach paid dearly. That's why he kept an assortment of antacid medication on a shelf that he and I shared for our toilet articles. Charlie's portion of the shelf contained other medicinal products, enough to make a drugstore-sized display of over-the-counter remedies. I didn't mind his collection, but I resented the fact that friends who came to our quarters automatically thought that the medications belonged to me. I didn't even have a bottle of aspirin.

Charlie was really upset by his brush with death. He took one dose after another of his assortment of antacids. I told him to take a shower and change into civvies and we'd go loosen up at the Red Bull Inn. He thought that was a good idea, and we soon were sitting at the bar enjoying our drinks. I suggested that a little dinner was in order, and Charlie agreed. He wanted to go into the city for a gourmet dinner at the Rex, a billet for officers at Military Assistance Command Vietnam (MACV). I explained to Charlie that it was too late and we wouldn't get back before curfew. Besides, I told him we were having trouble with our air conditioner and I wanted to talk to him about it. So we had dinner at the Red Bull and returned to the bar.

I had a gin and tonic and so did Charlie. I reminded him we were still connected to the local electric system, which was playing havoc with our air conditioner. The voltage was fluctuating so much that it threatened to burn up the motor; we needed more dependable power. He'd done an outstanding job getting the air conditioner, but we still were not wired into the hospital's system. Charlie said it wasn't easy to get into the hospital's grid. It could not be done legally; it would have to be on the q.t. The crew that maintained the generators were indigenous personnel and didn't understand English. I suggested that Charlie get help from the mama sans who did our laundry. They knew enough English to understand what we wanted and could explain the situation to the people who operated the generators. The mama sans could also help negotiate the payoff that the Vietnamese electricians would want for the hookup.

Charlie promised me he'd take care of it and let me know what developed. What we were doing wasn't exactly aboveboard, but it was the way things were accomplished in combat theaters throughout history. There were always things that people needed for which they were willing to trade items they controlled. In our case we were merely in need of air-conditioning and dependable electrical power. Scrounging and trading were necessary to exist in combat. The normal medium of exchange was booze, which was always in demand. At unit levels, trades had more of a businesslike and contractual character and were made for items such as hundred-kilowatt generators, lumber, and other building materials. I even saw paving jobs traded for items or favors of equally substantive value. It was a corrupt system, but it worked and kept the war effort going.

Charlie finally got us connected to the hospital's electrical system. There was an immediate improvement in our room's lighting, and the air conditioner never ran better. The cost for the arrangement was booze and a case of C rations.

The change in our quarters was noticeable, especially at night. The light shining from the windows of the other rooms was dull in comparison to ours. When the local power was off (which was often), our windows still glowed with their usual brilliance, and our air conditioner hummed reassuringly. The rest of the inn would be in darkness, so it was evident that Charlie and I had somehow pulled off a coup. No one was unduly concerned or raised a fuss about the situation, but I was asked by the command chaplain how it was that we had electrical power when the rest of the building was dark. I explained that we were subject to call at all hours to handle medical emergencies, and that made it necessary for us to be fully rested and refreshed. I apparently satisfied his curiosity, because the matter was never brought up again.

I was with the 283d less than a month when I was made an aircraft commander. The upgrade was no doubt due to my long-term aviation experience and my being the only aviator in the unit with extensive knowledge of instrument flight. I became the unofficial instrument pilot for the unit and instructed the other aviators.

Heavy rainstorms and the darkness of night made instrument flight necessary to reach evacuation areas. Once the lights of Saigon were left behind, it was like flying in a black void. The horizon and all ground references disappeared, leaving no other method of aircraft orientation.

Most helicopter pilots in country were not trained to fly in instrument conditions. The curriculum of army flying schools didn't address the subject until the problem and resultant casualties became known. Even when instrument flight instruction was brought into the training program, the effort was minimal and never achieved its goals.

Army aviators, being mission oriented, tried to operate in marginal weather, which too often deteriorated into instrument conditions. Many aviators became victims of spatial disorientation when they found themselves without ground references. Some were killed when they panicked and lost control after becoming confused and disoriented.

Although I wasn't formally trained in helicopter instrument flight, I had hundreds of hours of flying experience in all kinds of weather. So I applied fixed-wing instrument procedures and was able to fly through some of the worst weather in the world.

When I became an aircraft commander, I was given my personal call sign. The aircraft commanders of the 283d had call signs that ranged from 30 to 39. Major Williams decreed that because of my age and experience I was to have a special number. So he gave me the only three-digit call sign in the company. I was known as Dustoff 300.

We had frequent field standby duty as the 1st and 25th Divisions expanded the scope and frequency of operations. The big problem was the lack of dustoff assets to cover all operations. In addition to the divisions, we supported Australian, Korean, Vietnamese, and air force units including the Ranch Hands, which were C-123s engaged in defoliation flights. They sprayed large areas with Agent Orange to deny the Viet Cong cover for their clandestine operations and prevent ambushes of our forces. The Ranch Hands operated in flights of three aircraft escorted by a dustoff helicopter. If a C-123 went down, dustoff was there to recover the crew.

Due to heavy demands for medevac, the divisions couldn't be given more than one field standby helicopter for direct support during operations. When the workload of the dustoff standby crews became so great that evacuations were slowed, they contacted base and received augmentation. This operational flexibility enabled dustoff to evacuate the wounded regardless of the tactical situation. Above all, the wounded came first.

The first week of June 1966 was exceptionally busy for the 283d. The 1st Division units operating in the field frequently engaged the Viet Cong and had casualties to be evacuated. To compound the problems of the dustoff crews, the weather was atrocious. It seemed as if every morning was beset with low clouds and fog; then the afternoons and evenings generated heavy rains and thunderstorms. It was June 9, and neither the tactical situation nor the weather improved. Jim Lombard and I, along with Specialists Anderson and Granlee, were scheduled for night duty. Jim was the aircraft commander. The 1st Division was engaged in a concerted effort to clear the Viet Cong from Highway 13, the main artery north from Saigon to the Cambodian border. It was the direct route that afforded access to the South Vietnamese capital from the Viet Cong sanctuary in Cambodia. Its value as an infiltration route for the Viet Cong was diminished by pressure applied by American forces constantly sweeping the route and its environs. The Viet Cong continued to roam the artery and maintained a fluid presence, launching attacks and ambushes.

Shortly after dark our crew received an urgent medevac mission at coordinates Xray Uniform 736 095. This was the airstrip at Loc Ninh, the northernmost government and Special Forces outpost on Highway 13, just below the Cambodian border. Loc Ninh was the target of regular mortar attacks by Viet Cong forces, which melted back into the jungle or crossed the border into their sanctuary after the raids.

The flight to the outpost presented the usual night navigational problems. There was rain along the entire route, but turbulence was negligible. We had limited forward visibility and made the flight on instruments. Paris Radar (the area radar control center) gave us assistance, but coverage ceased after reaching the limits of its range. The rain intensified as we neared the outpost. Contact with the ground unit was established, and we were told that the area was secure—no enemy activity at the time. Identification with the ground unit was verified by signals from handheld flashlights.

We circled the evacuation site once and landed without incident as the rain temporarily abated. Four wounded litter patients were quickly placed on board, and we departed for the 1st Medical Battalion at Lai Khe. All four of our wounded were injured by enemy mortar fire.

The facility at Lai Khe had some of the best medical talent in Vietnam. I knew that the wounded would get the best of care. Although their wounds were painful, they were in no danger; all would survive.

We left Lai Khe and headed for the base at Tan Son Nhut. En route we received another urgent mission. This time we were given the coordinates Xray Tango 825 915. This plotted out at Quan Loi, another of the 1st Division's many bases strung out along Highway 13. Quan Loi was in the center of a huge French rubber plantation, the Terre Rouge Plantation, named after the red soil, which acquired its color from a high concentration of laterite. The plantation was about eight kilometers from An Loc, a much larger rubber-producing complex that was bisected by Highway 13. The 1st Division used An Loc and Quan Loi as bases. Both had airstrips that the division's aviation units used to supply its ground combat forces.

We had been on the go since reporting for the night shift as contact with enemy forces increased. After receiving the mission and plotting the evacuation site, we headed back up the highway. Jim was flying while I decoded the tactical information, call sign, and radio frequency. The weather continued to deteriorate; the rain increased in intensity as we flew in and out of clouds.

Jim said he couldn't see a thing and would have to fly on the gauges. I told him that the course was set on his VOR and I'd take over if he needed a rest. The turbulence also increased, and in the distance I saw occasional flashes of lightning. The weather was getting worse with each passing hour.

The course on the VOR was set for 358 degrees off the Saigon station. That put our route over Highway 13, which allowed us to make out a village now and then to check our progress toward the pickup site. Navigation for the pickup depended on a chance break in the clouds or a slackening of the heavy rain at the moment we were over a village we could identify. The lights we made out were kerosene lamps used by the villagers. Only the larger communities had electrical power. It was not high-tech navigation. Army helicopters, unlike air force aircraft, were not equipped with TACAN or other distance-measuring equipment, so we made do with what we had.

We were thankful that VOR stations were still available. At least they gave us the lines of position (LOPs) that put us on a direct course to the evacuation area. Approaching the pickup site, we called the ground commander to advise him that we were nearing his position. If he heard our helicopter he'd tell us; otherwise, we'd continue flying on course until he did. As we communicated with each other, the position of the aircraft and ground unit would be confirmed and the evacuation would go on.

I preferred to turn on the helicopter's navigation lights to help the ground commander direct me to his position. I'd also turn on the searchlight and if needed the landing light. He'd confirm sighting the lit-up chopper, then all unnecessary lights would be doused. No need to help the VC; on night pickups, the cards were all in their favor.

Identification of the pickup site during night operations was by light signals, usually flashlights. Often ground units used cigarette lighters or even matches when a flashlight wasn't available. One night when I made a pickup, the only light was a fire in the middle of a small jungle clearing. As I descended, my downwash scattered the fire about the area. The wounded were placed on board, and as I made a vertical takeoff the embers were scattered farther. The whole area was ringed by small fires. I'd made a mess, but the wounded were out of there.

Jim and I continued flying to An Loc. When we saw the dim haze created by the town's lights, we turned northeast for the few klicks (kilometers) to Quan Loi. We made contact with the ground commander and descended for the pickup. We came down through some scud and finally broke clear of all clouds. Visibility improved and we landed without difficulty. The wounded troopers were taken on board and the evacuation was accomplished in good order. Except for deteriorating weather en route, the pickup was a piece of cake. We retraced our route to the medical facility at Lai Khe, unloaded the wounded, and shut down to refuel. It was a good chance to "take ten."

While there we visited Capt. Orman Simmons, one of the surgeons on duty. He commanded D Company, 1st Medical Battalion. He and his crew of doctors and medical technicians were among the best in the world. Many of the wounded brought to his facility were barely alive but by some miracle were stabilized and taken to more advanced medical care. It was a rare soldier, no matter how traumatic his wounds, who didn't survive when treated by Simmons and his people. If the war had a positive aspect, it was the rapid response and delivery of the wounded to life-saving medical aid and treatment. The availability and dedication of dustoff crews in the midst of the operational area, the proximity of medical facilities staffed with highly competent professionals, and an excellent communication system made it possible to respond quickly to the wounded. It was my good fortune to be part of such a dedicated group.

Captain Simmons decided that the wounded we brought in should be kept overnight. He'd decide in the morning whether or not to evacuate them to one of the hospitals at Saigon or Long Binh. Jim and I made our adieus and departed for the base at Tan Son Nhut. As soon as we were airborne, we checked in with the unit radio telephone operator (RTO) and were told that all was quiet. It must have been the weather; even the Viet Cong weren't anxious to be out in it.

At the base we shut down the engine, secured the helicopter, and returned to the night crew's alert quarters. Anderson and Granlee welcomed the opportunity for a little rest. The unit was short of aidmen and crew chiefs, because replacements for those who finished their tours had not arrived. It was a typical cycle that all units encounter. Military people learned long ago that shortages are alleviated in due time and transformed into temporary overages. It's the military way. The people in personnel are the last to know there's a shortage, and after they "fix" the problem they're the last to know they've created an overage. So it goes ad infinitum.

Anderson and Granlee were already in their sacks about to enjoy some Zs when the runner came into the crew quarters with another urgent mission. The pickup site was at Xray Sierra 935 800, which turned out to be Nha Be, a riverside base that supported operations in the Saigon area. It was about ten kilometers south-southeast of the city. There was only one injured soldier to be evacuated, but he was in serious condition.

We rushed to our chopper, fired it up, and were on our way. In a few minutes we were in the pickup area, where location, identification, and verification were quickly established. The patient was taken aboard on a litter, and Anderson quickly determined that the man's injuries had been overstated. But he indeed suffered a painful injury; his right hand had been crushed by a piece of heavy machinery being loaded onto a flatbed truck. We agreed that it was best to take him to the 93d Evacuation Hospital.

On the way to the 93d, we heard radio chatter on the ultra high frequency (UHF) indicating that another dustoff had been launched for a mission up Highway 13. After we delivered the injured soldier and were airborne again, we asked the RTO why another aircraft was launched when we were nearby. He said an urgent mission was received shortly after we departed for Nha Be. Because we had already switched to the tactical frequency for our pickup, the RTO couldn't communicate with us. He didn't know how long we'd be on our mission and decided to launch the "second up" crew. All this happened in a space of about five minutes.

The other dustoff had asked Paris Radar for the latest weather along Highway 13. He was airborne only a minute or two when we heard his call, the bit of radio chatter we'd picked up when landing at the 93d Evac. Jim and I had been up and down that route all night and knew that the weather was steadily deteriorating. While our patient was being unloaded at the 93d, I mentioned that Captain Rothwell was the aircraft commander of the other dustoff and I doubted he could get through to the pickup site. He couldn't fly instruments. Jim agreed and added that for Rothwell to succeed, the weather would have to improve and that didn't seem likely. I suggested that because we were familiar with the weather, we would call Rothwell before he switched to his tactical frequency and volunteer to take the mission. We didn't know the exact location of the pickup site, but Jim still called Rothwell.

I was certain that Rothwell wouldn't be able to make it through the weather along the highway. If he persisted, he and his crew might not survive the night. I'd flown with Rothwell and knew he was a level-headed aviator, but he was not able to fly on instruments. There was no doubt in my mind that he welcomed the suggestion that we take the mission; he breathed a sigh of relief when he accepted our offer. He furnished us with the essential information for the pickup before he returned to Tan Son Nhut.

I plotted the coordinates, Xray Tango 695 752; it was on the road to the Minh Thanh Special Forces camp. My 1-over-50 tactical chart indicated in greater detail that the pickup site was a narrow dirt road running northeast to southwest near a small bridge. We knew where to go. Our problem was finding it after getting to the area through deteriorating weather.

We had slightly less than fifty miles to go, which would take about thirty minutes. The rain was heavy and steady. There were intermittent flashes of lightning ahead of our flight path and an even greater display of lightning to the east. The thunderstorms appeared to be moving east to west, and shortly the worst weather would be directly in our flight path. All indications pointed to continued degradation of the situation. It was not going to be easy.

The VOR was set on 358 degrees, which again put us on a course over Highway 13. The pickup site on the Minh Thanh road was about seven kilometers west of the highway. There wasn't a built-up area or town along that portion of highway to serve as a jumping-off point for the evacuation site. But I planned to make our approach from a definite position and selected Chon Thanh on Highway 13 about thirteen kilometers south-southeast of the pickup site. Hopefully we could make out Chon Thanh's few lights to verify our position, then fly northwest to the evacuation area. If we continued up the highway until we were due east of the site, there would be nothing but woods below and we would be uncertain of our position.

We couldn't rely on assistance from Paris Radar. It was too far away, and the weather and thunderstorms seriously impaired its ability to accurately track us. My plan was crude, almost harebrained, but it was the best that circumstances offered. Luck would play a large part in our success or failure to reach the wounded soldier.

I rechecked my computations and confirmed that the time to fly was about thirty minutes. We didn't have a backup course of action if the site wasn't located on the first attempt, but Jim and I agreed on the plan and pressed on. He flew on instruments while I and our two crewmen looked for visual clues to our position and progress. As we continued up Highway 13 the rain intensified, and there was considerably more turbulence. The lightning flashes I had observed to the east moved slowly toward our flight path, with the greatest display at our one o'clock position.

I checked on Jim to see how he was doing, and he said we were on course where we should be. I asked if he needed a rest, and he replied that he was doing fine. I knew he was concerned about experiencing spatial disorientation, the sensation that the instruments were not presenting an accurate picture of aircraft attitude; for instance, the pilot feels he is in a turn but the instruments indicate he is flying straight and level. An inexperienced aviator or one with insufficient training is inclined to trust his sensations rather than believe his instruments. Flying the aircraft and ignoring the instruments usually ends in loss of control and disaster.

I glanced back at Anderson and Granlee. They were looking intently out the sides of the aircraft and reporting occasional lights that came into view. The rain became extremely heavy and made it impossible to see anything ahead as the violent turbulence tossed us about. I saw the airspeed indicator as it danced around a hundred knots. I suggested to Jim that he slow to about ninety. "We don't want to tear this aircraft apart before we get to our destination," I said.

"Don't worry, Mike. I was thinking the same thing when I felt those last big jolts."

"It's the lightning that scares me," chimed in Anderson. "What if it hits us?"

"It's highly unlikely that we'll be struck by lightning," I replied. "If we were hit, it probably wouldn't damage the aircraft. But it could disable our radios and navigational instruments." Our conversation was interrupted by a bright flash of lightning just to the right of our ship, then a lesser flash ahead of us.

Jim didn't hesitate to voice his thoughts. "Damn that shit. That was too close. I hope you're right about the lightning, Mike."

"Trust me. It never hit my B-24s or B-29s, and they were a lot bigger and easier to hit than this little ole helicopter."

I didn't know if that flippant rejoinder eased the tension in the aircraft or not. No doubt about it, this would be a gut-churning flight.

I decided it was time to contact the ground unit and learn more about its situation. I wanted to know the condition of the wounded trooper and the weather at the pickup site. I checked my mission sheet for the tactical call sign and the unit's FM frequency. I set 68.5 into the radio and listened for a minute or so, but I didn't hear anything but static.

I made my first call. "Damage Charlie Three, this is Dustoff 34. Do you read me? We're about fifteen minutes from your location. Over."

Nobody replied. The lightning and rain continued without letup while our aircraft was tossed about by the unrelenting turbulence. Jim was sweating like a racehorse as he tried to maintain control. I didn't know how long he could keep it up before I'd have to take over. He was hunched over with his face close to the instrument panel. He was too tense; he needed loosening up.

"You're doing fine, Jim. I want you to know that with the lightning flashing so often, I'm keeping one eye closed in case you or I are temporarily blinded. When this is all over, I'll probably look like Popeye."

Jim didn't appreciate my sense of humor. "Call that damned outfit again. See if this trip is really necessary. I don't know if this weather will allow us to make the pickup."

I made two more calls without getting a response. On the third try, I finally received an answer.

"Dustoff 34, this is Damage Charlie Three. We're receiving you. Do you read me?"

"Damage Charlie Three, this is Dustoff 34. We're inbound to your location. We're encountering heavy rain, a lot of turbulence, and lightning flashing all around us. Is your wounded troop really urgent? Do we have to evacuate him tonight? Over."

"Dustoff 34, this is Damage Charlie Three. We have three seriously wounded soldiers down here, not one. All have multiple shrapnel wounds caused by a short round from one of our mortars. We're aware of the weather. It's not any better down here. There's a huge thunderstorm over our position and it's raining cats and dogs."

"Damage Charlie, this is Dustoff 34. How's the visibility at your location? We've got to have adequate visibility to locate you and make the pickup."

"Dustoff 34, it's hard to measure visibility here. We're totally without light, but I can see all around me whenever there's a flash of lightning above us."

"Roger, Damage Charlie Three. We're pressing on. We'll try our best but can't promise you we'll be able to punch through these thunderstorms. We'll give you another call when we're closer to your position."

"You heard the same shit I did, Jim. Now they have three urgent wounded, but that doesn't make it any easier to make the pickup. Did you get what he said about the visibility? He can see around his area whenever there's a flash of lightning overhead."

"Mike, I hope you realize that we volunteered to take this mission for someone else. What the hell were we thinking when we did that? We were in this area earlier and we both knew the weather was shitty and wasn't going to get any better. Imagine, hoping for a flash of lightning at just the right moment so we might be able to see our way to a safe landing. Well, what do we do now?"

At that moment the crew chief, Granlee, reported seeing dim lights ahead, almost below us. I barely made them out but recognized them as the lights of Chon Thanh. This was the place from which we were to make our run to the pickup site. We had thirteen kilometers to go. Jim was still on the gauges.

"We're over Chon Thanh," I told Jim. "I'll give you a new heading in a second." I checked the chart and, without benefit of measurement, eyeballed the course to our destination.

"Quick, Jim, turn left to three hundred thirty degrees and hold it as best you can. Forget about the VOR." Jim's question about what to do next had its answer.

Jim put us on the new course to the pickup site. We were in for a wild ride for the next thirteen kilometers. We wouldn't have any visual clues to check our position or the VOR radial to follow. The entire route from Chon Thanh to the pickup site was over dense, uninhabited jungle. We were over an area that only the Viet Cong dared to penetrate.

Jim struggled to hold the new heading as we penetrated another thunderstorm, probably the same one that was over the pickup site. We'd already reduced airspeed to ninety knots, but the turbulence was so severe that I had to help Jim right the helicopter whenever a strong gust hit us.

I suggested that we reduce the airspeed to eighty knots. The turbulence was so severe that I could almost hear the aircraft metal creaking from the strain imposed by the shearing action of the violent air currents. Flashes of lightning exploded all about us, occasionally bright enough to light up the inside of our Huey. Jim never wavered. He doggedly stared at the gauges and maintained a tight grip on the stick. I thought I saw his mouth move imperceptibly, as if he were praying. It won't hurt, I thought. Anderson and Granlee hadn't said a thing. Maybe they were praying too.

Suddenly a violent gust hit us and forced the aircraft into a steep bank to the left. I helped Jim right the bird. Then a brilliant flash of lightning detonated right outside Jim's door. It nearly blinded us. The rain slammed into us with such ferocity that it made a deafening noise when it hit the windscreen. I checked the heading and noticed that we had strayed almost twenty degrees off course to the left.

"Jim, turn right. Back on course to three hundred thirty degrees. That last blast of turbulence forced us off our heading. Keep it at eighty knots. I don't know how much more shit like that last jolt this bird can take."

"Okay, Mike, back on course now. Eighty knots airspeed. By the way, how long has it been since we left Chon Thanh? It seems like ages ago."

"I'm keeping track of the time, Jim. It's only been three minutes, but we're about halfway there. When we're able to make visual contact with the ground unit, it would be best if you remained on the gauges. I'll give you directions to keep you over the area and take over only when a landing is possible. I'm going to contact them now."

"Damage Charlie Three, this is Dustoff 34. We're about four miles from your location. Do you hear our aircraft? We're coming in from the south-southeast."

"This is Damage Charlie Three. Negative on hearing your chopper. All we're hearing is the heavy rain coming down on the trees, and the thunder. I'm sure we'll pick you up shortly. For your information, the trees on either side of the road are approximately a hundred feet high. But there appears to be sufficient clearance for you to land between them. There are some small trees and brush adjacent to and on either side of the road, but that shouldn't present a problem for you. I'm describing what I see during occasional flashes of lightning; otherwise, it's totally dark down here. Over."

"Roger, Damage Charlie. I received your latest. I'm sure we're flying through the thunderstorm that's over your location. Right now the rain is coming down so hard that we can't see a thing except the flashes of lightning. We're having a damn tough time maintaining control. We're being bounced all over the sky. We still have no forward visibility. Do you hear our aircraft yet? Over."

"Roger, Dustoff. I think I hear a chopper coming toward me now. It sounds as if you're coming right at me. I've only got one flashlight to signal you with. I've sent out word to my people that I need another one. Over."

"Roger, Damage Charlie. I've turned on my navigation lights. Do you see me?"

"Dustoff, I can't see you yet, but I can still hear you coming directly toward me."

"This is Dustoff. I've turned on my searchlight. Can you see me now? Over."

"Roger, Dustoff. I see you. I'm flashing my light at you. Do you see my signal?"

While this chatter was going back and forth, Jim was flying the gauges. We were still encountering severe turbulence. Occasionally we'd ride through strong updrafts, then equally powerful downdrafts. I had to help on the controls as we were rocked first to one side, then the other. It was not uncommon for our heading to be forced a good twenty degrees to either side of our intended course. It was all that Jim and I could do to keep the aircraft upright while trying to hold a reasonable heading.

We were in the worst part of the storm. It was going to be touch and go. I looked back for an instant and saw Anderson and Granlee hunched against the aft bulkhead. I gave them a thumbs-up to alleviate their fears. They hadn't said a word for five minutes or so. They really hadn't had anything to do since we left Chon Thanh. I knew they were worried and couldn't blame them. We knew what we were trying to do but didn't have time to explain our actions to them. It was a shitty situation, but we'd have to wait to explain everything when it was all over. For the time being they could only sit and trust in our judgment and ability to overcome the obstacles before us. This flight was testing their faith in Jim and me to the utmost.

I finally spotted a dim flash of light through the rain. I was elated; we'd found the pickup site. I had Jim set up a right-hand orbit and begin a slow descent while I kept tabs on the lone flashlight. Jim told me to make sure we didn't lose sight of it. He remained on the gauges and relied on me for directions to keep us over the evacuation area. I turned off all exterior lights. I didn't want the Viet Cong to be aware of our presence other than what they could deduce from the sound of our chopper circling somewhere above them.

I had Anderson and Granlee take their positions on both sides of the aircraft to guide me and clear the rotor systems when I made the approach and landing on the road. Having heard the chatter about the pickup site, they knew that the place was extremely tight and flanked by high trees and realized that even in broad daylight it would be a difficult pickup. But in the midst of a violent thunderstorm in the blackness of night, with lightning flashing every second and the chopper being bounced around by extreme turbulence, it would take our best combined efforts to pull off this mission. They knew their jobs and responsibilities. I knew I could depend on them.

"Damage, this is Dustoff. I still have your light. Give me a few quick flashes for confirmation. Point your light at the sound of the chopper. I've turned my lights off. No need for the VC to know everything that's going on."

"Roger, Dustoff. I'm flashing my light in your direction. I can't see a thing. Let me know if you see my signal."

"I see your flashes, Damage. I'll be descending slowly. I intend to come in along the road from the northeast. I've got to take it slow and easy. I can't see a thing except your light. The damn turbulence is still tossing the ship around. Damage, it would sure be nice if you could get another light. If yours goes out, I won't know whether it's your batteries or some obstruction to the line of sight. A second source of light would eliminate that problem for me."

"Dustoff, I have my men looking for another flashlight. I hope to have one soon. Sorry about not being better prepared."

"Well, we can be thankful we found you in spite of all the shit that nature has thrown in our way. Keep that flashlight pointed at the sound of the chopper. The lower we get, the more important it is for us to maintain visual contact. We'll make the approach and landing as soon as we get positioned and lined up with the road."

Jim had us down to a thousand feet indicated. He'd done a masterful job. It was time for me to take over and make the landing visually. According to our prearranged plan, I would take over the controls while he monitored the instruments. If I lost visual contact while trying to land, Jim would take over and make a maximum-performance instrument takeoff out of the area.

Anderson and Granlee were at their stations to lend assistance in clearing both sides plus the tail rotor during the landing process. I continued the right-hand, descending turn, keeping my eye on the light from the lone flashlight. As I maneuvered and descended, a series of rapid flashes of lightning illuminated the terrain below and I had an excellent view of the area around the pickup site. Most important, I got a good look at the narrow road cutting a straight path through the tall trees. Anderson reported that he too saw the road and it looked tight. Granlee confirmed the report. Jim also got a glimpse of the area and said he wasn't sure there was enough room between the trees for us to set down. I countered that we were too far out for an accurate assessment, and because we were here, after all our troubles we were not leaving without an attempt to land.

I called the ground unit. "Damage Charlie, this is Dustoff. We got a good look at your position during that last lightning display. Most of us up here are having doubts about the width of the area between the trees. We're not sure there's enough space for the main rotor to clear all obstacles."

"Dustoff, I know it looks tight and it is, but I'm sure you'll have enough room to make it. We were supplied this afternoon in the same general area. It was tight, but the choppers were able to land."

"Roger, Damage. Thanks for the information. Did you get another flashlight?"

"Dustoff, I've sent out the word. We're not able to move about with any speed because it's raining so hard and we can't see much. The place is covered with mud, and it's darker than the ace of spades."

Jim interrupted on the intercom. "Mike, my altimeter tells me we're about three hundred feet above the ground now. You better check your forward visibility. Besides, those trees might be higher than estimated."

"Roger, I'm going to turn on the landing light. You guys in the rear let me know what you see."

I turned on the light, but all I could see was the rain coming at me in huge drops. The landing light seemed to magnify each drop. So I turned it off and checked the ground unit's light, which was still flashing at me. I maneuvered so that in my continuing right orbit the light remained out to my side. The crew chief and medic reported that they couldn't see anything but rain. Jim concurred.

"You're supposed to be watching the instruments, Jim. Stop peeking."

Jim told me to pay attention to my flying. "Don't give me any bullshit, Mike."

There was another flash of lightning, but I couldn't make out any details. I was concentrating on the ground unit's flashlight and keeping it in sight. Anderson reported that he thought he saw the tops of trees below us. I had descended another hundred feet and turned the landing light on again.

Jim yelled over the interphone, "Trees! Trees!"

I stopped the descent. "I see them, Jim. We're okay. They're below us. I'm going to line up with the road for an approach. I'll be rolling out of this shallow turn in a second or so. Anderson, Granlee, keep an eye on my clearances when we get down to tree level." They rogered my directions.

I called the ground. "Damage Charlie, this is Dustoff. I'm about to line up with the road. I'll be coming in from the northeast and hope to make it in for the pickup. I'll have to use my lights to make the landing, so advise me of any Viet Cong activity you see or hear."

"Roger, Dustoff. I finally got hold of another flashlight. They're both pointed right at you. I hope that makes it easier for you."

"Thank you, Damage. That helps a lot, especially in this rain."

I asked Jim to turn on the windshield wipers and set them at high speed. I needed all the help I could get. As I maneuvered into position, I turned on the landing light and saw the treetops. As lightning flashed again, I could make out the general area of the evacuation site and pick up the narrow road. I didn't begin my descent immediately, because I wanted to get closer to the evacuation site and make a steep approach into it. My planned angle of descent would lessen the amount of flying between the trees and should be the safest approach under the circumstances.

The rain was heavy, but the windshield wipers on high speed gave me enough forward visibility to proceed with the landing. When I arrived at the proper sight angle, I began the descent.

"Okay you guys in the rear, be alert. Call out and let me know any time you think we're too close to the trees. We don't want anything to go wrong now."

A brilliant display of lightning that seemed to last a good five seconds enabled me to make out the area with a high degree of clarity despite the heavy rain. My position was confirmed. I was exactly where I wanted to be. For once I welcomed the lightning instead of cursing it. I continued my slow descent between the trees. There wasn't much room to spare on either side.

"You're looking good on the left," said Anderson. "You're close but clear of the tree branches on my side."

"Clear on the right," added Granlee. "You can continue your present heading. You're looking good on my side."

"Damage Charlie, this is Dustoff," I radioed. "As soon as we're down, all my lights will be switched off, so tell your troops to be extra careful around the chopper, especially if they're in the vicinity of the tail rotor."

"Roger, Dustoff. Understand. All of my people are familiar with your danger zones. You're right on target. Be sure to set down in front of me. Some of the trees behind me and to the side of the road could cause you trouble."

"I hear you, Damage. I have every intention of setting this bird right on top of you."

The rain came down in sheets, but the high-speed windshield wipers did the job. I saw all that was needed. Anderson and Granlee kept assuring me that my approach was fine, that we were clear of obstacles. Jim finally came on line and said it all. "I never thought we'd find this damned place. Then I never thought we'd fit into this damned confined area. But by God here we are about to land."

There was another strong flash of lightning just before I set the chopper down. As soon as I made ground contact, Anderson slapped me on the back and yelled into the intercom, "You made it! You made it! That was some kind of flying! I was scared shitless the whole time, but you made it!"

Just before setting down, I heard the main rotor make contact with some tree branches. "Damage Charlie, this is Dustoff. What did I hit just before landing?"

"Dustoff, you cut about a foot off some branches on small trees next to the road. They were a little higher than we thought. You cut through them like they were tall grass. I don't see that they caused you any damage, although they made quite a bit of noise."

Jim told Anderson and Granlee to hurry with the three wounded. "We don't want to spend any more time down here than we have to. Get them on board and let's get the hell out of here."

Meanwhile I swept the area in front of the chopper with the searchlight before switching it off. I saw the heavy growth of bushes and small trees that Damage warned me about. Farther ahead to the left and right of the road were the tall trees that were our main hazards. They were at least as high as Damage had estimated. We were in tight quarters. Any maneuvering for a better takeoff angle was out of the question. It was too dangerous. Our best course of action for departure was to make a vertical takeoff on our present heading. I planned to go without lights. Now that the Viet Cong were aware of our presence, I didn't want to give them any other clues as to our position or route of departure. I intended to use the ground unit's two flashlights for reference during takeoff. In that way I believed I'd be able to maintain a good heading and avoid contact with the trees.

Anderson and Granlee loaded the wounded, who were on litters. At last the call came from the back: "We're loaded. All ready for takeoff."

It was time to pull pitch. "Damage Charlie Three, have your flashlights positioned on both sides of the road facing the chopper. I'm ready for departure."

"Roger, Dustoff. We're setting up the two flashlights now. Are there any other instructions?"

"Damage Charlie, I want you to keep those two lights on and pointed at me as I lift off and during my climb out. You'll lose me in the rain, but keep pointing them at the sound of the chopper. I need them for reference to hold a constant heading and avoid the trees. When I call clear, you can turn them off."

"Roger, Dustoff. Understand. We'll have the flashlights on you all the way."

I told our crewmen to do the best they could to alert me of any deviation from my heading or of any drift toward the trees. "Ready, Jim, I'm pulling pitch." I pulled up on the collective.

As soon as I felt the ship get light on the skids, I glanced at the heading and increased power for a positive rate of climb. I maintained a vertical ascent while concentrating all my attention on the two points of light. It was seat-of-the-pants flying. The aircraft heading and attitude were determined by what I saw of the two flashlights.

The windshield wipers beat back and forth furiously as the rain pounded down with authority. Damage Charlie's two lights receded and diminished in intensity. There wasn't any word from the guys in the back, and Jim didn't say a thing. Either the men were satisfied with what they saw, or they were too frightened to say anything for fear they might break the spell.

I glanced at my attitude indicator and saw that it was steady. We were straight and level and still climbing vertically. I no longer saw the lights on the ground but noticed we'd climbed about 150 feet. We were above the trees.

"Mike, get some forward speed. We're high enough now," Jim said. "Damnit, that was one hell of a mission. That was some flying. I still can't believe we pulled it off."

I called ground. "Damage Charlie Three, this is Dustoff 34. We're clear of the trees now and on our way. You can turn off your flashlights, and thanks for your cooperation. We couldn't have made it without your help."

"Thank you, Dustoff. You guys have balls. I still don't know how you found us and made it into our position in the middle of the night with the thunderstorm and all going on. Our regular supply choppers had a devil of a time finding us this afternoon. I want you to know how much we appreciate your efforts. Again, many thanks, Dustoff."

After the climb out, I made a slow turn to the left, intercepted the 358 radial, and flew down Highway 13 to Lai Khe. We would deliver the wounded to the 1st Medical Battalion. In addition to their multiple shrapnel wounds from the short round, one had a broken leg. I wondered if Orman Simmons was still up and about. It was almost midnight and I knew he'd had a full day when we saw him earlier that evening. No matter, the wounded would be well cared for.

I looked over at Jim. He had his head way back in his seat; he was finally able to relax. "You want to fly back to Lai Khe?" I asked. "You could get more practice flying on instruments. You had a bit of trouble holding your heading and altitude while flying to the pickup site."

"Go to hell, Mike. You were no help at all. I did all the sweating and kept this bird right side up in the middle of those thunder busters. All you did was jaw-jack on the tac frequency. I've done enough flying for tonight."

A crew can be pretty flippant after all danger disappears. Anderson and Granlee chatted back and forth in the rear as they tended to the dressings and the IVs attached to the wounded. They were also in a relaxed mood.

I called the base and reported we'd made the pickup and were delivering the wounded to the 1st Med at Lai Khe. The RTO rogered my transmission and said there weren't any missions pending. I let him know we'd be most grateful if there weren't more calls for our services for the rest of the night. I also told him we'd be on the ground for about fifteen minutes and would call again when airborne.

The thunderstorms and lightning were behind us. It was still raining but with much less intensity. I was flying by reference to instruments but soon was able to go visual; the weather was clearing. We flew into the more built-up sections of the country where our military presence had given birth to numerous bases. Some had taken on the semblance of permanence. These places were well lit; all had excellent power-generating equipment. It was relatively easy for the Viet Cong gunners and mortar specialists to take advantage of such highly visible targets. Sneak mortar attacks in the middle of the night were not an uncommon occurrence.

We delivered the wounded to the med battalion, took time to answer the call of nature, and relaxed while the doctors assessed the condition of our patients. It was well after midnight when we were

told they'd keep the wounded overnight for observation and transfer them to the 93d Evac in the morning.

That was all we needed to know. Jim and I made our farewells and
headed to the chopper for the short flight to Tan Son Nhut. We reported to operations and were told there still weren't any missions
for us. We heaved a collective sigh of relief. Maybe there wouldn't
be any more activity for the rest of the night.

We returned to the alert crew quarters. "You've done well tonight,"
Jim told the crew. "You deserve a little rest."

"If another mission comes along," I said, "don't wake me unless
you feel you just can't do without me. Good night all." I flopped into
my sack exhausted.

Our efforts that night—June 9, 1966—did not go unnoticed. The
283d received letters from Lt. Col. Jack L. Conn, commander of the
2d Battalion, 2d Infantry, 1st Division; his operations officer, Maj.
Clair E. Porter; and platoon sergeant Harry Bruce Sherman. These
men were directly involved in guiding us into their position while
the thunderstorms raged. Their witnessing statements were responsible for each member of our crew being awarded the Distinguished Flying Cross.

I am shown here as a young cadet. This photograph was taken at Bonham Air Field, Texas, in 1942.

As a cadet in training I flew a BT-13 shown here in formation in 1942. My instructor, Lt. Atlee G. Manthos took the picture.

My test flight crew about to board a B-24 at Laredo Army Field, Texas, in 1944. On right note the two thick cushions near my left foot.

As a captain, with some of my combat crewmen as we prepare for a B-29 mission on Tinian in 1945. From left, Novosel, Peirent, Ackley, Baczynski, Kolbo, and Newman.

I am at the controls of my B-29.

I was maintaining the same spacing as the other pilots. When the formation leader singled me out and told me to "tighten it up," I placed my left wingtip inside his number three engine, my left wing directly behind his right wing. He never again told me to tighten it up.

A Japanese Zero in front of Clark Field base operations in 1946. The woven bamboo construction is typical of the buildings at the time.

Head wound. One of the 5,589 people I brought life-saving medical care in Vietnam.

Field pickup of 1st Infantry Division wounded in 1966. (Photo courtesy of Hoot Gipson.)

1st Infantry Division troops bring in more wounded in 1966. (Photo courtesy of Hoot Gipson.)

Guns-A-Go-Go (CH-47) shot down by the Viet Cong on July 9, 1966.
(Photo courtesy of Hoot Gipson)

Hoot Gipson relaxes with
a cigarette in Vietnam in
1966.

Unit patch—82d Med Det, 1969.

I am buckling up for a mission.

Major Don Bissell,
Commanding Officer, 82d
Med Det, Binh Thuy,
Vietnam, in 1969.

Navy Commander Conrad Jaburg, C in C, FASU, Binh Thuy, Vietnam, in 1969.

Si Simmons presents me with the Purple Heart medal after I flew thirteen hours. It was a tiring experience, and it showed.

Battle area where my aircrew and I rescued twenty-nine surrounded, wounded soldiers.

One of the numerous hummocks the Vietcong used as firing positions during the battle of October 2, 1969.

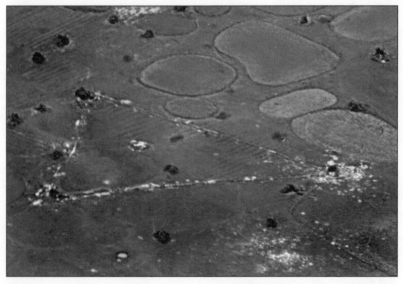

The triangular fort where I made two abortive attempts to rescue a soldier, October 2, 1969.

My wife Ethel and my son Mike at his graduation from flight school in 1969.

My son Mike, Rex Smith, and I at Binh Thuy, Vietnam, in 1970.

Official Army photo-
graph of me wearing the
Medal of Honor.

"Present the Command." The flag honor guard at my retirement ceremony at Fort Rucker on October 31, 1984.

10 Military Operations Increase

The summer of 1966 saw a gradual buildup of forces in III Corps as the 1st and 25th Infantry Divisions kept the pressure on the Viet Cong. The preponderance of my flying was in support of units of the 1st Division that mounted simultaneous operations throughout the corps area. They were involved in Operations Paul Revere, Fillmore, Fresno, Santa Fe, and El Paso. Our rescue mission on the Minh Thanh road was in support of 1st Division units during Operation El Paso. By the end of June 1966, enemy losses as a result of the operations were 685 killed, 29 captured, and 124 weapons seized. The operations continued into July.

To keep pace with increased military operations, dustoff units were reorganized when the 254th Medical Detachment was formed and placed at Long Binh. The 57th and 283d Medical Detachments were given more space in a large hangar at Tan Son Nhut. The move increased the efficiency of operations despite the rotation of many of our pilots to the States.

The 283d lost its commander, Major Koch, as well as Captains Colbert, Borth, Lombard, and Rothwell and Lieutenant Sawyer. They were replaced by Majors Bill Briot (the new CO), Floyd (Flood) Coddington, and Warren (Punchy) Hoen; Captains Charley Webb, Joe Fulghum, John Hosley, and John Colvin; and Lt. Mel Ruiz. Coddington and Hoen were aviator retreads—that is, they returned to flying duty after years of ground assignments with the Medical Service Corps. The others, except for Charley Webb, were relatively recent graduates from the army's flight training center at Fort Rucker in Alabama. None had any practical instrument flight experience.

Despite the reorganization and replacement of so many aviators, dustoff detachments maintained full support of the 1st Infantry Division and its units widely deployed in the field. Operation El Paso kept pressure on the Viet Cong in Binh Long Province in the same general area where we had made the night extraction on June 9. One of the units sweeping through the province was C Troop, 1st Squadron, 4th Cavalry, commanded by Capt. Stephen M. Slattery. C Troop was patrolling up and down the Minh Thanh road and was supported by B Troop of the same squadron.

The road stretched southwest to northeast through the Minh Thanh rubber plantation. To the northeast the road intersected Highway 13 just south of An Loc. To the southwest it went to Tay Ninh. The Minh Thanh road, so designated by the troops for lack of a formal name, covered about forty miles between the two sites.

An Loc was about sixty miles due north of Saigon; Tay Ninh was about fifty miles northwest of the capital city. Control of this artery by our forces contested Viet Cong access to Saigon and greatly interfered with their terrorist operations. The enemy's willingness to respond against the 1st Division for control of this pathway was an indication of its importance.

The Viet Cong maintained a fluid presence along the road and periodically struck with ambushes and mortar attacks on the nightly encampments of our troops. They would emerge from concealment to attack, then melt back into the jungle, only to strike again at another location. The ongoing fighting produced a never-ending demand for dustoff support, and the 283d remained in the thick of the action.

On July 9, a classic battle erupted in the area, one I shall never forget. Viet Cong forces at near regimental strength clashed with B and C Troops, 1st Squadron, 4th Cavalry. The troops were supported by a Mustang helicopter fire team, a CH-47 Chinook helicopter (Guns-A-Go-Go), Dustoff 39, my crew (Dustoff 300), and air force F-4s armed with 500-pound bombs and 20mm cannons.

Steve Slattery was up before dawn preparing his troop for its reconnaissance in force along the Minh Thanh road. He and his men had the usual C-ration breakfast. It was possible to tolerate Cs and find them suitable for human consumption only when nothing else was available. C rations tasted better and were easier to eat if heated.

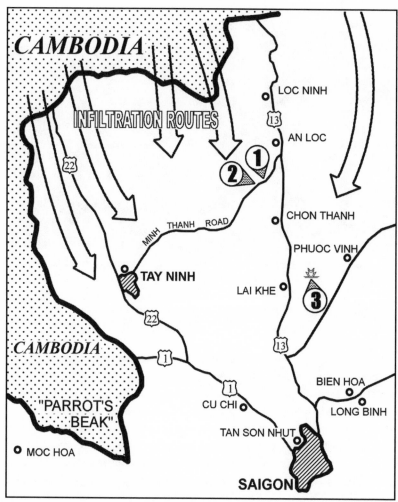

The "Minh Thanh" road sits astride the Viet Cong infiltration routes to Saigon and major bases at Tan Son Nhut, Bien Hoa, and Long Binh. Ambushes and firefights along Highway 13 produced a never-ending stream of casualties. Highlighted position "1" indicates the night mission of June 9.

A can of the rations could be brought to a boil in a few seconds over a small piece of C-4 explosive that had been ignited. This didn't produce smoke or give away the position to the enemy.

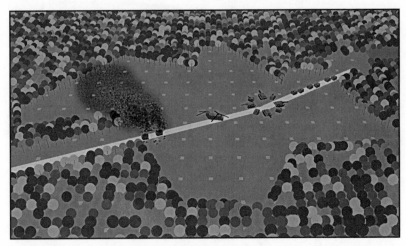

Computer-rendered scene of the Minh Thanh road ambush on July 9, 1966. It shows the approximate position of the burning armored personnel carriers, the crashed Guns-A-Go-Go helicopter, and Slatter's "hedgehog" armored perimeter.

The Viet Cong were deployed in their ambush site, ready and waiting for the Americans. They had prepared well, and their confidence level was high. Their breakfast was probably the usual issue of cold rice. Their supply system didn't allow such luxuries as the use of explosives for anything other than their intended purpose.

The Mustang fire team, operating out of the Lai Khe airstrip, was also getting ready for the day's missions. It was commanded by Capt. Billy J. Slusher. His wing ship was commanded by CW2 Frederick W. Fields.

Dustoff 39 was CW2 Thomas C. "Hoot" Gibson Jr., and his copilot was my roommate, Charlie Wilson. They were on field standby at the 1st Division's Quan Loi airstrip. I was preparing for flight with my crew—1st Lt. Mel Ruiz, copilot; SP4 Salvatore Parisi, medic; and SP4 Harley W. Graham, crew chief. We were scheduled first up and saw no reason to expect anything but business as usual.

The air force F-4 pilots, operating out of Bien Hoa Air Base, were also preparing for their missions, knowing that before the day was over they'd be called into action.

The Guns-A-Go-Go guys were in country to try out a novel concept of helicopter fire support. These people flew heavily armed Chinooks—transports a good bit larger than our UH-1 Hueys. The Chinooks were said to be able to do everything the Huey gunships could but with greater authority and for longer periods of time. They were armed with .30- and .50-caliber machine guns and 20mm cannons and carried literally tons of ammunition. This big bird could deliver an awesome amount of firepower on enemy forces while remaining out of range of counterfire, or so the press releases declared.

Midmorning found Steve Slattery and C Troop reconning the Minh Thanh road. They were within yards of the site where Lombard and I had made our hairy pickup in the middle of a thunderstorm. This time it was not a short round from one of our weapons that caused trouble. It was a Viet Cong (VC) force, part of a regiment, waiting on both sides of the road in a concealed and well-entrenched ambush position.

Slattery's troop made its way down the road, crossed a small bridge, and, after moving forward a couple of hundred meters, came upon an open area. It was almost clear of trees for about a kilometer on both sides of the road and extended ahead of the troop for about two kilometers before the woods closed in again. Unknown to Slattery, the VC had set up the site for an ambush.

The VC were entrenched in camouflaged bunkered positions on both sides of the road and in the woods with unobstructed observation and fields of fire. The VC had no doubt been observing C Troop patrolling the Minh Thanh road for some time and decided that this time and place were ideal for a confrontation.

Slattery and his troop were about to be severely tested. But he was an experienced commander who had met the Viet Cong in a number of earlier firefights. C Troop entered the clearing with nine armored personnel carriers (APCs) and three tanks. All were armed to the hilt. C Troop was not a pushover; it would be a hard nut to crack.

The open area didn't have the usual characteristics of an ambush site. The VC liked to attack where dense trees and jungle crowded both sides of a narrow roadway, which limited the maneuverability of the ambushed force. This was an exceptionally large clearing, but the enemy had planned well and was ready. The Viet Cong's long-range weapons (recoilless rifles) were in the trees facing both sides of the road, their positions impossible to detect. They also had several mortars in place ready to hit the armored column. Troops with automatic weapons in well-camouflaged bunker positions were situated throughout the clearing. In other positions Viet Cong soldiers, highly trained in the use of rocket-propelled grenades (RPGs) and other antiarmor weapons, waited for a signal from their commander to strike.

C Troop moved steadily through the clearing at normal speed, not slowing or stopping for a more detailed recon. There was the usual radio chatter throughout the column, and the troop proceeded as if nothing was amiss. The presence of the well-concealed ambush went undetected. The troop's lead element approached the southwestern edge of the clearing. At the same time, the rear emerged into the open area at the other end. More by chance than by design, the clearing was large enough to accommodate the stretched-out armored column. Slattery and his troop faced their moment of truth.

As the two lead APCs neared the far end of the clearing, a thunderous barrage erupted from both sides of the road. The column was engulfed in a raging concentration of high explosives. Heavy mortar and recoilless rifle rounds exploded along the length of C Troop. Shrapnel from the exploding shells slammed into the sides of the APCs and tanks. Tracers from numerous enemy automatic weapons crisscrossed the battlefield.

The leading APCs were the first casualties, hit just as they came to the end of the clearing. They were simultaneously destroyed by well-timed, well-directed RPGs. Both APCs were immediately engulfed in flames, their fuel systems ignited by the antiarmor charges. Their ammunition exploded, set off by the RPGs and the intense heat of burning fuel. Nothing could be done for the soldiers manning the vehicles. They were killed instantly by the penetrating explosive charges, and their bodies were incinerated.

Slattery was riding in the operations track when he saw the fury of the enemy barrage. He saw the impact of the RPGs on his lead tracks, and it hit him as if he had taken a hammer blow to the solar plexus. He knew the damage done by the RPGs to the interior of the vehicles and the fate of his men. These were his troops, and he knew them well. They were excellent soldiers who in an instant were gone.

There was no time for regrets; this was a granddaddy of an ambush. Slattery had to think fast. He quickly maneuvered his armor to form a hedgehog position. The rapid repositioning of the armored force was reminiscent of John Wayne circling the wagons in the days of the old Wild West. C Troop's APCs and tanks laid down murderous fields of fire across both sides of the clearing and into the woods as they maneuvered to form their defensive perimeter. Their fast reaction and the withering defensive fire prevented further loss of vehicles, but not without taking additional casualties.

The enemy continued laying down a furious barrage on C Troop as Slattery set up his circular position. Had the ambush been set in a tight area where the trees came close to the road, he couldn't have maneuvered into his hedgehog formation. The Viet Cong's selection of the open area was the tactical error that permitted the successful defensive maneuvering and was instrumental in saving the day for Slattery and C Troop. The issue settled down to whose firepower would outlast and outgun the other's. C Troop had taken heavy casualties; it was sheer luck that Slattery was not hit, because he was exposed atop his track while directing his force into its defensive perimeter.

The Mustang fire team was the first aviation unit on its way to assist the ambushed force. Dustoff 39 was at Quan Loi airstrip, only ten miles away, when he was alerted to evacuate wounded. My crew was sent to the area when informed that additional dustoff support was needed. In less than half an hour, we were on station.

I called Hoot on the tactical net and discovered that he hadn't had the opportunity to make any evacuations. Slattery was too busy directing the support of the Mustang fire team and a bevy of air force F-4s. The jets were hosing down the Viet Cong positions with 20mm cannon fire and hitting them with an occasional 500-pounder. The concentrated air strikes in such a confined area made it difficult to coordinate a medical evacuation at the same time. Furthermore, a half-baked scheme produced an incident of near catastrophic proportions. It happened while I was en route to the area.

Shortly after the Mustang fire team initiated offensive operations against the Viet Cong, but before the air force F-4s arrived, the Guns-A-Go-Go guys came on the scene. It appeared they came to "save the day" for the embattled armored force and would do it "their way."

In a mindless course of action, they proceeded down the Minh Thanh road, flying at less than a thousand feet, blazing away out both sides of the aircraft at the VC positions. It looked good; in a John Wayne movie it would have been great. But this was not Hollywood, and the VC were reading different cue cards.

Guns-A-Go-Go was lumbering down the road and blasting away at the VC until they were directly over the encircled troop. The problem was that they were in range of everything the VC had except hand grenades. Any clear-thinking person could have predicted what would happen next. The VC opened up with automatic weapons on the Chinook and immediately shot it down. It crashed about a hundred yards from C Troop's defensive perimeter.

What a waste! The heavily armed Chinook could have taken a position half a klick away from the ambush site and laid down a murderous barrage on the VC. At that range, Guns-A-Go-Go would have been extremely effective and still been beyond the reach of the Viet Cong. Instead, the Chinook lay a crumpled mass of metal on a dirt road with a wild battle raging all around it. Miraculously, none of its crewmen was killed. The Viet Cong leadership was no doubt giving one another their version of high fives, laughing and congratulating themselves on such a coup. They had no idea that the crew survived the crash. Imagine their surprise when they saw the downed airmen hauling ass for Slattery's defensive perimeter. The VC were asleep at the switch and let the crew escape. Any producer of slapstick comedy would have relished the scene.

When Slattery directed his force to form the hedgehog position, he created an armored circle with enough space inside the perimeter to land a Huey. We waited impatiently to begin evacuating the wounded. At last Slattery contacted us on the tactical net and said he had many seriously wounded troopers ready for evacuation.

Hoot coordinated with Slusher, the Mustang leader, for escort into the perimeter. It would require a vertical landing and takeoff to extract the wounded, which would make the helicopter extremely vulnerable to enemy fire. The plan was to have the Mustangs cover Hoot on both sides as he made a low-level, high-speed run into the evacuation site. At the last instant, Hoot would make a strong flare, come to a halt over the circle of armor, and descend into its center. The plan sounded good. It had to be.

The dustoff would be exposed to enemy fire flying over the open area until setting down inside the perimeter. Leaving was the reverse of the procedure and just as dangerous. After Hoot completed his evacuation, I would have my chance to do an encore.

Hoot and the two Mustangs maneuvered into position over the road for the run into the evacuation site. I circled above the trio to observe the plan in action. The gunships with Hoot in between proceeded down the road. When they reached the clearing, the gunships opened up on the tree lines to the right and left. I heard Slusher call out, "We're taking fire from the left."

Fred Fields answered, "On the right too."

Hoot called out, "I'm breaking off—taking too many hits. Let's try again."

The trio returned to the starting point and began another run into the site. The gunships poured a steady stream of fire into the trees while Hoot flew to the circle of armor and made a strong deceleration. The fire team's gunships broke left and right. Hoot came to a hover for an instant, then descended quickly into the defensive perimeter. He made it in for the pickup. How would he do coming out?

The dustoff was on the ground for half a minute or so while the wounded were loaded. Hoot didn't waste time. I saw his ship rise out of the circle, hover for an instant, and accelerate out of the area. I noticed that his helicopter rolled right, then left in a jerky manner. I called to ask if he was okay. He answered in a strained voice that his hydraulics were shot away when he came out of the defensive perimeter and it was all he and Charlie could do to keep their ship under control. I escorted them to the aid station at Quan Loi, where the wounded were off-loaded. Hoot said he would have to shut down. I understood his situation; there was no way he could continue the mission with his hydraulic system inoperative.

I returned to the battle area, where the firefight continued hot and heavy. As I circled to join the Mustangs for my run into the pickup site, two F-4s flew past about two hundred feet above me on their way to bomb and strafe the VC. I contacted Slattery to tell him I'd be coming in to get his wounded. I also told him that Dustoff 39 was out of action due to battle damage and at least for a while I was his only dustoff. I didn't know if another was available.

"Dustoff 300, Dragoon Charlie," he replied. "I understand. Let's get with it."

I formed up with the Mustangs for a run into the perimeter. I started at treetop level with the gunships on my flanks and slightly above me. As we came to the clearing, I dropped down until I was skimming the ground. Slattery's perimeter was dead ahead. Slusher's voice came over the radio: "Picking up fire from the trees."

My medic, Salvatore Parisi, reported, " I see all kinds of gun flashes in the tree line on my side."

I acknowledged the calls as we rapidly closed on the pickup site. At the last second I decelerated with a slight climb and a hard flare, simultaneously throwing the tail around and facing the direction I'd come from. The flare and flip of the tail put me directly over the opening in the armor, and I slammed the helo down into the hole. Parisi and the crew chief, Graham, with help from the troopers, loaded three litters and four wounded ambulatory soldiers. In less than a minute we were out of there.

In the short time we were on the ground, which seemed an eternity, I saw and heard the vicious barrage that Slattery's troops were laying on. The .50 calibers were especially loud. Their booming reports were in sharp contrast to the staccato of the smaller .30s.

As we flew to the aid station at Quan Loi, I told Parisi and Graham how much I appreciated their fast action at the pickup site. They did well; they were excellent soldiers. There was no need for orders or directions; they just instinctively responded to the challenge of the situation. They heard the incoming and outgoing firing as well as I but went about their tasks with what looked like utter disdain for the dangers of the moment. I couldn't have been prouder of them.

We left the wounded at the aid station and returned to the battle for another pickup. Ordinarily, dustoff pilots alternated flying duties, and the next pickup would have been Mel Ruiz's turn. But Mel was new in country and this was his first taste of combat, so I decided it was best to overlook the custom. I'm sure that Mel did not object. He had a whole year to go, and he'd have countless opportunities to take his turn.

When we returned for another evacuation, I contacted Slusher and his Mustang team to tell them I was ready for another try. I also contacted Slattery, and he said that the wounded were piling up. I told him to be ready for another pickup within the minute.

We formed up with the Mustangs as before. I was as low as possible, and the gunships were slightly higher on my flanks. Using this technique, the Viet Cong could see the guns but had a harder time picking me up. It worked well. Despite considerable fire directed at us, we made it into the perimeter without taking any hits. I used the same hard, fast flare and flip of the tail to get on the ground.

While Parisi and Graham were loading the wounded, I noticed the machine gunner on the APC directly in front of me. He was hammering away at the Viet Cong when an enemy round blasted the front of his vehicle. It was probably a mortar round, and its explosive force hurled him backward. He was obviously wounded and tried to drop down inside the APC. His comrades inside the vehicle, unaware of his condition, wanted him on top to continue laying down fire on the enemy. They literally threw him back up. He again tried to squirm down into the APC, and again the crew abruptly muscled him back on top. The din of continuous firing made it impossible for him to make his condition known. I noticed blood on his face; it appeared that the exploding round had blinded him. He was still positioned in the hatch, half in and half out of the vehicle. He didn't try to fire his weapon but was wiping the blood off his head and face with the sleeve of his fatigues. I saw him try again to squeeze back into the APC.

Before any more of the sequence was repeated, I got on the interphone with Parisi and told him to get the trooper before he was maimed by his "friends." Graham saw Parisi having difficulty removing the wounded soldier and went to his assistance. They got the wounded man loose as another trooper's head popped out of the hatch. He looked around, no doubt wondering where his gunner had gone. Then he saw Parisi and Graham loading the wounded soldier onto the dustoff aircraft. At that instant another round exploded in front of the APC, and the inquisitive trooper ducked back inside.

I got on the net with Slattery. "Dragoon Charlie, this is Dustoff 300. I've got as many of your wounded as I can take. I'd appreciate an extra effort with the outgoing fire as I depart. Victor Charles [the VC] is hitting uncomfortably close to my position."

"Roger on the extra effort, Dustoff. We'll pick up the tempo ASAP. We want you to return for the rest of our wounded."

Dragoon Charlie was as good as his word, and his response scared the hell out of me. Just as I lifted up and out of the tight armored circle, the tank on my right let loose a volley with its .50 caliber, and the APC to my front did likewise as I crossed over it. The noise was deafening but reassuring. I called Slattery. "Thanks for the send-off, Dragoon Charlie. Be back in a few minutes."

Parisi, Graham, and the medics at Quan Loi unloaded the wounded. Many were desperately in need of lifesaving medical attention. I looked back at the rear of my ship and saw that the deck was red with blood. We didn't have the time or facilities to wash it down. That had to wait until we finished with Slattery's wounded.

When we returned to the battle area, the Mustang fire team was gone. Dragoon Charlie told me that the guns had returned to the base to rearm and refuel. However, the air force was still overhead laying down the heavy stuff. I decided not to wait for the guns and called Dragoon Charlie to tell him I'd be coming in for another evacuation and needed covering fire. He rogered and I low-leveled down the road toward the defensive perimeter. The VC had me under fire as soon as I came into the clearing. Slattery's troopers countered with a heavy barrage as I hopped into the ring of armor. We got in okay but took a few hits. The wounded were placed on board, and we were out of there. The extraction came off as planned.

While we were off-loading the wounded at Quan Loi, I learned that Lieutenant Oaks, aircraft commander of another dustoff, had arrived to get the wounded whom we had brought out earlier. They were stabilized and headed for more sophisticated medical treatment at the 93d Evacuation Hospital at Long Binh and the Third Field Hospital at Saigon.

While we refueled, I got out of the chopper to stretch my legs. Oaks came over to me and said he was taking my mission and I should take the wounded to the rear. Colonel Dalton, the 1st Division surgeon, came out of the aid station just as I was adamantly letting Oaks know that I had no intention of handing over my assigned mission unless told to do so by the unit commander or the operations officer. Colonel Dalton heard my declaration and told Oaks in a forceful manner, "Everything is running smoothly, *Lieutenant*. I don't want anyone screwing up the situation. Mike, carry on with what you're doing."

I threw the colonel a highball and went back to my chopper. Oaks was a perpetual pain in the ass, a screwup who required a lot of supervision and an officer who could often be an embarrassment to the detachment. It seems as though every unit in every war is issued one like him.

I returned to the battle area and completed the evacuation of Slattery's wounded. The firefight had run its course; the Viet Cong broke off the engagement and melted back into their jungle sanctuary. All in all, I made six flights into Slattery's armored circle and evacuated thirty-one of his wounded troopers.

I thought that my mission was completed when Slattery called and told me that B Troop was currently engaged with the same Viet Cong force that had ambushed him. B Troop was in a supporting role in the operation and was positioned as a blocking force to prevent an unopposed withdrawal by the Viet Cong. The troop took several casualties when it engaged the retreating VC and needed immediate dustoff support. Its evacuation site was a small clearing about five hundred meters north-northeast of C Troop's location. I couldn't hug the terrain during my approach into its pickup site, because it was surrounded by huge trees.

An examination of B Troop's location from altitude showed that I had to use a high, overhead, tactical approach. I'd fly toward the troop's position and, when almost over it, point the nose of the helicopter at the ground and dive toward the evacuation site. This would set up a rate of descent of about three thousand feet per minute as I altered direction left and right, simulating a falling leaf. This made the chopper hard to hit. I'd be in the diving mode from about two thousand feet, so it would only take a few seconds to reach the ground. At the proper instant I'd stop the dive by making a last-second flare and be on the ground ready to take on the wounded.

The army gunships and the air force fighters had not returned, so we continued the evacuations alone. I coordinated the pickups with Lt. John Morrette, B Troop's executive officer. We encountered heavy concentrations of enemy fire on three entries into the area while Morrette and his troopers covered us with supporting fire. Departure from the confined evacuation site was my greatest problem. The area was about 400 meters long, averaged 150 meters in width, and had an obvious slope on the long axis.

The UH-1 gives up a considerable amount of its maneuvering capability when heavily loaded, and I'd definitely be loaded during departure. It was best to accelerate downslope and with the increased speed make a cyclic climb out of the area. The trees around the site were about a hundred feet high, but once I was clear I'd be out of the enemy's reach.

On my first pickup we had three litter patients and four ambulatories. I checked the amount of power necessary to pick up the ship to a hover. I'd have about five additional pounds of torque to make the takeoff and clear the trees at the far end of the clearing. I accelerated toward the trees and, with a combination of cyclic climb and application of the remaining power, cleared all obstacles—but with less room to spare than good sense and safety dictated. We evacuated nineteen wounded soldiers out of B Troop's position and finished the job with little damage to our aircraft.

All in all it was a productive day for our crew. Mel Ruiz got his first taste of combat, and in the lexicon of aviators in Vietnam, the Viet Cong got his "cherry." Parisi and Graham worked with their characteristic quiet and dedicated efficiency. The ambush and ensuing fighting cost B and C Troops twenty killed in action (KIA). Our crew evacuated fifty of their wounded. There were some traumatic amputations, a few sucking chest wounds, and some severe head wounds. I was amazed how many of the wounded could walk and get on board the chopper without assistance. The VC losses were reported as more than two hundred killed, but I saw only twenty-two enemy bodies after the battle. We logged five hours of flying time in support of B and C Troops.

Hoot Gibson and Charlie Wilson were put out of action when their hydraulic system was shot away, and they and their aircraft were airlifted back to the base. After my mission was over, I completed the afteraction reports. My last official act of the day was to recommend the two crews for Distinguished Flying Crosses.

Charlie Wilson was in the shower when I returned to our room. I yelled to let him know I was back from the wars. I wasn't aware that he had been wounded in the burst of fire that put his ship out of action. It was a simple flesh wound but good enough for him to be awarded the Purple Heart.

Charlie wanted to go into Saigon to get a good meal, and after a quick cleanup and change of clothes we were ready to go. We walked the few yards to the main drag, where we boarded a tricycle-like, open-air vehicle that the GIs called a cycelo. The Saigon area had thousands of these contraptions, each of which could handle two passengers and the operator, who sat and steered it from the rear. There was no windscreen or any other protection from the elements. When it rained, passengers got soaked. It was usually a wild ride as the driver made his way through traffic with the highly maneuverable but flimsy vehicle. I felt safer in combat than riding on them. They'd flip over in a heartbeat if the driver turned too sharply. Their only redeeming value was that they were always available, whereas regular cabs were not.

We decided to go to the Rex Hotel, which served as an officers' billet for the people assigned to MACV. The top floor of the building served as an officers' club, where one could relax, have a few drinks, and enjoy a good meal while being entertained by a string ensemble. Later in the evening there was a floor show and a modern band. The dining area contained a huge salad bar, a wine bar, and a lounge area with several slot machines. It was a place to escape the humdrum pace of paperwork or, in our case, the carnage and horror of the battlefield.

We were freshly scrubbed and in clean clothes only a few hours after we had been under fire as we extracted lift after lift of bloodied, traumatized, wounded troopers. Their comrades were still in the steaming jungle searching for the enemy, looking for another confrontation. It was unreal; it was, to say the least, insane.

Charlie and I hadn't eaten since breakfast, so the first item on our agenda was food, preferably a huge steak. We lucked out on a table. The place was usually packed, and getting seated quickly was rare. We ordered drinks, a couple of New York strip steaks, and a bottle of Mateus for the meal, then filled our plates at the salad bar. While waiting for our steaks, a major came to our table and asked if he could join us. Of course we said yes, and he accepted Charlie's offer of wine. We were enjoying our salad as our guest studied the menu. We were shocked when he suddenly slapped the menu on the table and exclaimed, "Same old shit. This place sucks."

Charlie surprised me. He reached over and took back the wine he had poured for the major. "I've never seen or heard a more ill-mannered and ungrateful act in my life," Charlie said. "Just who the hell do you think you are? You'd better leave." With that the major stood, threw his napkin on the table, and left.

I could see where Charlie was coming from. He'd been in the boondocks for five days and drawn fire from the Viet Cong as he picked up the wounded. He didn't eat regularly; when he did get a meal, he ate it out of a greasy mess kit or had cold C rations. He couldn't shower or bathe, and when he slept it was likely on a blood-encrusted litter. He didn't have time to undress or remove his dirty boots. Earlier in the day Charlie's helo was shot up and he was wounded. As he graciously poured the major's wine, he was in a dream world, enjoying the good life, which was shattered by the man's vulgar behavior.

Unfortunately, this major was typical of many who infested the commands scattered about Saigon. They made you wonder where the mold was that created such nematodes. I know that rear-echelon personnel were an important part of the military establishment; the war could not be fought without them. But their numbers in Vietnam were out of proportion to their contributions to the war effort. They fed upon and were nurtured by the administrative machinery and multiplied as they built their empires. Too often they were the pot-holes on the road to military success. Yet they garnered the medals and told the wildest and hairiest war stories. Individuals such as this major made you wonder how the system could create such selfish and inconsiderate bastards.

Our steaks arrived, and I looked over at Charlie. "You feel better now?"

"What do you think? The son of a bitch was lucky I didn't deck him. The nerve of that ungrateful bastard. He damn near ruined my day."

I told Charlie to forget what had happened. "Don't work yourself up. You know what that does to your gut. Besides, I noticed that your supply of antacids is getting low. Enjoy your steak, Charlie. Have some more wine." Then I added, "I've got to admit, you sure cut that pompous bastard off at the pass."

Finished with our meals, we went to the bar for an afterdinner drink; I had a brandy and Charlie had a crème de menthe frappe. We looked around for our "friend," but he was not in the bar. Most likely he was back in his air-conditioned room writing letters home, describing the terrible ordeals one endures while fighting for one's country. If not, he was probably complaining about his bedsheets not being smoothed out sufficiently by the "gook" maids, who he likely thought never did anything right.

It was getting late and curfew would soon be upon us, so we decided to return to quarters. We got lucky, found a cab, and were soon back in our compound. I went to bed immediately and lay there reflecting on the day's activities. My crew had extracted planeload after planeload of wounded soldiers, some who would have died in the jungle without timely medical attention. We were fired on during every mission and took several hits but escaped without a scratch. After the work was completed, I wined and dined as a gentleman of leisure, albeit with a distasteful interruption. All in all it was a fine day, and I soon fell asleep.

The next morning I was back at the same old grind. The two divisions were still conducting operations, and we were constantly on call for support of the 1st or the 25th. One week we operated out of Lai Khe supporting elements of the 1st Division. Then the action shifted to the 25th Division and we operated out of Cu Chi. We flew just about every day. During one stretch, I flew fifteen consecutive days.

Later that summer our aircraft were fitted with hoists that enabled us to make extractions from areas without landing zones. The added capability brought with it a new hazard. A helicopter at a stationary hover with a litter being lowered a hundred feet or so, then loaded with a wounded soldier and slowly brought back up, was more than a Viet Cong gunner could resist.

The hoist was used with the jungle penetrator and Stokes litter. If the penetrator was used, the wounded soldier had to be conscious and hold on while being raised to the helicopter. The navy-developed Stokes litter was a long, narrow, reinforced-wire basket configured to accept a person in the prone position. It worked well aboard ships for transfers between them. But in a jungle environment it presented problems; it could get snagged in tree branches as it was raised to the helicopter.

Because hoist operations presented more risks than the usual dustoff missions, I developed a procedure that I found effective. When preparing for a hoist mission, I'd lift off vertically and climb to two hundred feet before initiating forward flight. I wanted to know how much power was needed to hover at such height and how much was in reserve for the hoist. It was best to discover limitations that could prevent me from completing the mission while we were at home base rather than waiting until we were in contact with the enemy.

After I arrived in the evacuation area, I'd slowly move toward the pickup site just above the trees to see the exact position where the rescue was to take place. I'd circle the spot at about twenty miles per hour, giving the Viet Cong every opportunity to fire at me. If they did and hit the ship, I still might get away. My purpose was to get a feel for the enemy dispositions and determine if they could interfere with my operations. I wanted the VC to make their move before I settled into a stationary hover. While hoisting I made a lucrative target. If the Huey were hit and disabled without forward speed, I'd crash down upon the troops I was trying to help. No hoist mission could be classed as typical; all were rough.

I was flying with Charlie Wilson, who was on his first hoist mission. I could tell he was on edge. Nearing the extraction area, I went through the usual procedures: radio contact, call signs, a rundown of the tactical situation, and popping smoke. I circled the extraction site and found a small opening that permitted me to nestle into the treetops and make my helicopter difficult to observe from the ground. As I settled into position, a salvo of artillery from 105s impacted about fifty meters to my left.

The ground commander asked if I wanted the artillery lifted. "Hell, no," I replied. "If you need it that close, I do too." Then an F-100 flashed by and fired a long burst that passed me about fifty meters away at my five o'clock position. I was impressed with the coordination and accuracy of the artillery and the air force. It seemed that the F-100s were using my tail fin as a reference point when hosing down the Viet Cong positions. The fighter-bombers had to be using explosive rounds, because at the end of the day we noticed that the tail of my chopper was riddled with small holes. We probably picked them up when the shells exploded upon impact with nearby tree branches.

The jungle below was thick, and I could hear the ground commander voice his frustration at being unable to make progress through the area. I think the same condition hampered the Viet Cong trying to bring effective fire on our troops. It was probably the reason that the VC didn't fire on my aircraft during the extended hover period.

At first I was told that only one wounded soldier was to be hoisted. It was an agonizingly slow process; it took about ten minutes to bring the casualty up to the ship. Meanwhile, the ground troops reported a second man seriously wounded, so we lowered the hoist for another extraction. Before we got him on board, another soldier was hit, this one reported as life or death. The ground commander was anxious to evacuate all three. I sympathized with him but told him it might not be possible to retrieve the third casualty because of weight limitations, plus I was low on fuel. Then I realized that the low fuel condition made my aircraft lighter, so I decided to try for the third man too.

The medic told me that the two wounded troops on board were in serious condition and needed more medical attention than he could administer. I gambled and continued with the third extraction because the litter was on its way back down.

The dustoff aviator frequently faced unpleasant decisions dealing with life or death; it was part of the job. It's called triage: determining which casualty lives or dies according to a system of priorities designed to maximize the number of survivors. If I ordered the third hoist, one or both of the wounded aboard might die before reaching critically needed medical care. If I aborted the third hoist, the man left behind might not be alive when I returned for him.

I was motivated by the ground commander's statement that the third casualty had a serious sucking chest wound plus other wounds about the body. It was a critical decision. While we were hoisting, the artillery kept impacting to our left, and F-100s continued hitting the Viet Cong on our right. I'd given the controls to Charlie after the second hoist and was getting some rest. The crew chief operating the hoist said that the wounded soldier was almost up to the aircraft and was completely naked. The ground medic had probably stripped him to fully determine the extent of his many wounds.

Suddenly I heard a lot of radio chatter among the troops on the ground and a heavy volume of automatic weapons fire, which I assumed was not all ours. I took the controls and told the crew chief and medic to hold onto the litter; we were getting out of there.

Ordinarily we took the time to bring the litter into the ship, but I considered it essential to move out and did just that. The crew chief and medic steadied the litter against the side of the Huey as we picked up speed. The medic saw that the wounded man had stopped breathing. He quickly secured the bandage over the chest wound and in that awkward and dangerous position began administering mouth-to-mouth resuscitation. He was half in and half out of the helicopter as we clipped along at 120 knots. It was only a few minutes to the forward aid station at Dau Tieng, and the medic kept up the mouth-to-mouth effort. He dismounted the aircraft and continued with the resuscitative efforts to keep the wounded man breathing even after the litter bearers arrived and carried him into the aid station.

As the aircraft was refueled, I expected to be called back for more extractions, but I lucked out; there were no more hoists that day. I checked on our third patient and was told he was being treated by two doctors and finally breathing on his own. He soon would be sufficiently stabilized to be transferred to a hospital in the rear area.

I found out later that the increased firing and radio chatter I'd heard at the pickup site was the arrival of additional friendly troops. Their added firepower was all it took for the VC to break contact.

My medic on the hoist mission was a black soldier, Specialist Fourth Class Baker. He had joined the 283d fresh out of medic training at Fort Sam Houston in Texas. He'd been on a few combat evacuations, but this mission was the first time he saw concentrated firepower. It also was his first hoist mission. If I had any concern about his performance under pressure, it was gone by the time the mission was over. He passed the test with flying colors.

"Baker," I said, "you did well today. That last casualty would never have made it if you hadn't given him mouth-to-mouth resuscitation. It took a lot of nerve to lean over that litter outside the aircraft while in flight and give him breath. I wonder if the situation were reversed, would he have done the same for you?"

"Thank you, Mr. Novosel. I only did what I figured had to be done. It was strange at first, but I kept reminding myself to do what they taught me at the medic's school. I ain't never had my lips touch white lips before, and a grown man's at that. I hope my folks back home in Louisiana will understand."

"I'm sure they will," I responded. Until Baker made that statement, I had no idea he came from Louisiana. I lived in New Orleans for a while and knew the social and racial attitudes that prevailed there. The politicians in the statehouse in Baton Rouge did nothing to elevate the moral and intellectual climate of the times.

The evacuation missions increased as the 1st and 25th Divisions continued applying pressure on the Viet Cong. It was the middle of summer—hot, humid, and unusually wet. The troops in the field knew we could perform hoist missions and requested many that would never have been considered in the past. Now any small opening in the jungle sufficed for a pickup site. We were often called for hoist missions when ground troops with a little effort could have reached a landing zone where a normal evacuation could be made.

Hoist missions were never easy; too many things could go wrong. I witnessed a mission where the hoisting aircraft experienced control difficulties. A Stokes litter with a wounded soldier aboard was being raised when a second casualty was thrown on the litter. The sudden increase in weight on one side of the helicopter compounded the problems for the pilot. In his effort to bring the ship under control, he pulled pitch. The cable was extended about 150 feet and, as the pilot applied power, the helicopter was forced sideways by its unbalanced condition. The litter was dragged through trees and at any moment could have been snagged by a large branch. It pulled free of the trees and somehow the two wounded troops were not dislodged. The pilot still didn't have the situation under control; the aircraft drifted sideways because its center of gravity limits had been exceeded. The pilot kept his cool, descended over a clear area, and placed his load on the ground. When the helicopter became controllable, the cable was cut and dropped to earth. The evacuation was completed using regular procedures.

On another occasion, Jim Lombard was on a hoist mission about two hundred meters from a sizable clear area. The ground commander apparently considered the soldier's wounds serious enough not to take the time to move to a more suitable extraction site. Jim's hoist operator had the wounded soldier within ten feet of the aircraft when Viet Cong gunners opened up on the ship and scored hits on the engine area. Jim glanced at his instrument panel and saw that the readings were all in the normal range. The litter was being pulled on board when the entire engine area erupted in flames. The VC's rounds severed a fuel line and caused the flammable liquid to be ignited by the heat of the engine.

There was little Jim could do except try for the clear area nearby. When he got there he slammed the helicopter onto the ground and ordered everyone out. His medic and crew chief carried the litter away from the flaming ship, which they expected to explode at any minute.

There was nothing more they could do except await pickup by another dustoff. Setting up a perimeter for security wasn't worth the effort, because the crew had only personal weapons. Jim had managed to send a distress call before setting down, and in less than a minute another dustoff landed and took the crew and patient out of harm's way.

As the rescue ship departed, Jim saw a huge ball of fire go skyward when the fuel cell exploded. He thought about the incident and remembered he didn't have time to remove the ship's logbook. Soon the chopper was a pile of gray ashes. On top of the pile was the helicopter's stabilizer bar, a solid metal part situated above the main rotor. That mound of ashes stayed right there. We saw it every time we passed the area. It served as a vivid reminder of the dangers of our missions, especially when a hoist was involved. But despite the problems and dangers it created, the hoist served us well. I'm certain that many people are alive today because of it.

Flying dustoff was extremely fatiguing and demanding. Dustoffers departed on their missions without flight plans or weather or intelligence briefings. They flew when nobody else did, even when the air force's big stuff stayed on the ground because of weather. When the concept of aeromedical evacuation was developed, nobody thought it would spawn such dedicated, heroic efforts to save human lives. Yet this is what happened, and dustoff became legendary. The pilots flew missions that spanned the spectrum of imagination. Details of their exploits regularly approached the unbelievable and often surpassed it. Their missions were the most dangerous, brought about by combat action, weather, and fatigue. To get the job done, they had to disregard their personal well-being, set down in the midst of battle, and stand by under enemy fire while the wounded were loaded. No wonder the medical evacuation detachments sustained more casualties than other aviation units in Vietnam. Despite all hazards, dustoff crewmen carried with them a strong determination and a deep-seated confidence that they would get to the wounded and bring them to safety.

But I was in a world that seemed to be getting nowhere. Every day I'd fly to a new battle and pick up new wounded. There seemed to be no end to it. It was not pleasant to see so many torn bodies, so many traumatized soldiers who too often were still in their teens. The compensating factor, the reward, was knowing that I could help ease their pain and start them on the road to recovery.

There was no letup in the frequency of operations as the summer wore on. The missions came with monotonous regularity. At least once a week I'd be on the night shift, which gave me the opportunity to use my instrument flying experience. A Viet Cong attack on a Special Forces unit gave me another chance to use that experience.

The 283d, which covered the III Corps area, was given a mission that required unique solutions to defeat the elements. The Special Forces troops at Nhon Co in II Corps had been attacked the previous night and sustained heavy casualties. They desperately needed blood. A dustoff detachment in II Corps normally took the mission but couldn't because of the weather. The unit didn't have instrument-qualified pilots able to fly through clouds and dense fog, which covered the route to the outpost. Bill Colbert was still with the detachment, and he and I more or less volunteered for the mission.

We plotted the destination on the operations chart and quickly marked off an LOP from the Tan Son Nhut VOR. The course to the airstrip at Nhon Co was along the forty-degree radial, a distance of ninety-one nautical miles. I picked up a 1-over-50 chart covering the area around the airstrip, and after the blood supply was loaded we were off. If all went well, we'd be there in about an hour.

The weather was not bad in the Saigon area, but as we proceeded on course the clouds below us got thicker and finally we were flying above a solid overcast. The course deviation indicator was set on forty degrees, and we continued along the radial. I studied the 1-over-50 tactical chart and told Bill that the elevation approaching the airstrip was 1,500 feet above sea level. There was a "candy stripe" (a narrow road so named because the tactical chart displayed it as alternate red and white segments, much like a peppermint stick) that approached the Nhon Co airstrip from the same direction as our route of flight.

The road rose rapidly as it came to the airstrip, where the elevation was 2,300 feet above sea level. There were numerous hills throughout the area that were even higher. We were still over a solid overcast when our planned time en route was up. We had to descend and penetrate the cloud cover to find the airstrip, if we could. Bill and I decided to go into the clouds at sixty knots airspeed at a rate of descent of 500 feet per minute. He would make the descent while I monitored the instruments and altitude. We intended to descend to an indicated altitude of 2,500 feet, which should place us about 200 feet above the level of the airstrip and most of the hills around it. The higher hills in the area should be about five miles away, according to the chart. If all went well, we'd penetrate and break out of the overcast and continue to the airstrip.

The descent went as planned, but when we arrived at our decision altitude we still were in the clouds. Bill hesitated for a second as if he were deciding whether to descend farther or climb back on top of the clouds. In that instant I caught sight of the ground and told Bill, and he continued the descent in a tight circle to maintain visual contact. We were about a hundred feet above the ground when I spotted the candy stripe to our left. I pointed it out to Bill, and he followed it to the airstrip. Our plan could not have worked better. We were right where our instruments and our time of flight said we should be. It was a flight accomplished by primitive methods, but it worked.

We didn't waste time at the airstrip. The blood was delivered to the waiting medics, and we took off for Tan Son Nhut. When we got back and were asked how the mission went, Bill and I said there hadn't been any problems. We lied. Like many others, that flight was just one example of the many facets of dustoff.

Operations against the Viet Cong didn't let up in the summer of 1966. It was a rare day when we weren't scheduled to fly. When I had a day off I'd catch up on my correspondence, then spend the rest of the day in Saigon. Trips into the capital were a welcome change of pace. I'd shop around for gifts for the family and finish with a visit to one of the better restaurants. There were several excellent establishments where one could dine in style and enjoy fine cuisine and wine. Such relaxing days and evenings passed so fast that they often were remembered more like dreams than reality. The next day was a return to normal duty: hauling men who had been bloodied in battle to the nearest medical facility so that they might live and then take off to repeat the process.

Mid-August brought no letup. The missions continued, and the weather remained hot and humid. The long duty hours and the weather were debilitating. My crew was on field standby with the 1st Division for days at a time. The mosquitoes were especially bad, and many cases of malaria required evacuation.

As usual I didn't take the prescribed issue of Atabrine and for the first time wondered about the wisdom of my method of malaria control. While in the field my crew slept in the helicopter with the doors closed to keep out the mosquitoes. I loved my crewmen, but after so many days without a shower or change of clothing they became downright gamey. So I'd sleep on a litter underneath the helicopter. At least it kept me out of the rain, and although the mosquitoes got to me I never contracted the dreaded disease.

On one standby assignment, I received a mission in the early morning hours. A soldier was the victim of a powerful Viet Cong land mine and had suffered a traumatic amputation of his right leg below the knee. When we got to him I was surprised and impressed by the fact that he was wide awake and aware of the extent of his injury. Ordinarily a person with such a severe wound would not be as lively. We took him to his unit's medical facility on the north side of Bien

Hoa Air Base at about two-thirty in the morning. As his litter was unloaded from the chopper, he raised up on one arm and looked at
his missing limb. I had no idea what was going on in his mind, but
he knew what was happening. Then I saw a diminutive female handling one end of the litter. She certainly knew how to take care of
her end of the chore. Then I realized that it was Martha Raye, the
actress and singer who was in her third war visiting troops. I'd heard
she was in Vietnam but had no idea she was so well versed in the duties of medical people. Later I heard she was a qualified nurse. In
our line of work we never knew what to expect, but I appreciated the
presence of people such as Martha Raye.

On August 24 I returned to the unit after four rough days of field
standby duty. All I wanted was to shed my muddy, filthy fatigues,
shower, and get into clean, comfortable clothes. I was so tired that
after I showered I took a short nap and forgot about everything else.
When I awoke it was almost nine in the evening. The dining room
had stopped serving, but the bar was still going strong. I had a few
gin and tonics and returned to my quarters, where I slept until five
in the morning. I was scheduled to fly that day with Mel Ruiz, Sal
Parisi, and Harley Graham.

When I arrived at the flight line, Mel said he'd preflighted the
chopper and it was ready to go. Parisi was loading his medical supplies and Graham was wiping off excess grease from the head of the
helicopter. Though we were ready for action, we didn't get a mission
until ten o'clock. I suppose that even the Viet Cong needed to rest
once in a while.

The mission involved a trooper suffering from heat exhaustion.
We'd been getting quite a few heat cases since the 1st Division embarked on Operation Amarillo. The temperature reached the mid-
nineties every day while our troops, loaded down with combat gear,
were constantly on the move. When we finished the extraction I
thought it would be a slow day, because we had only three missions
by early afternoon and none was pending.

At about two-thirty in the afternoon, the 57th Detachment received a mission in the general area of Phuoc Vinh, about thirty-five
miles north-northeast of Tan Son Nhut. We received a mission in the
same area at coordinates Xray Tango 845 390, tactical call sign Dra-

goon Charlie Six. The mission was urgent. I knew who'd be in the thick of the action. Dragoon Charlie was C Troop, 1st Squadron, 4th Cavalry; it was the Quarter Horse. Dragoon Charlie Six was the commander, Capt. Steve Slattery. He had his ass caught in a Viet Cong wringer again. I hoped he was all right.

I checked my 1-over-50 and saw that the coordinates plotted out to a position about four miles east of Lai Khe. When I approached the site, I saw a lot of smoke in the area. The tactical net was loaded with all kinds of chatter, including a good bit of cursing, which meant that things were going hot and heavy. I saw a pair of gunships in action and a number of F-4s bombing and strafing the area immediately north of the battle site. Artillery firing from bases at Phuoc Vinh and Lai Khe impacted to the south. All indications pointed to a fierce battle generating a lot of casualties. We were going to earn our combat pay. Incidentally, combat pay was $65 dollars a month, which averaged about $2.15 a day. It was evident we needed a more powerful lobby in Washington.

The raging firefight had started earlier in the day when 1st Battalion, 2d Infantry, made contact with the Viet Cong Phou Loi mainforce battalion. The VC had established a well-fortified position about four miles east of Lai Khe and seven miles southwest of Phuoc Vinh. The 1st Battalion, 2d Infantry, was sweeping from the northeast when its lead elements took fire from the Phou Loi battalion. Eventually the battle involved four battalions of the 1st Division; A and C Troops; 1st Squadron, 4th Cavalry; two Mustang helicopter gun teams; several air force F-4s; an air force Pedro helicopter; and four dustoff crews. The division's battalions were the 1st Battalion, 2d Infantry; 1st Battalion, 16th Infantry; 1st Battalion, 26th Infantry; and 2d Battalion, 28th Infantry.

When I arrived, artillery was impacting, bombs were bursting, tracers were crisscrossing, an APC was burning furiously, and an air force Pedro was burning and smoking where it had crashed. I heard Dustoff 39 reporting; he was on his way from Tan Son Nhut. Hoot Gibson's crew, my crew, and Steve Slattery's C Troop were caught in another hot battle.

The 57th Medical Detachment had already committed Dustoff 76 (Capt. Ed Preston) and Dustoff 78 (Warrant Officer Sanchez) to the battle. They were on station waiting to initiate the evacuations. The 57th Med was the first dustoff unit dispatched to Vietnam, and each of its helicopters displayed a sign on its doors reading THE ORIGINAL DUSTOFF. The folks in the 57th were extremely proud of their history and accomplishments. One of their earliest commanders, Maj. Charles L. Kelly, was the first dustoff pilot killed in Vietnam. He left a legacy of devotion to duty that every dustoff pilot tried to emulate.

Slattery and his Quarter Horse set up a landing zone similar to the one they had on the Minh Thanh road in early July. After they cleared an area in the dense jungle, they positioned their armored vehicles and tanks in a large circle. The ring of armor was bigger than the Minh Thanh defensive perimeter but still not large enough to accommodate more than one Huey at a time.

The first evacuation from the site was attempted by Sanchez (Dustoff 78) and his crew. As he flew over the circular perimeter, he came to a hover, intending to descend into its interior. But the Viet Cong opened up on his chopper. His aircraft was hit repeatedly, and his copilot and one of his crewmen were seriously wounded. Sanchez pulled out quickly and in a highly excited voice shouted that his copilot had been killed. Although Sanchez didn't know it at the time, the copilot was immobilized by his neck wound; he could hear Sanchez's transmission but couldn't speak to make his condition known. Fortunately he and the other crewman survived; both recovered completely from their wounds. But it was not a good start for what was to become an exceptionally long, hot day.

Ed Preston was the next to attempt a pickup. He made it into the perimeter but was having difficulty taking on the wounded. The 57th was still equipped with B-model Hueys, which with their small passenger compartments couldn't take on as many wounded as the more spacious D models. I heard Dragoon Charlie report to the command and control (C&C) ship that the "Original Dustoff" was in the landing zone and the chopper was being loaded. Slattery must have uttered the term "The Original Dustoff" three or four times during his exchanges with the C&C.

I was getting impatient because of the delay and came on the tactical net. "Original Dragoon Charlie, get that damn Original Dustoff the hell out of there and let the Original Dustoff 300 come in."

"All right, Mike," Ed Preston replied. "I'm lifting off now."

As soon as Ed departed, I initiated my entry into the area. As I came in with a fast, low-level approach over a road leading to Slattery's position, I saw artillery impacting ahead of my flight path. Ruiz reported artillery impacting outside his window and a squad of Viet Cong running away from the area being hit by the barrage. Hoping for the best, I continued the run into Slattery's defensive perimeter. When coming close to his position, I flew past an impacting round. I couldn't tell if it was friendly or unfriendly. It really didn't matter; it was just too close for comfort.

I hopped over the perimeter's armor, flared hard to a stop, and in a second slammed the chopper onto the ground. I surveyed the defensive position and noticed that the APC outside the perimeter was still burning furiously; nearby the downed air force Pedro was still smoking. I had no idea what had happened to the Pedro's crewmen and wondered what they were doing away from their base at Bien Hoa. They had probably stumbled on the scene and tried to help. I hoped they survived the crash.

Parisi and Graham quickly loaded four litter patients and an ambulatory and we were ready to get out of there. I applied power to lift the chopper up and over the armor. The torque meter indicated near maximum power as I came to a hover, and I still had to get over the armor. If I tried to get more out of the engine, the rotor revolutions per minute (rpm) would probably deteriorate and I might not be able to continue flight. I should have reduced the load, but I allowed good sense to be overruled by the criticality of the moment: The wounded had to be flown out of there. I made it over the armor but noticed the rotor rpm winding down. It was clear that this helicopter was not going to fly.

If I tried to keep going, the rotor revolutions per minute would continue to deteriorate and I'd soon be out of control. I had to set down, but there wasn't a clear spot ahead of me. Fortunately the trees in front of me were not too high, so I decided to settle down into them. I yelled for Parisi and Graham to give me directions to clear my tail rotor, then called Slattery and told him we were going down. He rogered and said he'd send a force to cover us. We weren't down more than a minute before the covering force surrounded our downed chopper. I sent three litters and the ambulatory back to the perimeter and kept the most seriously wounded soldier aboard.

I applied power, slowly nursed the chopper out of the trees, and noticed that I was hovering with about a pound of torque to spare. Even then the revolutions per minute fell slightly as I cleared the last of the obstacles in my flight path. My bird had a sick engine, so I called the RTO at the base and told him I needed another aircraft.

I dropped off the wounded soldier at Lai Khe and hurried to Tan Son Nhut to pick up a replacement helicopter, which I didn't bother to preflight. Slattery had more wounded to evacuate, and his dustoff support was dwindling. The only one left at the scene was Dustoff 39—Hoot Gibson and his crew. Sanchez was down because of battle damage, and so was Ed Preston. I called Slattery to tell him I was returning. He said he had a lot more casualties standing by.

The violent firefight hadn't abated one bit. Both sides kept up a continual stream of automatic weapons fire while artillery and mortar rounds impacted throughout the area. The Viet Cong were experts in the use of mortars, but the heavily wooded area prevented full exploitation of their capabilities. Our artillery continually raked the VC positions. The troops had excellent communications and adjusted fire from batteries at Lai Khe and Phuoc Vinh. Meanwhile, the air force F-4s continued attacking with bombs and 20mm cannons, and army gunships poured it on from close range.

Mel Ruiz made the next run into Slattery's circle. He was an excellent student and quickly learned the ropes of the dustoff trade. Mel came in fast, made a hard flare to stop at a hover, and settled into the defensive perimeter. His descent was slower than I wanted to see under the circumstances; we drew a lot of fire during the pickup. Mel was trying to put the chopper down gently; showing a degree of displeasure, I let him know that I wanted fast, sure contact with the ground—no wasting time trying to be gentle. The safest medevac pickup is one that takes the least amount of time. Landing a helicopter smoothly and gently takes time and gives the enemy a chance to boresight and get in a lucky shot that could be an aviator's undoing. If the skids are damaged by a hard landing, they can be replaced; that's easier and costs less than new pilots.

As the afternoon wore on, it was evident that we were in for a substantial engagement. The Viet Cong were well entrenched, and it was

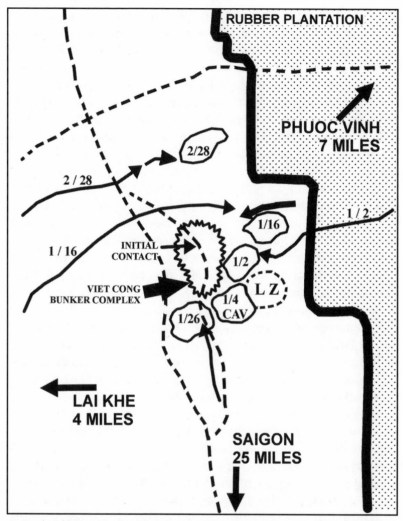

A fierce battle with the Viet Cong (VC) Phou Loi main-force battalion occurred August 25, 1966. After a patrol from 1st Battalion, 2d Infantry, made contact, the rest of the battalion engaged the VC and was joined by the troops shown in the map.

going to take a determined effort to eliminate them. The Phou Loi battalion was well known to the troops of the 1st Infantry Division. Superbly trained and well equipped by VC standards, it was an outfit dedicated to its cause and had its share of heroes. Many of its troops held their positions until death. They were the kind of men that officers were proud to command. The soldiers of the 1st Division were just as dedicated and intended to get rid of the Viet Cong.

Slowly the superior firepower of our combined forces began to tell on the Viet Cong. Our casualties were evacuated from the battlefield, but theirs had to remain and interfered with the VC's ability to continue. There wasn't any shortage of armaments or ammunition for the American forces, but the VC had to make do with what they had accumulated in their underground hideaways. When their supply of armaments was gone, it was either surrender, or disengage and withdraw into the jungle. How they always managed to regroup was a mystery. It was an unbelievable task, but the Viet Cong did it time and again. That was one reason this war was so difficult to fathom. The enemy had the characteristics of the legendary Phoenix, able to rise out of the ashes of defeat in a rebirth of renewed vigor and ability to resume the fight.

As the battle raged during the afternoon, Hoot and I continued our evacuation missions. Four battalions of the 1st Division and A and C Troops of the Quarter Horse were deployed in a semicircle facing the Viet Cong and were slowly tightening a gigantic noose around them.

The 1st Battalion, 26th Infantry, anchored the line on the southern flank and was joined by the 1st Squadron, 4th Cavalry, on its right. The skirmish line continued north with the 1st Battalion, 2d Infantry, to the right of the Quarter Horse and 1st Battalion, 16th Infantry, on the northern flank.

The Viet Cong's firing pattern changed after a while, indicating a repositioning of forces and possible preparation to disengage and attempt to distance themselves from the Americans. Lai Khe and the division's 2d Brigade were to the west. A huge rubber plantation only a kilometer to the east offered little cover; Saigon and other American forces were to the south. The only chance of a successful disengagement was to the north. To prevent such an uncontested withdrawal from the battle area, the 2d Battalion, 28th Infantry, was airlifted by the division's choppers to a blocking position about a kilometer to the north.

Our forces continued to take casualties, and requests for additional medical evacuations kept coming in. Hoot and I flew mission after mission throughout the afternoon. The air force kept bombing and strafing while the artillery shelled the enemy. Later in the afternoon the helicopter gunships ceased operations, and soon after the F-4s did likewise. But the artillery kept at it, even past nightfall.

Time after time I made my fast, hedge-hopping entries past impacting artillery into the evacuation perimeter. It was already a long day and wasn't close to being over. I made my last extraction from Slattery's perimeter just before darkness settled over the area. Then the action shifted slightly to the north, and my next evacuation took place in a small clearing; I was guided in by flashlight. The area was also lit by flares sent up by the artillery. It was not unusual to see two or three flares at different altitudes suspended from their small parachutes floating to earth. As soon as one was doused as it landed, another flicked on with a pop and temporarily brushed aside the darkness.

It was an eerie scene as flares cast shadows where no shadows should have been. The intensity of the light emitted by the flares increased and decreased in time to the swaying of the descending parachutes. Haze and smoke from the flares, bombs, tons of munitions, and exploding rounds hung over the area. The pungent odor of cordite permeated the air, heavier in some areas than others. While I looked down on the scene, I couldn't help but think that I had come upon another planet, maybe the moon. The explosives created a panorama that resembled land worked over by a giant machine that processed the soil into a grayish, powdery ash. The flickering light of the flares danced and played on the undulations of the talclike loess covering the earth and made it look like rippling waves on a body of water.

The intensity of fire subsided but the casualties kept coming in. We were sent from one sector to another to make evacuations as the emphasis of the fighting shifted. The battle may have changed but the pain and agony of the wounded had not. I thought the fighting would never end, but at long last we made our final evacuation of the day. I checked my count with that of the medic, Parisi. We agreed. We had extracted sixty-six wounded soldiers of the 1st Infantry Division during the afternoon and night.

We had gone in and out of the battles sixteen times, drawing fire almost every time. We filled the forward medical stations of Lai Khe and Phuoc Vinh with more wounded than either had ever treated before. The medics at both facilities worked tirelessly throughout the day tending the wounded. The doctors, nurses, and attendants went without food that day; they were unable to leave their stations. I hadn't eaten since breakfast, but for some reason I didn't feel the least bit hungry.

It was half an hour before midnight; I'd been on duty for eighteen hours. By the time I returned to dustoff operations, it was the next day. I completed the afteraction reports, returned to my quarters, showered, and tried to relax with a shot of Scotch before hitting the sack. I was not sleepy even though I'd been on duty for hours on end and had flown for ten and a half hours. I poured another drink, this time almost three fingers. It was almost two in the morning when I finished the drink and went to bed.

Instead of falling asleep, I was surprised to find myself reliving the day. The more I thought about the day's events, such as the runs into Slattery's perimeter, the more I was exhilarated. I experienced a postcombat high. I'd had similar sensations after other battles, but nothing like the high I experienced that night. The stimulation peaked when I recalled flying through artillery barrages, the heavy concentrations of enemy automatic weapons fire, and the hits we took. I could almost smell the cordite again as thoughts of the action flashed through my mind.

Slowly, ever so slowly, fatigue finally overcame the hypnotic effect of the sensations and I fell asleep. That was not the only time I was consumed by such an experience. The high often returned and dominated my mind as I vividly relived the harrowing encounters. I wondered if others experienced similar reactions after being engaged in fierce battles. I was afraid to ask; I didn't know if I'd like the answer.

All dustoff crew members who took part in the action of August 25, 1966, were awarded Distinguished Flying Crosses for their heroic actions. Considering the number of aircraft damaged, crewmen wounded, and soldiers whose lives were saved, it was the least they deserved.

11 Beating the System and Getting Short

I'd flown combat missions for almost nine months without time off. It was army policy to grant a week of R and R (rest and recuperation) to soldiers during their year of duty in Vietnam. Most R and Rs were taken during the latter six months of a person's combat tour. The most popular spots were Hawaii, Hong Kong, and Sydney, Australia. Other excellent locations were Taipei, Manila, Bangkok, and Kuala Lumpur. Most of the married men tried to get to Hawaii, the ultimate spot for a second honeymoon.

I came up with a plan for my R and R after talking with air force friends. I found out that medical personnel routinely accompanied and assisted the wounded on air force evacuation flights to hospitals in the States. My air force contacts considered my dustoff assignment as proof of my medical qualifications and said I could be assigned to one of their evacuation flights as a crew member. All I needed was the approval of my commanding officer. There was no reason why I shouldn't take advantage of the situation, so I went to see my boss, Maj. Bill Briot.

I explained the situation to Briot and reminded him that I'd been most helpful to the detachment, putting forth a lot of extra effort giving instrument instructions—and I was due an R and R. Briot reminded me that an R and R was only seven days and I couldn't possibly get to the States and back and have any time to visit with my wife and family. I replied that I was asking for two weeks' leave, which he had the authority to grant.

"*Two weeks!*" he exclaimed. "That's not possible. What will the other pilots say when they find out?"

I suggested he tell them I was on temporary duty with the air force, which would be partly true. He thought the matter over. "Let me get this straight. You're going to be a medic on an air force evacuation flight, right?"

"Right," I replied.

"You'll go home to the wife and kids for a few days and return to Vietnam, right?"

"Right."

"You expect me to believe that shit, Mike?"

"Look," I replied, "I've always been straight with you. I've always done my job and never crossed you up. Give me my leave and I'll be back in two weeks."

"You wouldn't be pulling a shitty on me, would you, Mike?"

"No way, Bill. I'll do my work as a medic, deliver my patient, go home for a while, and be back for duty as promised. The only reason I wouldn't make it back on time would be delays by the air transport people or maintenance problems."

Briot didn't say a word as he mulled over my proposal. "Okay. I must be crazy to believe all the shit you're putting on me. You can go, but I'm not going to put any of this on paper. If I did, it would be a matter of record for the Morning Report. Then everyone would know I gave you two weeks' leave."

I hadn't counted on this turn of events. "What kind of proof do I give the air force people that you've given me permission for the trip?"

"That's your problem. No paperwork on this deal."

I decided to give it a try. I told my air force contacts that everything was all set and I had my commander's permission. I was given the time of the flight and told to be at operations two hours before departure, ready to go. No one bothered to ask for any written orders or proof that I had permission for the flight. It was unbelievable that everything was going so smoothly. I was about to travel halfway around the world, spend about a week at home with my wife and family, then fly back to Vietnam—all without documentation, leave orders, or written authorization. I thought back to my days as a lieutenant colonel performing reserve duties. I couldn't even get a local, one-hour flight in a C-47 Gooney Bird without a set of orders. This trip was based on verbal orders of the commanding officer (VOCO). I thought to myself that the Lord, the army, and now the air force all move in mysterious ways.

I arrived at operations with my luggage, a briefcase containing my original orders assigning me to Vietnam, my immunization record, and a few personal items. I wore a flight suit, so I fit right in with the aircrews. The wounded arrived in a bus specially configured to handle litters. The airplane was a C-141 designed to handle the medical needs of the wounded during the long flight to the States. All crew members (me included) assisted the nurses and medical people with the loading. I was shown the patient I'd be escorting to Walter Reed Medical Center in Washington, D.C. This fit right in with my plans, because my wife and family were in Fayetteville, North Carolina, a short flight from Washington.

There was something vaguely familiar about my patient, who was recovering from a severe abdominal wound. By coincidence, only two days earlier I had evacuated a young, nearly unconscious trooper with the same type of wound. He was in a huge bomb crater dotted with tree stumps and saplings, all charred by the explosive force of the bomb. I remember that the landing area was uneven, and I had to keep the helicopter light on its skids to keep it level. I saw a hulk of a sergeant carrying a young soldier with blond hair to my helicopter. While watching him carrying his wounded comrade in his arms, I momentarily relaxed my grip on the cyclic and the aircraft tilted forward slightly. The main rotor hit a small sapling, and there was a loud report similar to that of an artillery round going off. It startled me for an instant before I leveled the ship.

I asked the young soldier on the plane when he had been wounded. He said it was two days earlier when a land mine detonated near his position and he was hit by a large piece of shrapnel. He said his unit was sweeping an area that was bombed earlier by the air force, and the ground was covered with craters.

He was amazed when I told him that it was my crewmen who had rescued him from the bomb crater. Then I told him that I'd seen his sergeant carry him to my helicopter. He remembered that but couldn't recall who carried him. I asked him how old he was, and he replied, "Nineteen."

I told the soldier that the war was over for him, that he'd be going to Walter Reed and I was his escort. He smiled weakly and said he was from Maryland; the hospital was close to home. I checked his dressings and could tell he'd been subjected to drastic abdominal exploration. There were a lot of sutures plus two metal clips holding the incision in place. He said he was still weak but wasn't in pain. He was anxious to see his parents. He wasn't married.

Toward the end of the flight home, I was surprised to see my patient get up and slowly walk to one of the lavatories. I rushed to assist, but he wanted to try it alone. I had seen this soldier close to death only two days earlier and couldn't believe his recuperative powers. He clearly proved that there was more to the human spirit, the ability to survive, than I ever dreamed possible. He was a genuine inspiration to me.

The flight and delivery of my patient to Walter Reed took almost twenty-four hours. At Andrews Air Force Base, another of the special hospital buses met our plane. I escorted my patient to Walter Reed, where I said good-bye and wished him a speedy recovery. The size of his grin made it clear that he was happy to be home. From all indications, his recovery would not take long.

I made the trip to Fayetteville on Allegheny Airlines aboard a prop jet Fokker F-27 and was home within four hours. The week with Ethel and the children went much too fast. But in many ways it was as if I had never left home. For example, I had to make a court appearance with my son, Mike Jr., who would turn seventeen in a few weeks. I had left him in charge of the family car while I was gone and, like too many of his peers, he had driven too fast too often. He was in court to take care of a speeding ticket (I paid the fine).

My daughters were growing up and were a special delight. Patty was fourteen and Jean twelve. They displayed signs of beauty inherited from their mother. Little John was three and didn't understand why I'd been gone and why I had to leave again so soon. Ethel was of like mind. But I had given my word, and there was nothing more sacred than that. My old-fashioned cadet training was still with me: "An officer's word is his bond."

Because of the unique arrangement I'd made with Bill Briot for my time off, the return from Fayetteville to Travis was at my expense.

Even so, I insisted on going back first class. I wondered what the air force people at Travis would say about the flight to Nam. I didn't have orders or any other authorization covering my return. When I entered operations, I went directly to the highest-ranking noncom behind the desk and asked when the next flight was scheduled to depart for Saigon. He said the aircraft was boarding passengers and would leave as soon as that was completed. The sergeant said there were a few spaces available due to scheduling foul-ups. I said, "Put me on board. I've got to get back to my outfit within the next two days and I don't want to be late."

"Let me see your orders, sir," he said.

At this point things could have gotten sticky, but I bluffed my way through. "All I have with me are my original orders assigning me to Vietnam. My new orders haven't caught up with me. I've been on a special project."

"These will do. No one in his right mind would be returning to Nam unless he had to."

"You're absolutely right, Sergeant." After that short exchange, I was on my way back to Saigon and the 283d Medical Detachment. I wasn't even asked to show my military ID card, and this time I had one. I couldn't believe it was so easy. It reminded me of the days when I'd first reported for duty with the army. But now I was wearing a uniform and had orders to show, even if they were more than nine months old.

The flight to Saigon was monotonously long. There wasn't anyone like Bob French to help pass the time and make the trip interesting. I called the detachment as soon as I disembarked; I got out of the new arrival orientation by telling the sergeant in charge that I was returning from emergency leave. Within half an hour Charlie Wilson and Hoot Gibson arrived with a jeep. Charlie said Briot wanted to see me as soon as I got in, and we had to stop at the orderly room before going to our quarters.

The gang at the 283d and the 57th were happy to see me and greeted me warmly as I walked in. Briot was at the door to his office, asked me inside, and shook my hand. "Have a seat, Mike," he said. "You've surprised the hell out of me. I really didn't expect you back. I let you go knowing you would have served more than ten months overseas by the time your leave was over, enough to give you credit for a full year's tour. I wouldn't have been angry with you if you had stayed home."

"Look, Bill, I gave you my word I'd return. I'm from the old school—my word is sacred to me. We old-timers might screw around with the system, but we don't screw each other. You knew you didn't have to go along with my scheme, but you did. What we did was somewhat irregular, maybe even illegal, and we knew that. It sure as hell was not in compliance with army regulations. Now, aren't you ashamed of yourself?"

Bill grinned. "Get your ass out of here and get some rest. I don't want to see you again till you've overcome every bit of your jet lag. Seriously, Mike, we missed you. I'm glad you're back. Now get!"

"What the hell did Briot want with you so soon?" Charlie asked when I got to the jeep. "You haven't even had a chance to get into fresh clothes, and you sure as hell haven't had any rest."

I told him that Briot just wanted to know how my family was and whether or not I had a good time on leave.

"I think you're putting some crap on me," Charlie said. "He never calls me or anyone else into his office just to chew the rag."

I laughed and told Charlie to get me back to our quarters, that I really needed to relax and get some rest.

Too tired to shower, I flopped onto my bed without undressing. Although it was midmorning, I told Charlie to leave me alone and not to make any noise for the rest of the day. I was dead to the world for the next eight to nine hours. When I awoke it was almost dark, but there was still plenty of time to clean up and get something to eat. There was even time (if I hurried) for a few drinks at the bar.

I had a steak for dinner in the company of my dustoff friends. Someone had the bartender bring me a bottle of Mateus, which I didn't expect but consumed with the help of others at the table. After dinner I went to the bar and ordered my usual gin and tonic. Briot was there, as was big John Hosley. They told me that operations had slacked off a bit while I was gone, but the scuttlebutt was that the 1st Division was resting and regrouping for more action—maybe even farther north into II Corps. Meanwhile, the 25th Division was operating along the Cambodian border north of Tay Ninh.

It appeared that the two divisions were preparing a strong sweep of their respective northern sectors. If successful, the operation would seriously hamper the Viet Cong's ability to operate close to Saigon. In due time these operations would have a decided effect on dustoff units.

Bill Briot, John Hosley, and I rehashed earlier operations of the two divisions and our missions in support of them. It was a good bull session, but I got the impression that they were telling me to be careful. They joked about my short-timer's status, and Briot said it wouldn't be long before my tour was over and I'd be going home.

I stayed at the bar with Briot and John and had a couple more drinks. The jet lag, the Mateus, and the three or four gin and tonics had the desired effect. I was tired and went to my quarters, albeit somewhat unsteadily, and slept until noon the next day.

Late that afternoon I reported to operations and said I was available for duty. I was put on the flight schedule for the next day and did my first flying in nineteen days.

Things were slow for about a week, but I managed to pull one field standby at Lai Khe. Captain Joe Fulghum was with me as my copilot. We got quite a bit of rest, which was highly unusual. There wasn't much enemy activity. One evening after dinner, Joe and I were talking to Mickey Runyon, the battalion dentist, and Father Michael J. Queely, one of the division chaplains. We decided on a game of bridge and set up a table in the 1st Medical Battalion officers' club, which was nothing more than a corner in the battalion mess tent. The area had a table with a few bottles of hooch and some mix. Payment was on the honor system.

Mickey and Father each had a drink and Joe and I had Coke. Father Queely had no sooner taken his seat when he asked me and Joe to change positions. We took our new seats, and I immediately noticed why Father wanted the change. He'd been facing a part of the tent that was adorned with centerfolds from the latest *Playboy* magazines. The wall was studded with all shapes, sizes, and colors of mammary glands. Even with the distraction we had a good game, called it a night, and retired for the evening. It was one of those rare occasions in the field when nothing happened—not one evacuation mission. We were able to sleep through the night for a change.

The next day Joe and I had a mission that took us away from Lai Khe for more than an hour. In our absence an urgent mission was answered by Briot and his copilot, Hosley. The operation we all expected started and produced the inevitable results. The 2d Battalion, 16th Infantry (commanded by Lt. Col. William S. Hathaway), halted its sweep through the jungle as nightfall approached and set up a sizable defensive perimeter. Everything went according to plan, but at first light Viet Cong forces hit Hathaway's encampment with everything they had. The attack was launched against the battalion while it was being resupplied by the division's helicopters. One of the ships was riddled by automatic weapons fire as it lifted off from the perimeter. Two of its crewmen were seriously wounded, but the pilots managed to fly out of the field of fire and make their way back to the base. Briot and Hosley were the first dustoffs on the scene and had their hands full evacuating the wounded. Joe and I arrived as Briot was making his second extraction. The perimeter was being pounded by mortar rounds and a steady stream of automatic weapons fire. Briot called to let me know that Father Queely was inside the perimeter giving last rites to the dying and consoling the wounded. On the next lift I was told that a chaplain had been hit in one of the VC assaults and was killed. I didn't have to ask who the casualty was.

After the battle ran its course and all the wounded were extracted, I flew back into the then quiet perimeter to get the body of my friend. Father Queely did not have to go into the battle area, but that was the way he operated. He felt that his presence was needed, and he had hopped on Briot's ship during one of the extractions.

Father Queely had flown with me many times. When he saw or heard my ship cranking up, he'd run and get on board so he might help at the scene of action. His death didn't make any sense. One of his chaplain associates took care of his personal effects. A pack of four cigars was found among Father's things and I was asked what should be done with them. "Give them to me. I'll smoke them for him," I said. I remembered how Father enjoyed his cigars during his rare moments of relaxation. I tried to put his death out of my mind, but ensuing events made that a difficult task.

Shortly after Joe Fulghum was made an aircraft commander, he took his turn on field standby at Lai Khe. One night he received an urgent life-or-death mission, and Mickey Runyon volunteered to go with him. Lights were needed to make the pickup, but Joe made it into the extraction site even though it was under constant fire. He was making his departure when the VC shot him down. The ship went out of control, crashed, and exploded on impact, instantly killing all on board. Joe's copilot on that fateful mission was 1st Lt. Alan Zimmerman, the detachment's latest replacement. He had been in country less than two weeks. Only a short time earlier, Joe, Mickey, Father, and I had enjoyed a game of bridge. I was the only one left.

Casualties have a way of accelerating in war, especially in flying outfits. There is an old saying in aviation: "Fatalities come in threes." Dustoffs in our area went through a time when the KIA numbers went off the charts. I remember stopping for fuel at Long Binh at about three in the morning. It had been raining continuously since midnight and my missions required a lot of instrument flying. Majors Kent Gandy and Harry Phillips, who were first up in their detachment, came out of their operations building to chew the fat while I refueled. They especially wanted to know what kind of weather I'd encountered during the night.

I'd flown with Kent Gandy in the Dominican Republic about a year earlier. He was a level-headed officer and a good pilot. The short conversation about the weather was the last I enjoyed with my two friends. They were killed within the hour while on an urgent evacuation mission. Then WO Edward Bush and his copilot, 1st Lt. Jack Lichte, were on a critical night mission. They and their crew and patients were killed when they slammed into Nui Ba Den, an extinct volcano, while flying through a thunderstorm. The dustoff crews of Fulghum, Gandy, and Bush were lost while on night extractions in stormy weather. The losses of my close friends were hard to accept. But we could not afford the luxury of taking time to mourn. The wounded were still with us every moment of every day and every night. Their plight was uppermost in our minds. The dead were remembered, but the mission came first.

Not long after I returned from leave, we took time out to celebrate Thanksgiving Day. It was a reminder of a special time of year when families draw closer and pleasant moods seem to embrace the soul. Christmas and New Year's were coming—indicators of my combat tour coming to an end. I'd soon be going home. I was getting short.

Some pilots grew edgy as their rotation dates approached. Survival instincts took on increased emphasis and created their own priorities. This often made the pilots dangerous to themselves and their friends, because they let distractions take over and no longer concentrated on the job at hand. Some lost confidence in their abilities and substituted odds or percentages to situations. In other cases pilots on the ragged edge expected everything to go wrong, and of course everything did. They thought the engine would quit, and invariably it did. In the worst case they thought that the next mission would be their last, and it was. Survival in combat requires an attitude likened to omnipotence: The bullet meant for me has yet to be cast. As for the engine quitting, it wouldn't dare. A positive attitude is absolutely necessary to survive long in combat. I resolved to continue to the best of my ability, keep my head clear, and work in my usual style. I wanted to be in excellent shape for the trip home.

December was my last month of combat, and I took my turn on the duty roster as usual. The mission of the 283d hadn't changed, so I still spent time in the field and flew as much as ever. I lucked out on Christmas Day; I wasn't scheduled for field duty. The Viet Cong and the Americans had declared a truce for the day, but some people (as always) managed to get their signals crossed and found themselves in trouble. We flew a few missions going to their assistance. We completed one north of Lai Khe and were headed back to the base when we overflew a perimeter of our troops. It was an element of Col. Sidney B. Berry's 1st Brigade of the 1st Infantry Division. A call came over the dustoff universal frequency: "Hey, Dustoff, Merry Christmas. Come on down."

"Be glad to oblige," I answered.

I saw a large tent within the perimeter, an unusual sight in the middle of the jungle. I landed within the enclosure but as far from the tent as possible. I didn't want my downwash to disturb the activities. Colonel Berry greeted us and offered us a glass of champagne—a hospitable greeting in a combat zone. I thought, what the hell, it's Christmas and we don't have a mission pending, at least not at the moment.

Colonel Berry directed us to a long table that was loaded with an assortment of food not normally found in a tent in a combat zone defensive perimeter. We ate our fill, finished our champagne, thanked the colonel for his gracious hospitality, and prepared to leave. Colonel Berry said he appreciated all that we had done for him and his troops. He added that it was unfortunate that circumstances hadn't given him more time to display his gratitude in the past. I thanked him and assured him he could expect the quality of dustoff support to remain unchanged. We returned to the base and thankfully didn't have any more missions. It was a different Christmas, one that I hoped was my last in combat.

There was little time left on my tour when I drew standby duty on New Year's Eve at Papa Victor (Phuoc Vinh). The combatants again had declared a truce. There must have been a conscientious attempt to comply, because there was little dustoff activity. The troops at Papa Victor were preparing to bring in the new year in style. They were barbecuing a pig and had a few GI cans loaded with ice-cold beer and sodas. Some had already sampled the beer. At the rate they were going, they'd soon be drunk as skunks.

After dark we went to see how the pig was coming along. It was being turned slowly on a huge metal spit. I'd eaten a big dinner but was determined to have some of the barbecue when it was done. It looked so good, and the aroma made my mouth water. I told my crew that if we didn't get a mission by the end of the day, they could have a beer. I didn't expect any action after that. We'd had champagne with Colonel Berry on Christmas, so we ought to be able to have a beer on New Year's Eve.

I opened a beer and managed to get a serving of the barbecue on a slice of bread. It was delicious. The troops took care of the pig in short order and celebrated the coming of the new year as best they could. They didn't have Guy Lombardo to play "Auld Lang Syne," and there was no champagne, no fancy nightclubs, no tuxedos, and, unfortunately, no wives or girlfriends. That would have to wait for another new year.

We stayed at Papa Victor until we were relieved on January 3. My flight home was scheduled for January 7, 1967. I made my last dustoff flight on January 5, when I delivered six ambulatory patients to an area hospital. That closed out my flight log. My next flight would be on the Freedom Bird. There followed the usual farewells and a gathering of fellow dustoffers at the Red Bull Inn. I received a plaque attesting to my outstanding performance: 631 hours flown, 760 combat missions, and the evacuation of 2,001 wounded soldiers. To my knowledge I had neither offended nor harmed anyone in one year of combat flying. I was ready to go home.

12 My Plans Go Awry

I was ecstatic. I was home at last and everything was just as I expected. Ethel had done well with the children. Mike Jr. was seventeen and a senior in high school, Patty was fifteen and a sophomore, Jean was twelve and in grade school, and John would be four in two months. Ethel asked if I was through with my war games.

"I promise you I won't go into combat again. Let someone else go. I'm through with war. When my service with the army is over, we're going back to Atlanta, and I'll be happy to return to the life of an airline pilot."

Ethel observed that she'd heard of men and their midlife crises and how they usually went through such phases by chasing women. "But you! You go out searching for a war to fight. You're not normal. I almost wish you had opted for chasing after some floozy. I wouldn't have worried so much."

"First of all," I replied, "I did not have a midlife crisis. But if I had, would you really want me to go chasing women?"

"Try it and you'll wish that the Viet Cong had you," she remarked. As usual, Ethel had the last word. I was in a blissful period enjoying my family. The joy of returning home after a year of combat is a high that only a select few can appreciate.

The army was preparing to take over Hunter Air Force Base at Savannah, Georgia, and I was one of a handful of officers assigned to effect the transfer. My family went with me and we settled into housing on the base. Our small group of army aviators was tasked with setting up a new flying school to augment the facility at Fort Rucker in Alabama. It was the type of assignment that I expected when I volunteered for duty with the army. Now after traveling all over the world and being in combat for a year, I finally was going to work where my experience could be used.

The number of aviators being graduated at Fort Rucker each month was not enough to support the war effort. We were to establish the flight school at Hunter, have training begin by July 1967, and attain the capability to graduate two hundred students a month by fall.

My job was to establish an instrument trainer department. The most difficult and time-consuming part of the task was getting equipment. Specifically, I needed Link trainers. These primitive trainers, which dated back to World War II, were the only ones used by army aviation. Their age revealed the low priority that army aviation planners gave to instrument training. But the senior staff at Hunter was determined to organize a creditable instrument program. Instructors at Hunter had to be instrument qualified. Colonel Cabell commanded the army takeover and Lt. Col. Julian Anderson coordinated the project. I worked closely with Lt. Col. "Dutch" Ebaugh; he gave me the task of setting up the instrument trainers.

I didn't have a budget dedicated to the project but had unlimited authority to scrounge, so I was constantly on the phone trying to get Link trainers from stateside army installations. It was slow work. Even though most airfield commanders were not using their trainers, they were reluctant to let them go because there was always the possibility they'd need them in the future.

When I was told that a trainer was available but not in working condition, I had it shipped and put aside as a source of spare parts. When the supply of Links in the States dried up, I contacted the army's overseas installations. I finally got enough trainers for Hunter, and in two months the instrument training facility was operating.

We were a hard-charging, hardworking group that had a job to do and a deadline to meet. Most of the officers working on the project were Vietnam vets. Talking with Dutch Ebaugh, I learned that he was with the 1st Infantry Division at Lai Khe and we were involved in the same battles but weren't aware of each other's roles at the time.

As the war progressed, more aviators returning from Vietnam were assigned to us. One was Capt. Mike Chastain, who moved into the quarters next to ours. We became close friends. Mike was with the 25th Infantry Division; in discussing our service in Vietnam we discovered that we were in the same firefights. It was a strange war. Its mobility was appreciated when offhand conversations revealed that individuals who operated from different bases with different missions were involved in the same battles. One of the latter arrivals at Hunter was Maj. Don Bissell, a fellow dustoffer just back from Vietnam. He had been Chuck Conselman's executive officer assigned to the 82d Medical Detachment at Soc Trang, in the delta.

We worked six-day weeks in the early days at Hunter, and it paid off. We'd have the school ready to accept its first students ahead of schedule. I didn't feel any pressure but was caught up in the spirit of getting the job done. Meanwhile, I was happy working to produce instrument instructors for the army.

Our job as instrument method of instruction (IMOI) teachers was to school aviators just returned from Vietnam in the fine art of instrument flying. Then we showed them how to impart those skills to future aviators who were to be assigned to Vietnam. My work couldn't have pleased me more.

Our heavy work schedule finally eased off. This was the first assignment I'd ever had that allowed me to relax, enjoy life, and play golf. Mike Chastain and I were usually off duty at the same time and played regularly. Our wives didn't play but often accompanied us.

It was an enjoyable period, and Ethel and I knew we'd miss our friends when my military service came to an end. It was late April 1968 when I wrote to Everett Martin, vice president for personnel at Southern Airways. I told him that my discharge was scheduled for September 1 and I'd be ready to return to work. Southern was flying new airplanes and routes, including daily flights to New York City and Miami. I was anxious to get into the new equipment.

One afternoon while I was at the club, I bumped into Don Bissell. He expected to be picked up on the lieutenant colonels' list and return to Vietnam for another tour. I was happy to hear about the promotion, and the news about returning to combat didn't surprise me. I had many friends who were serving second tours in Nam. The usual period between combat assignments was about two years, but aviators in critical specialties returned in eighteen months or less.

Don said he didn't mind the impending assignment. He was pretty sure he'd get command of one of the medical detachments when he returned to Nam sometime after the first of the year. I told him he was looking too far ahead; the war could be over by then.

"Don't hold your breath," he replied.

"Well, I'm scheduled to be discharged on the first of September, and I expect to be back in the cockpit of my airliner shortly thereafter. I've already informed the company's director of personnel. I expect to hear from him any day now." With that exchange of personal plans, we went our separate ways.

A short while later I heard from Everett Martin. I was surprised when he asked me to request an early discharge so I could undergo retraining beginning on July 22. I went to see Dutch Ebaugh and told him about Martin's request. He told me to write and ask the Department of the Army (DA) for an early release. There was no reason for them to refuse. After all, the new discharge date would be only a month and a half earlier than originally scheduled.

Meanwhile, I received notice of promotion to chief warrant officer three. I sent my letter to DA asking for an early release effective July 15, 1968, and declined the promotion because of my upcoming departure from the army.

Everett Martin's letter had reached me in early May, and my letter to DA was on its way a week later. By the time a decision was made at DA, it was almost the middle of June. My request for an early discharge was approved, and I notified Everett that I'd be in Atlanta ready to attend classes on July 22. My return to civilian life meant taking off a uniform that I had grown to love and putting on one more attuned to my age and experience. I was almost forty-six years old.

My orders arrived and I notified Dutch. He set the administrative machinery in motion and I proceeded to clear post. My separation physical was scheduled for July 12. I didn't expect problems; I had completed my last flight physical six months earlier and everything was fine. I arrived at the post hospital and got into the exam routine.

The final part of the exam was my session with the flight surgeon. He looked over the results of the examination and said he had to check my eyes again because there appeared to be some error. I wore reading glasses and thought I might need a new prescription. He stretched me out on the examination table and rechecked my intraocular tension. I wasn't unduly concerned, because the primitive measuring device was subject to error if not applied properly. The flight surgeon said the readings in both eyes were too high and more tests were necessary. I told him that my last physical was six months earlier and the tension in both eyes was satisfactory then. But the flight surgeon said his readings for both eyes were above thirty. I was to return in the morning and have the tension rechecked. I said that this was my separation physical and I was to report for work in ten days. He said he understood but the additional tests were necessary.

I went home that night not knowing what to tell Ethel. The situation had me worried. When she asked if I had completed my physical exam, I told her I had to see the flight surgeon in the morning because he hadn't had time to complete the examination. I was not being entirely candid but didn't want her to worry, especially because the eye checks could have been in error. I spent a fitful night and didn't get much sleep.

In the morning the flight surgeon checked and rechecked my intraocular tension. It still was above thirty in both eyes. The countenance of the flight surgeon was not reassuring. He didn't say anything for a few seconds, then made the statement that changed all my plans and my life: "I'm not certain, but all indications point to glaucoma. We'll have to make more tests and schedule a consultation with an ophthalmologist."

"Does that mean that my separation from the service might have to be put on hold?"

"There's a strong possibility that all the tests might not be finished by the time you're scheduled for separation. Meanwhile, you're grounded."

His last statement shocked me. "How long will I be grounded? Can I return to flight status later? What's the FAA policy with a situation such as this?" I asked.

"It's possible you might get a waiver for your condition. I'm not certain about the army's policy concerning glaucoma. As for the FAA, you'll have to call them."

"What do I do now?"

"You've got to inform your boss that you're grounded. I'll make the arrangements for your consultation with the ophthalmologist. If possible that will be sometime tomorrow. I'm sorry it has to be this way, but there's nothing else I can do. If it is glaucoma, and I'm almost certain it is, you're better off knowing it now than sometime in the future. Untreated, glaucoma can lead to blindness."

That was it. There was nothing more I could do, so I went to see Dutch Ebaugh to give him the news. I had no idea what his reaction would be. I was confused by all that was happening. A few days earlier everything was fine. My early release had been approved and I had received my separation orders from DA. My retraining with Southern at Atlanta was on the agenda, and I was looking forward to getting into the DC-9. But suddenly everything was on hold and looking mighty grim.

I knew that nothing in life is guaranteed and that one must be prepared for occasional reverses. But this was too much, like getting a hard kick in the teeth. I remembered how I felt when I received the phone call years before notifying me that I'd been RIFed by the air force. The blow delivered by the flight surgeon was just as hard. This was the second time that my career was abruptly terminated. If my life had been a crap game, I would have been rolling snake eyes when I needed a natural.

I had to stop dwelling on my reverses; self-pity wouldn't change a thing. After all, I had a beautiful wife and four fine children and they came first. I knew that it would all turn around somehow. It was my responsibility to make that happen. I had glaucoma and was grounded by the army. Getting back on flight status was my first priority.

I had to be certain of the FAA's position regarding glaucoma. A call produced a quick strikeout; a waiver for an airline captain was out of the question. That ruling terminated my airline career.

I told Dutch I was grounded and unloaded my problem on him. His response was more than I ever expected. He promised to do everything in his power to have the separation orders revoked and get me flying again. His quick response to my situation turned my day around. I thanked him and went to see my friend Don Bissell.

I told Don my story and that I was sure the flight surgeon's diagnosis would be confirmed. I felt better when he said it should be possible to get a waiver and get me back to flying. If anyone could do it, Don and his Medical Service Corps people could. They knew the rules and regulations and how to cut the red tape. I was in good hands, and getting a waiver for glaucoma, although not routine, was possible. My hopes were up.

I dreaded my next task, which was to tell Ethel. She was looking forward to returning to the Atlanta area and the routine of civilian life. I couldn't think of a way to tell her that wouldn't upset her. Once again doubt clouded our future. I still might be medically discharged and again have to suffer the indignity of being booted out of the service, although this time it would be for an entirely different reason. There also was the loss of a terrific job as an airline captain and the possibility of being through with flying forever. We had been young parents with our first child when the air force RIF caught us. Now we had four children; I was almost forty-six years old and could be out of a job. I even feared that it was all my fault, that my condition was the result of something I'd done. I decided to come straight out with the bad news and tell Ethel what had happened.

When I got home that afternoon, Ethel was watching John playing in the yard with Chastain's son and daughter. She asked me how everything went and whether or not I had finished clearing post. I didn't hesitate: "You're not going to like what happened. I stopped clearing post and I'm not going to be discharged, at least not now. The flight surgeon says I have glaucoma. He's set up a consultation with an ophthalmologist tomorrow and I'm sure he'll confirm the diagnosis. Ethel, I'm so sorry I have to give you such bad news. I'm sorry I can't tell you in a more gentle manner, but there's no use holding back or denying what's happened. I wish with all my heart that it wasn't so. One other thing you should know: I'm grounded."

She came over to where I was standing and hugged me tightly. "Mike, I'm so sorry for you," she said in her gentle way. "It's not fair. I know how much you were looking forward to going back to the airline and working with the new jets. I know how much you enjoy flying. It's been your life and you're so good at it. It just isn't fair."

I was surprised by Ethel's attitude. I thought she would voice her disappointment at not being able to return to Atlanta and her concern that I might be out of a job again. She thought only of me and my feelings. "What is the army going to do with you now that you're grounded?"

"I've already talked to Dutch Ebaugh and Don Bissell. They're going to set the machinery in motion to stop my discharge and obtain a waiver so I can continue flying. I've talked to the people at the FAA. There's no way they'll let me fly as an airline pilot. Let's face it, my airline career is over. I have to stay in the army, if they'll have me."

Ethel was still holding me tightly. "I don't know how you can take such devastating news and still maintain your composure. Most men would lose all control. But you appear to treat it all in a matter-of-fact way, as if you've just missed the bus and you're waiting for the next one."

"Do you reckon it might be that most men don't have a wife as tolerant, as steady, and as pretty as you?" I said. "Every time I've been knocked down, you've been there to help me. You never ran. You could have, but you didn't. You've been more than understanding. Besides, I don't know of any wife who would permit her husband to leave a cozy airline position and an air force lieutenant colonel's billet to be an army warrant officer. That reminds me, you know it had always been my intention to return to the Air Force Reserve after my army commitment was over, but I'll have to forget that. I've got to stay with the army and give up my air force commission."

We expected the children to be disappointed by the bad news, but they surprised us. Their response was, "Good, we won't have to move and make new friends again." Mike Jr. was recently graduated from high school and worked at the officers' club, where he had many friends among the young aviators. He didn't want to move either.

The next day the ophthalmologist confirmed that I indeed had glaucoma, and I was put on pilocarpine. Subsequent examinations indicated I responded well to the medication. The therapeutic regimen caused minor, temporary blurring of my vision, but the doctor said there was "no impairment in aviation ability." That opened the door for Dutch Ebaugh and Don Bissell to get me back on flight status.

Meanwhile, my separation orders were still in effect and had to be revoked. When my glaucoma was confirmed, I signed documents stating that due to my medical condition I elected to remain on active duty, but DA wasn't yet aware of the action. I was in Dutch's office when he called Warrant Officer Branch: "This is Colonel Ebaugh at Hunter. I want CWO Novosel's separation orders revoked immediately. There's a change in plans and he'll be remaining on active duty. As you know, he declined the promotion to CW3 because he was leaving the service. But because he has elected to remain on duty, I want his promotion reinstated and his date of rank and all pay and allowances to be effective on the original date. I expect all documentation to that effect transmitted to CW3 Novosel without delay."

If Dutch tried to make me feel better because of my recent medical problem, he succeeded. For me it was a positive declaration of confidence in my ability and my contribution to the mission of the organization. The support I received from my friends, associates, and superiors was more than I expected. Incidentally, DA and Warrant Officer Branch did as Colonel Ebaugh directed.

Meanwhile, Bissell and his Medical Service Corps friends greased the skids for my waiver. The flight surgeon's declarations attesting to my fitness for flight duty were appended to the request for waiver, which had numerous positive endorsements from the chain of command. The final approval required the signature of Brig. Gen. Frank Meszar, the commanding general of Hunter Army Aviation School. He signed the waiver without question and I was back in the saddle again. This army was all right.

I saw Bissell often but was still surprised when I got a call from him one day telling me he was going back to Vietnam. He'd expected it. I recalled we had talked about it before I had my eye problem. "When do you think the army will be sending our aviators back for their third tours?" I asked facetiously.

"That's not as far-fetched as you think," he said. "This war could go on forever. But that's not why I called. Arleigh Price wrote to tell me he's commanding the 45th Medical Evacuation Company at Long Binh. He said he wants me to command the 82d Medical Detachment at Soc Trang."

"So why are you calling to tell me all the latest about the army's assignment policies?" I asked.

"Look, Mike, I don't have a departure date yet, but I'm sure I'll be leaving just after the first of the year. You and I returned home about the same time, so I figure you'll be alerted for your return to Vietnam also."

"I'll cross that bridge when I come to it," I said. "Besides, I've got glaucoma. The army doesn't need a half-blind aviator over there."

"Cut out the bullshit, Mike. The people at DA don't delve into details unless it suits their interests. You'll get a call from your branch shortly. I'll bet on it."

Don didn't tell me anything I didn't know. A number of our instructor pilots had already departed for second tours after being back in the States for a couple of years. A few received orders after less time than that.

"Mike, I'd like you to join me in the 82d when you return to Vietnam. I need an aviator with your experience to ride herd on all the new warrants we'll be getting—and the young commissioned guys as well. They'll listen to you when you tell them to do something. I know how you operated with those jokers in the 283d."

I thanked Don for his call and invitation to join him. He was a tireless worker, an officer who always got things done, although he could display a fractious temperament. When things or individuals displeased him, he threw tact out the window. He'd say just what he thought and didn't mince words. But I liked Don and was willing to work with him. A tour of duty with him wouldn't be dull. I told him I'd let him know when I got my orders and that it would be a real pleasure to join him in the 82d.

That evening I told Ethel about Bissell's call. I was surprised that she already knew he'd been alerted to return to Nam. One thing about being stationed on a small post such as Hunter—nothing is new or secret for long. She asked if I'd get orders soon, and I reminded her I'd been back two years.

Chastain and I had returned at the same time, and it wouldn't have surprised me if we both got orders. Ethel said that she and Sandy, Mike's wife, discussed moving when Mike and I went overseas; the wives would have to leave Hunter. They decided when the time came they would go to Green Cove Springs, Florida, where government housing was available for families of servicemen ordered to

Vietnam. The housing wasn't luxurious, but it was adequate and roomy. Most importantly, it was not far from Jacksonville Naval Air Station, with its commissary, exchange, and hospital facilities.

We knew what was in our future: another trip to Vietnam for me and a year of separation from the family. The only thing we didn't know was when. I was surprised how Ethel took it all in stride even though she had most of the responsibility on her shoulders. Mike Jr. was still around to drive her and the family for shopping and occasional outings. The problem was that he was eligible for the draft. He knew my views regarding service to the country and planned to enlist. It was only a matter of time before both of us would be leaving, and it was not certain who would go first. Still, Ethel and the children would not be alone. There would be other wives whose husbands were at war living close by. They knew how to rely on one another and handle their problems with grace and self-reliance, in a manner hard to explain to people who didn't know military wives.

I asked Ethel if she remembered what I'd said to her when I returned from Vietnam almost two years earlier. She said she did but wouldn't hold me to my promise. "I know you meant every word when you said you were home to stay and wouldn't leave again. I know you had every intention of returning to the airline, and I know how much it hurt you to learn you had that horrible eye disease. I felt the hurt myself. I'm so sorry for you. I'm so sorry for all that happened to you. You're too good a person to deserve that. When you have to go, don't worry about us. We'll get along."

It was early December 1968 and I hadn't yet heard from Warrant Officer Branch. It seemed as if Mike Chastain and I were the only Vietnam veterans at Hunter who had not been alerted. About the middle of December, I got a call asking if I was interested in a fixed-wing assignment when I returned for another combat tour. I told the caller that I had not received orders for another tour. The joker at the other end of the line said, "What do you think's the purpose of this call? You'll be getting orders soon. We're trying to give our aviators returning to Vietnam the opportunity to select, where possible, the types of assignments they might prefer. Your records indicate considerable experience in heavy, long-range aircraft, and we're offering you a nice, clean, safe assignment. I'm calling about a billet flying the P-2V. The missions are flown at relatively high altitude, all in South Vietnam, and average about ten hours. It's a good assignment and should be right up your alley."

I told the caller I appreciated his concern for my safety and well-being but was not interested. I'd heard about the P-2V missions. They were safer than crossing the street in most American cities but boring as hell. Each mission was the same: taking off, climbing to altitude, flying an orbit for about ten hours, and landing. I also told the caller that if I had to return to Vietnam, it might as well be in my old specialty as a dustoff pilot. If I had to bore holes in the P-2V for a year in Vietnam, I'd turn in my wings. The caller said I was nuts but if I wanted another dustoff tour, it was mine.

The deal was done. I didn't have my orders but would in a few days. That afternoon I told Ethel about the call but didn't mention the P-2V offer. I merely said I'd been alerted and my orders for another trip to Vietnam would be coming shortly.

"From all indications you're not going to contest the assignment because of your glaucoma," she stated.

"I just don't feel right about doing that, not after so many of my friends were involved getting me back on flight status. The army allowed me to continue in my profession. Any other service would have grounded me forever. I don't know what others would do, but I feel obligated to take the assignment."

"I should have known better than to ask," Ethel replied. "You have a rare sense of duty and honor that would be strange to most people. They wouldn't do it your way. I hope you understand that. You've served your country in three wars."

That was as close as Ethel got to suggesting I not go back to Vietnam. She believed I had the option of contesting the assignment because of my waiver for glaucoma. I had to take eyedrops every six hours, and meeting the need for constant medication might not be possible in combat.

"What you say is no doubt true, Ethel, but I wouldn't be honest if I said I couldn't perform my flying duties in Vietnam. After all, I fly every day at Hunter. True, I need medication four times a day, but I'll be around medical people. Getting my drugs shouldn't be a problem."

We didn't talk about it anymore, because the greater problem was another long year of separation. I don't know how she handled everything with so much grace. I never saw her lose her temper or break down in frustration. She was an extraordinary woman, the bravest I've known.

Two days later, Sandy told Ethel that Mike had also been alerted for his second tour in Nam. The plan was for the two women to leave at about the same time to set up housekeeping in Green Cove Springs.

Chastain and I finally got orders detailing our assignments. As predicted, we'd report for duty overseas within a day of each other. We moved our families to Green Cove Springs and took up residence a few doors apart. I had about two weeks at home before leaving for Vietnam. By then, Mike Jr. had enlisted in the army, so Ethel would have to depend on Sandy and the other wives for transportation.

Mike, who was at Fort Polk, indicated in his letters that he'd applied for flight training. That gave Ethel another worry. She knew that flight training could be dangerous, and her fears centered on her firstborn. It was a strange development. I knew she'd also be concerned about me in combat, but because I had survived a year of that kind of flying before, she fully expected me to do it again.

I made the necessary arrangements for my return to Vietnam, including the usual first-class passage to San Francisco. My outlook and habits had not changed.

13 Vietnam: The Second Time Around

Travis Air Force Base hadn't changed one bit. The "blue suiters" were at their stations working with flight schedules and manifests. The passengers, mostly army, milled about the terminal waiting to board their flights. It wasn't long and we were soon airborne.

We were taking the southern route, and our first stop was Honolulu. We disembarked while the plane was refueled but were restricted to a cordoned-off area. I recalled that Bob French and I had loaded up on rum miniatures the last time we'd been here; the drinks eased the burden and monotony of the flight.

As I was reminiscing, an elderly couple strolled by. The gentleman asked why so many men in uniform were about. I told him we were going to Vietnam and would be on our way as soon as the airplane was refueled. He said that he and his wife had been on vacation in the islands and were waiting for their flight to the mainland.

A brilliant idea flashed through my mind, and I asked the man if he knew where the liquor store was. He said he did, so I asked if he'd mind purchasing four miniatures of rum for me. I gave him a twenty-dollar bill and hoped the flight wouldn't be called before he came back. As luck would have it, he returned with a paper bag just as the announcement to board the plane came over the public address system. He said my change was in the bag. I thanked the man, shook his hand vigorously, thanked him again, and departed for the airliner.

I took my seat and was pleasantly surprised when I checked to see what brand of rum the gentleman had purchased. There were six—not four—miniatures, and my twenty-dollar bill. I didn't even know my benefactor's name, but his kindness was one of the bright spots of my return trip to Vietnam.

It was mid-March when we arrived at Tan Son Nhut, and the heat and humidity were the same as during my first time in country. The place teemed with individuals in uniforms—American and Vietnamese. There was the usual complement of military police and the ubiquitous White Mice (local police in their all-white outfits).

It was late morning when I got to the replacement depot, where I could call Lt. Col. Arlie Price. He was to pick me up and expedite my assignment to the 82d Medical Detachment. I went to the depot office to use the phone but was told by the officer in charge, a second lieutenant, that "transient personnel" were not permitted to use the office phone.

"But I only want to call the 45th Medical Company. It's a mere couple of hundred yards from here. I won't take long."

This officer was in charge. "No transient personnel are permitted to use the phone. There can be no exceptions."

Arguing with second lieutenants was (and is) a waste of time. The rank gives them their first experience with authority, and they are apt to display it to the utmost. I told him what he could do with his phone and went to the depot gate, which faced the road that went past the 45th Medical Company. I watched the traffic pass by, and eventually a cracker box (army ambulance) came into view. I flagged it down.

"Do you know the location of the 45th Medical Company?" I asked the driver.

"Yes, sir."

"I want you to deliver a message to Colonel Price, the company commander." I wrote a short note that read, "Arlie, HELP. I'm being held a prisoner of war at the replacement depot. Come save me. Mike Novosel."

I gave the note to the driver and told him to go straight to the 45th and deliver the message to Colonel Price. "This is very important. You sure you know where to go?"

"Yes, sir. I'll see that the colonel gets the message."

I wasn't sure how long it would be before Arlie could help or if the ambulance driver could deliver the note. I was feeling the effects of jet lag, so I returned to the replacement depot to rest. I dozed off for what seemed barely a minute when I was awakened by someone repeatedly kicking my cot.

"What's the idea of being in bed at this hour? We have work to do. Get up." It was Arlie Price.

"Arlie, you old son of a gun. Do you usually give incoming dustoff pilots such prompt service, or are you guys so desperate for good help that you'll do anything to get your quota?"

"Cut out the bullshit, Mike. Get your ass out of bed. Gather your gear and let's get out of this flea trap. Don's already called wanting to know if your flight arrived. He'll be sending a bird for you the first thing tomorrow morning. In the meantime you can rest in my trailer."

With that, Arlie and I loaded my two bags in his jeep and headed for the 45th. We didn't even bother to tell the officer in charge, the second lieutenant guarding the phone, that I was leaving. It would not surprise me if he's still looking for a CWO army aviator who went AWOL from his replacement depot.

When we arrived at the 45th Company, I saw that the place had been completely transformed. Two years earlier it was a muddy mess still under construction. Arlie even had an air-conditioned trailer for his domicile; the officers and enlisted men occupied less opulent, but quite adequate, quarters.

Arlie made me feel right at home. He directed me to a bedroom and put a bottle of Chivas Regal at my disposal. I thanked him for his generosity and for springing me from the replacement depot. I had to catch up on some much needed rest and get back to normal. "Arlie, I know my way around the place. You don't have to worry about me. Thanks a million for all your help."

I awoke at seven o'clock the next morning and headed for the 45th operations building, where I was told that the chopper that would take me to the 82d Medical Detachment was on its way from Binh Thuy. Don Bissell was not wasting any time getting me located down in the delta. While the chopper was refueling, I returned to Arlie's trailer, got my gear, and thanked him for his help and hospitality. He said he was within a month of completing his tour and would be returning stateside shortly. He added that he'd see me again when he visited the 82d before leaving for home. "Give Don my regards when you see him," he added.

"Roger," I replied, then left for the waiting chopper. Our destination was the navy base at Binh Thuy. We flew over terrain I vaguely remembered from my last tour.

Bissell was on the flight line waiting for me, and as soon as the chopper was parked in its revetment he had one of the men take my gear and deliver it to my quarters. I noticed that Don's room was next to mine. I told him that Arlie had a whole trailer all to himself at Long Binh and asked why he had only one room. He said the navy had allotted only twelve rooms to the officers of the 82d and he couldn't take another without leaving someone homeless or causing two pilots to double up. He was not prepared to do either. Don said he was working with Captain Beckwith, the navy commander of the Fleet Air Support Unit (FASU), to get more quarters, but space was at a premium. Anyhow, he was satisfied with the navy's support.

"The galley in the officers' mess is still serving breakfast," Don said. "Let's go have some, unless you've already eaten."

"No, no. Let's go, I'm starved."

The FASU officers' mess was a wonder to behold. Philippine mess stewards in fresh white jackets attended huge, round tables covered with immaculate white tablecloths. My army eyes had a hard time comprehending the scene.

A steward poured a cup of coffee for me and asked if I would like breakfast. I said I'd appreciate a couple of well-scrambled eggs and dry toast. I was in a state of disbelief when he added, "Would you care for bacon, ham, or sausage with that?"

Half jokingly I said, "I'll have one of each."

When my order arrived, the plate contained a strip of bacon, a piece of ham, and a sausage patty neatly arranged around the eggs. "Do these people know there's a war going on?" I asked Don.

"Wait till you see the shower and latrine facilities. They use potable water."

After our sumptuous breakfast, Don and I went to his quarters and had a serious discussion about the work ahead of us and the 82d Medical Detachment. Don surprised me when he said he was not pleased with the way the outfit was operating. Having just arrived, I hadn't seen the detachment or its people in action. In the past, the 82d had a reputation for being one of the best dustoff units in Vietnam. Don said the aircraft commanders lacked discipline, and he didn't appreciate their cavalier attitude toward their responsibilities. He thought the reason might be the recent transfer of the 82d to its new location. Many of the aviators were not happy about leaving Soc Trang, their original base, and were highly critical of the small size of their quarters at Binh Thuy.

The 82d Medical Detachment had been based at Soc Trang since 1964, and there had been ample opportunity to develop quarters and furnishings considerably better than average for a combat outfit. I could see why the people in the detachment might not view the move favorably, but they should have been more understanding. The relocation placed the 82d at a more centralized base and facilitated the evacuation of wounded from all parts of the delta. Yet the hardline objectors' mulishness prevailed.

Don said the change in location was just one of the factors that generated the attitude problem. Another was his arrival as the new commander. He replaced a popular detachment CO whose method of operation was different and who allowed the aircraft commanders greater autonomy in the unit's operation. As an example, the aircraft commanders organized a committee to decide who among the unit's pilots would be appointed aircraft commanders. Don also told me he heard rumors that one of the pilots who landed at Soc Trang during an evacuation mission had gone to the officers' club for a beer. I interjected, "Don, I can't believe that any dustoff pilot could be guilty of such an outrageous act. You'd be better off to forget that."

"Well, Mike, you can see we have problems. We have to get this outfit running right, and I'm going to need your help. You know that the 82d always dispatched two aircraft on each night mission. Well, I've changed that. All missions, night or day, are treated alike—one chopper only. There was considerable displeasure concerning that decision, but I had to make the change. We need the choppers for more productive work. Besides, in all the years we've flown night missions, we haven't suffered a loss that a second aircraft might have prevented. When we lost an entire crew during a recent night mission, the other aircraft commander couldn't give us any information about it. He didn't even know that the other aircraft had gone down."

"I'm sure you did the right thing," I said. "I never believed that the 82d accomplished much by dispatching two ships on each night mission. The other dustoff units didn't operate that way. There may have been a rationale for such operations years ago, when the military presence in the delta was widely scattered. But the situation is dramatically different today. What else is on your mind?"

"Mike, the 82d doesn't have a training officer. The ACs [aircraft commanders] act as instructor pilots when the mood strikes them. Some of them are only six months out of flight school and still don't know how to fly on instruments. We've got to take back control of this detachment. Tomorrow I'm going to appoint you and me ACs. The 'committee' is a thing of the past—it's gone. I'm also appointing you the 82d training officer. You'll be responsible for all unit training. As the commanding officer, I'll make all new appointments of aircraft commanders after consulting with you."

"I've got to tell you that for a while you're not going to be the most popular officer in the outfit, Don, and I'm certain that the resentment of some of the ACs will be directed at me as well. The old clique will look upon us as a cabal that's out to destroy their creation, which they figured was a good thing. You've been here long enough to know that something is amiss and correction is needed. You can count on me to help set this detachment on the proper course. You know my attitude toward a unit's mission. I can't stand to see an outfit operate in a half-assed manner. I'm sure everything will turn out all right, and it shouldn't take long."

Don smiled. "Why do you think I asked you to join me down here in the delta? I knew how screwed up this outfit was before I got here. Arlie Price kept me posted on the situation while we were still at Hunter. You're right, we'll make the 82d an organization that will be second to none."

The next day Bissell acted just as he said he would. He published orders appointing the two of us aircraft commanders. We were given our call signs: He was Dustoff 86 and I became Dustoff 88. For a few days there was great weeping and wailing among the aircraft commanders. Some came to me and asked what was going on. I said that the commanding officer was asserting his authority and running the detachment his way, that commanders operated with different styles, and Bissell thought that some changes were needed. I also stated that the commander wanted to streamline the operation of the unit and make it more efficient and productive. I didn't expect other operational changes and emphasized that they should give him their unqualified support.

The 82d continued its mission without adverse manifestations as a result of the changes. In due time Bissell's coup had its desired effect. He was in charge of a military organization completely dedicated to its mission. Major Bissell was satisfied.

The command problems that Bissell had encountered were unique to the detachment. But the war had produced other changes since my first tour, and most didn't enhance the efficiency of the combat units. For example, getting command time had become part of the ticket-punching ritual in the officer corps. A command assignment became a career-sustaining part of an officer's dossier. It was considered so important that it drove the assignment policy of the army. It resulted in officers being given command of combat units for six months, then being replaced by others for a like period. It had a deleterious effect on the efficiency of combat outfits and their conduct of operations against the Viet Cong. It was no way to fight a war.

Another deterrent to combat effectiveness was the unbridled growth of the administrative apparatus. In my early exposure to officer education, administration was listed as one of the Principles of War. During the Vietnam War, too many high-ranking officers made administration *the* principle of war. In 1966 monthly recurring reports were a mere handful, but what I saw in the commander's office was a list of reports that had more than quadrupled in the ensuing years.

The combat units had become the unwitting tools of the empire builders at Long Binh and Military Assistance Command Vietnam (MACV). There were too many field-grade officers who attempted to justify their existence by developing new reports or expanding existing ones. Another advantage of being empire builders was that their positions kept them out of harm's way.

One example of their inane efforts was called the hit report. Every time one of our helicopters was shot up, a special report was forwarded to higher headquarters. The report required a form designed specifically for that purpose. It displayed the outline of a helicopter centered in a circle, where the hits were marked on the aircraft representation. Several questions were included in the report, such as "From which direction was the fire received?" and "Was it enemy or friendly fire?" It was difficult for a combatant to see how such data was going to advance our cause. To my knowledge, we never received feedback as a result of the information submitted. More than one combatant observed that our real enemy was Long Binh and MACV, not the Viet Cong.

Our outfit was saddled with so many meetings and orientation sessions that just preparing the reports on them became a major production requiring hours of effort. If every orientation requirement had been honestly and legitimately met, our outfit couldn't have performed half of its missions. So we winged it with the old soft-shoe routine. We invented replies to their stupid reports and kept the paper pushers off our backs. If the Viet Cong brass had engaged in such wasteful endeavors, they'd have been eliminated.

One of the most cockeyed acts occurred when six officers and a senior noncommissioned officer suddenly appeared in our detachment area. Fortunately for all, Don Bissell was not around: He had gone into Can Tho to attend a social function with local Vietnamese political and military leaders. The visitors were directed to my office. They informed me they were to inspect the detachment. In plain military jargon, it was a visit from the inspector general (IG).

In all my wartime experience, I had never been confronted by inquisitors whose sole purpose was to evaluate a combat unit's administrative procedures. The members of the team didn't appear to know or care that our business was saving lives. They thought our mission centered on the reports that their superiors conjured up. They spent the afternoon checking our files and records and never ventured to the flight line, where they might have seen the battle damage our helicopters had sustained. In the previous day's action, five of our six helicopters had been so badly damaged that they were not flyable. Our people had worked all night and, with assistance from the navy, managed to get one flyable. Another chopper was borrowed from a unit at Soc Trang, and that gave us three flyable aircraft.

The inspectors recorded several "gigs," deficiencies that required written confirmation of corrective action taken. One was the lack of documentation of our soldiers firing for record. I pointed out that five of our aircraft were not flyable due to battle damage, that the crew members fired their weapons in defense of their mission the previous day. The IG's reply was, "There are no paper targets on file to document the scores or the fact that your people fired for record as required by regulations."

It was indeed fortunate that Don Bissell was away. He would not have been pleased. If he had seen the gig about firing for record, he would have exploded. And I'd bet dollars to doughnuts that the IG team would have been hustled out of there. It was impossible to talk sense to these people; their mission was to fight the war in an administratively correct manner. "I hope your filet mignons are prepared exactly to your specifications tonight in Saigon," I said as they left.

"You warrants all think the army has to bend its regulations to suit your fancy," one of the officers replied testily.

I could have mentioned that I was flying B-29s in combat while he was still messing his diapers but thought better of it. We were at least rid of the clowns and their circus.

I was (and am) critical of the brass at Long Binh and MACV because, from a soldier's point of view, they were impediments, not contributors, to the war effort. I'm especially critical of Long Binh, which had grown to the size of a city in the States. Thousands of people were stationed at the enormous complex, and there was seldom an individual there who fired a shot in anger. They continued to send message after message to units in the field outlining new reports, programs, and training requirements that had nothing to do with winning a war.

The Long Binh bureaucracy couldn't be satisfied with the usual officers' and noncommissioned officers' clubs. They demanded more pizzazz for their entertainment and ample leisure time. They had restaurants built that pandered to the varied palates of the "warriors." As a change of pace from the GI mess halls, the gourmands could sample foreign cuisine in newly constructed establishments. They cited their presence in a "combat theater" and their austere existence as justification for the "minor luxuries." But some still demanded more diverse facilities after a grueling day "facing the enemy" and capped their efforts by bringing in massage parlors for exotic relaxation and relief.

From my perspective, the war degenerated into an exercise that bordered on corruption. It was not corruption associated with illegal acquisition of wealth. It was corruption of the spirit. Too many officers went to Vietnam merely to have their records embellished. They weren't there out of a sense of duty or service to the country. They knew that time spent in a combat theater enhanced any dossier placed before a promotion board. Once in Vietnam, these officers looked for plush assignments that put distance or barriers between them and the line of fire. There were plenty of administrative nooks where they hid and survived—and a year later returned home as "heroes." Of the more than half million men that the United States had in Vietnam at the peak of its involvement, 90 percent were in support roles.

Our politicians and their policies were criticized for their conduct of the war, but they shouldn't have caught all the heat. Many—too many—of our military, officers and enlisted, also deserve a share of the criticism.

The 82d Med's mission didn't get easier in 1969. Instead, that was by far its most active and intense period. Casualties peaked as the enemy stepped up operations, especially in the delta. The Tet Offensive of 1968 may have been a disaster for the Viet Cong, but any evidence of that was gone a year later. It was rare when an aircraft of the 82d Med was not airborne. From March 1969 to March 1970, every pilot of the 82d logged well over a thousand hours of combat time. I knew that the flight schedule was murderous, because I prepared the duty roster and trained the pilots. I made certain that my schedule was at least as heavy as any aviator's. My leadership style was based on the premise that I wouldn't have any of my charges do anything I wasn't prepared to do.

It was also a rare day when the 82d had an aircraft that escaped battle damage. During my year with the unit, five of our helicopters were lost in battle. Considering that we had only six choppers, that was a high percentage. But on the plus side, we didn't have any crewmen killed in action during my tour. True, most of our crew members were wounded, but only one was so severely injured that he had to be evacuated to the States. I attribute the 82d's outstanding record to Don Bissell's leadership and policies. He made it into a crackerjack outfit. The troops in the delta knew that if they had wounded to be evacuated, they could count on the dustoff crews of the 82d Medical Detachment. I was proud of my part in the development of that reputation.

A big factor in our success was the close relationship with the folks of the Fleet Air Support Unit, Binh Thuy, commanded by Captain Beckwith. He and his men saw to it that all formal agreements of support were met. They often went beyond the letter of the contract to keep our birds in the air.

The gunship squadron that supported the navy interdiction and patrol effort throughout the delta, HAL-3, was also based at Binh Thuy. The pilots flew old B-model Hueys obtained from the army's surplus stores. They were not the best aircraft for the mission, but they were adequate. The Seawolves of HAL-3 and the dustoff pilots of the 82d developed a special rapport. The navy's aviator-to-aircraft ratio was personnel heavy, so monthly flying hours didn't present crew rest problems. On the other hand, the 82d was adversely affected by its aviator-to-aircraft ratio. There wasn't a thirty-day period when the detachment pilots could comply with the army's crew rest guidelines. The 82d had six helicopters and twelve pilots, including the unit commander, to cover more than thirteen thousand square miles of the delta twenty-four hours a day.

The Seawolves were aware of our manning problems, and many volunteered to fly with us. They were a great help to the dustoff mission. Army and navy aviators in our section of Vietnam developed a camaraderie that put to shame the antics of their respective leaders sitting in plush offices in the Pentagon.

After completing his tour, Captain Beckwith was replaced by Comdr. Conrad Jaburg, who continued the level of support and then some.

Beckwith and Jaburg had totally different personalities. The former was quiet and reserved, even reticent. Con Jaburg was the opposite, almost another Don Bissell. I liked him the first time I met him, and we became great friends. He took the 82d under his wing as if it belonged to the navy. When he learned about our crew rest problem and how it affected our operation, he set a personal example and volunteered to fly with the 82d. He was my copilot on his first mission and volunteered many more hours of combat flying with the detachment.

Another of Jaburg's naval aviators who flew with us regularly was Lt. Buddy Barnes. He logged a minimum of 250 hours of combat with our dustoff pilots. Buddy did most of his flying with the 82d at night when he was off from his regular navy duties. It was gratifying to see officers of another service pitch in to help their army counterparts. They were nearly indispensable.

Whenever Con Jaburg could break away from his duties, he'd let me know he was available to fly. But this man was a magnet ass. I can't recall any mission when we flew together that we didn't take fire. On one of his first flights with me, we had come into the pickup site and were sitting on the ground waiting for the wounded to be placed on board when the Viet Cong opened up on us. Con was doing the flying on this lift, and I felt his pull on the collective. I resisted his control movement. "Not yet," I said. "We have to wait till all the wounded are on board."

"But they're shooting at us. Can't you hear those automatic weapons?"

I saw small geysers erupting where enemy rounds were impacting the rice paddy water around us. I knew that our medic and crew chief were still out of the ship and taking fire while they hurried to load the wounded. It was difficult for a pilot to turn around to see what was going on behind him. He was constrained by the seat and shoulder harness and weighted down by the chest protector, and often his view was obstructed by the aircraft armor, the walking wounded, or equipment. He had to rely on the medic or crew chief to give the order to leave. It was a necessary arrangement. He didn't dare think of lifting off until the call came from the rear that everyone was aboard.

Before I had time to answer Con, one of the crewmen yelled, "They're all on board. Let's get the hell out of here."

On that mission Con learned the importance of a certain posterior muscle that was often exercised in the dustoff trade. Con also learned what being a dustoff pilot was all about. There had been an incident when a dustoff pilot took off after heavy fire raked his pickup site. Unfortunately the medic was left behind and killed in the ensuing action. As a result of that action, dustoff aircraft commanders declared themselves honor bound never to take off until they knew that all crewmen were on the helicopter.

In all fairness to Con, pilots are used to having their machines moving, especially when under fire. Waiting on the ground while the wounded are loaded and the enemy has you in his sights requires a lot of willpower.

Dustoff pilots wouldn't have been surprised if our navy counterparts found things to do besides flying with us. But that was not the case; they were undeterred and stuck with us. Con Jaburg, however, never lost his status as the world's greatest magnet ass. He and I continued to draw fire every time we flew together.

Even with the navy's welcome help, we couldn't keep our flying time within the limits of dustoff standard operating procedures (SOPs) and the army's crew rest guidelines. The 82d set a limit of 140 hours during any thirty-day period even though the army recommended 90 hours. Every month, I was on the phone to the 45th Company advising that I was prepared to fly each dustoff pilot 160 hours if we didn't get more aviators to help us. The answer never changed: "You know you can't fly your people more than a hundred forty hours in a thirty-day period. And we can't spare any pilots."

My reply was always unequivocal: "You know we can't shut down operations, but that's the only way our pilots won't exceed the max of a hundred forty hours."

After the exchanges, I'd receive the suggestion that we could be more efficient by delaying the evacuation of routine patients until they could be sandwiched in with an urgent pickup in the same general area. The suggestion was inane. We operated within the guidelines of patient priorities, and the person giving us suggestions knew it.

When there was no further reason to continue the discussion with the 45th, I'd finish with the reminder: "We'll just do the best we can.

We might have to disregard some flying time or forget to log it. But all requests for evacuations will be covered." I don't know why we went through that drill every month. Within a week or so we'd receive the assistance requested. Usually the 45th Company would send about four aviators to help us. When we asked the aviators if they had been busy, we were not surprised to learn they hadn't flown for three or four days. They would remain with us for a week or two, during which time they'd log as many flight hours as they did in a month at Long Binh. They certainly experienced more combat.

Our missions produced new experiences and new challenges. The vastness of the delta contained more than subtle differences in geography and terrain. Most of the area was monotonously level and crisscrossed by numerous canals. It was one huge rice paddy interrupted by thin wood lines and minor streams and waterways feeding into the canal system. Most of the inhabited areas hugged the shores of the canals, which connected the few villages and minor cities. The few roads were nothing more than lanes of packed-down dirt. Paved roads were rare, although some in the cities were blacktopped.

As flat as the delta was, there were two isolated mountainous complexes that broke the monotony of the miles of paddies. One known as the Three Sisters consisted of three abrupt, craggy granite hills just north of the small port of Rach Gia. The port was situated on the Gulf of Thailand in the extreme western part of the delta. The Viet Cong used the Three Sisters as a base for operations. Our forces occupied the tops of the hills to interdict the forays of the VC, who had burrowed into the hillsides and were impossible to dislodge. They moved from one burrowed bunker complex to another when assaulted and occasionally launched small raids and counterattacks.

During my year in the delta, we were unable to eliminate the Viet Cong on the Three Sisters. Daily incursions by both sides produced a steady stream of casualties that required evacuations. Landing zones on the mountains were exceptionally restricted—so small, so sloping, and so full of huge boulders that our choppers couldn't make normal landings. We had to execute a sort of semihover, nudging the front of our skids onto the sloping terrain while holding sufficient power to keep the skids level.

The Viet Cong never failed to harass us during our approaches to the landing sites and continued to fire on us while we made the pickups. Threat of fire from the VC positions necessitated the use of gunship escorts. This usually resulted in delays. Once I waited for the guns for such a long time that I had to refuel at the Rach Gia airstrip. When I returned for the pickup, the guns still had not arrived. Because one of the wounded soldiers was in critical condition, I went in to get him without the guns and made the extraction. After that success, I left it up to each aircraft commander to decide whether or not to wait for gunship support. This change in procedure resulted in more timely evacuations and didn't produce additional casualties among the dustoff crews.

The other mountainous area, known as the Seven Mountains, was situated along the Cambodian border in the northwestern sector of the delta. It was some of the more forbidding territory in the delta and one of its most dangerous. Like the Three Sisters, it was never completely cleared of the Viet Cong. The Seven Mountains covered a considerable part of the border, but unlike the Three Sisters it didn't jut out of the ground. These hills were covered with trees and thick brush and presented maneuvering problems for the troops. Our soldiers made forays into the area to clear out the VC but got their noses bloodied every time. It was the rule that evacuation missions in the Seven Mountains would be tough. Heavy enemy fire was always expected.

Once while operating in the Seven Mountains area, I was asked to drop off some ammunition during the pickup. This was an improper request of a crew flying the red cross. As a dustoff pilot I was not to resupply forces engaged with the enemy even if they were hard pressed and low on ammunition. But because the Viet Cong were firing at me during my evacuations, I ignored the SOP and delivered the ammunition. I don't know if two wrongs made a right, but I told the embattled unit commander that I was dropping off some preventive medicine.

Another bad area was the U Minh forest, which was situated south of Rach Gia and stretched along the Gulf of Thailand to the Ca Mau peninsula. Dominated by the Viet Cong, it was lightly populated and in most places highly inaccessible triple-canopy jungle. There weren't any roads, towns, or cities, and its strategic possibilities were limited. The Viet Cong didn't have a great prize with the U Minh; in a way, they were prisoners of their own success there. They were kept under constraint in their enclave by control of its perimeter.

In an attempt to eliminate the jungle cover, air force C-123 Ranch Hands flew frequent missions spraying Agent Orange. They were always accompanied by a dustoff helicopter. Nobody warned the crews of the danger of contamination by the toxic chemicals, so it was not uncommon for our aircraft to occasionally fly into the spray while staying close to the C-123s. I don't know of any dustoff crews contracting health problems, but they were definitely placed in danger by the unknown threat to their safety.

In the limited forays into the U Minh, our forces suffered unrealistic casualties, so evacuation missions into the area were never greeted with enthusiasm. We had one mission into the area to evacuate four soldiers wounded by VC land mines. The friendly force had hacked out a clearing in the dense jungle and set up a base camp. The clearing was the only nonwooded spot within hundreds of meters. Such a huge open space in the midst of miles of solid jungle was a clarion call to VC gunners and mortar specialists to zero in on with their weapons. Under the circumstances, my only entry into the pickup site required a diving approach. The wounded were loaded, and I left as fast as my machine would go. I pulled up on the collective for maximum power and was climbing as best I could when I saw a line of tracers shoot past the nose of my ship. They seemed so close that they appeared to flash between my legs. I said to myself, *aha, missed me.* Back at base I saw fuel dripping from a bullet hole in the bottom of the chopper. They hadn't missed me after all. In fact, there were six more bullet holes in the bottom of the ship.

A day's flying in the delta presented considerable variety. We flew missions to mountains, rice paddies, woods, canals, streams, rivers, islands in the Gulf of Thailand and the South China Sea, and ships operating in those waters. During an aviator's twelve-hour shift, he could easily cover the entire gamut.

On occasion a pilot would log thirteen to fourteen hours of flight time in a scheduled twelve-hour day. All our aviators experienced days when they'd be airborne soon after reporting for duty and wouldn't shut off their engines all day. The crewmen would use hot refueling (taking on fuel with the engine running) to save time, then proceed on the next mission. If a pilot had a distant medical evacuation near the end of his shift, it could be an extra hour or two before he got back home. Even then it was not unusual to be diverted to another mission while returning to base, further delaying the end of work.

Mission variety and flexibility for dustoff pilots was typified by a mission flown by Chief Warrant Officer Whitehead. He was to locate and pick up two air force pilots who ditched a Bird Dog (Cessna O-1) observation airplane at night in the Gulf of Thailand. The only information Whitehead received was the coordinates of the Mayday reported position of the downed aircraft. But dustoff helicopters weren't equipped with radio navigational equipment compatible with the system installed by the air force. Whitehead plotted the reported coordinates of the downed airplane on his map, drew a reference line to Rach Gia—a place he could identify on the coast— eyeballed the direction, and flew a timed course from there to what he hoped would be the ditching. He began an ever-expanding orbit over the search area. He had one advantage: There was no enemy interference. So he used his search and landing lights to illuminate the water as he and his crewmen looked for the downed airmen. Miraculously, they spotted the two pilots, wearing Mae Wests, clinging to the floating wreckage of the Bird Dog. It was a well-executed mission accomplished in spite of the equipment, certainly not because of it. It should be noted that dustoff aircraft and crewmen were not equipped with flotation gear or Mae Wests. As an indication of how commonplace that mission was, neither Whitehead nor the 82d received any press coverage for their rescue. Saving two pilots from drowning was reward enough for our men.

When dustoff missions involved the navy, a variety of landing platforms were to be expected. Even the smallest river patrol boat (PBR) dedicated to operating with helicopters had platforms to accommodate our Hueys. Some of the boats were so small that the skids of the chopper nearly overlapped the structure. But with care, safe landings were routine.

Medical evacuations required coordinated efforts between dustoff crewmen and the navy people on the PBR. The wounded had to be raised up to the helicopter so the medic and crew chief could lift them aboard. Operations with a PBR proved delicate at times because of the power differential between the boat and the chopper. Because the helicopter had considerably more power, the chopper pilot's cyclic control could overpower any maneuvering by the boat captain. So the chopper pilot had to be watchful of his control movements.

Operations off a landing ship tank (LST) were the easiest. The ship's helicopter landing area accommodated two choppers. The navy crewmen could refuel our aircraft; meanwhile, if there was enough time, good food and drink were available in air-conditioned comfort. If a third helo needed to land, one of the two helos on the ship had to take off and land elsewhere or orbit until the "visitor" landed, accomplished his mission, and departed.

It was my habit when operating with ships of the navy to conform to their traditions. After communication was established and before landing, I used the standard navy procedure: "Request permission to come aboard." I would not land until I received the reply, "Permission granted." My navy friends were much amused by my adherence to their protocol. I also joked with them about not seeing an "ensign" aboard to salute.

We received an interesting mission with a destroyer under way in the South China Sea. The ship was on patrol about ten miles offshore when I was dispatched to evacuate a sailor with a smashed hand. I couldn't contact the ship on the tactical net because I was given the wrong frequency. I didn't see a helicopter landing pad on the destroyer and wondered if I had the right vessel. Fortunately, I was able to contact one of the LSTs that I had worked with earlier in the day. They communicated with the destroyer and relayed the correct frequency to me. I established radio contact with the ship and found it to be the right vessel; my observation of its configuration had been correct. It did not have a landing pad, but the injured sailor was standing by for evacuation.

I carefully examined the ship, which continued under way, and determined that there was a portside structure on the forward section where I could maneuver the helo and make the pickup. It appeared to have been a gun mount at one time, probably an antiaircraft position, but now contained no armament. It was encircled by a metal railing about three feet high. The gun mount didn't look strong enough to support a helicopter. I approached it and determined that I would have clearance from the structures and fittings of the ship while hovering alongside. I asked that the injured sailor be brought to the mount and we'd effect the evacuation from there. The sailor seemed in great pain but was ambulatory. His injured hand was wrapped in a huge bundle of bandages, and he was in no shape to help himself get aboard the helicopter. He stood in the center of the gun mount with a sailor on each side to lift him onto the chopper.

I hovered over the outside edge of the gun mount while my medic and crew chief took positions on the skids to lift him aboard. They used hand signals to the sailors to hoist the man onto the skids, then they lifted him into the helo. As soon as I heard, "We have him, move out," I maneuvered the Huey away from the gun mount and the ship. We had little margin for error but pulled it off. If the sea had not been so calm, it probably would have been a different matter. We refueled at Ca Mau and took the sailor to Binh Thuy.

Missions flown in the delta were full of unusual twists and encounters. For example, in the rice paddies just across the Bassac, the river that flowed past our Binh Thuy base, we conducted an evacuation that involved a unit of Vietnamese soldiers and their American adviser. There were two casualties suffering from minor wounds inflicted by a VC mine. Identification was routine, and there were no enemy forces nearby to frustrate the evacuation. As we were about to leave, the American adviser asked if we had any foot powder with us. He said he had a bad case of trench foot (the troops were in water that was knee-deep) and was in dire need of some of the medicated powder that was standard issue for troops with his problem. I told him we didn't have any but would try to bring him some later in the day. I didn't think that in his condition the powder would help. What he really needed was dry ground, but that was not his call.

We didn't have another mission when we got back to the base, so I sent the medic to the 3d Surgical Hospital for foot powder. When he returned with the medication, we still didn't have a mission. We boarded the chopper and flew to the area where we last saw the adviser. I got him on his tactical frequency and learned he was in contact with a VC force of unknown strength but had not taken additional casualties. I rogered his transmission and informed him I had his foot powder and would drop it to him if he'd throw smoke to identify his position. He did, we did, and he got his powder. It was no big deal, but it was of immense significance to an infantryman stuck in the rice paddies.

Night evacuations in the delta offered many challenges. Too often the weather was a greater danger than the enemy. All missions, day or night, were flown without flight plans, and we never received weather or intelligence briefings. Simply put, missions were received, given to aircraft commanders, and left with them and their crews to carry out. In some strange, almost unbelievable fashion, the missions were successful. If an aviation expert had examined our operations and noted our choppers' inadequate instrumentation and lack of operational radio navigation equipment, and if he took into account the low experience level of our aviators and the hazards they faced, he surely would have classified our jobs as missions impossible. Whitehead's night flight into the Gulf of Thailand to find two ditched pilots, with only his compass to guide him, ranks high among our "missions impossible."

Priority number one was always the mission, and so it was during a night evacuation involving a small boat, a Boston Whaler, on a stream. The American adviser directing the evacuation by radio said the area was alive with VC activity. He wanted the pickup to be under blackout conditions until lights were absolutely needed. The outline of the stream was dimly visible due to lights coming from the huts on the shores of the waterway. The adviser was able to direct the dustoff into the area by the sound of the chopper, then fine-tune his directions when he picked up the aircraft's navigational lights. At the last moment he told the pilot to turn on his landing light; miraculously the Boston Whaler was right there in the glare of the light. That was simplicity itself, using the visual and aural senses to bring about a rendezvous.

There had to be a hitch, though, and there was. The dustoff hovered just above the water while the adviser in his Boston Whaler maneuvered toward the chopper. As he neared the helicopter, its downwash was so strong that it kept the boat from getting near enough to transfer the wounded. Radio transmissions from the adviser were almost drowned out by the chopper's noise, and he had difficulty telling the dustoff why he couldn't get closer. The message finally got through to the pilot, who lowered the helicopter until its skids were in the water. This produced less downwash, enabling the boat to reach the chopper and the wounded soldier to be evacuated.

Our missions produced emotional highs and lows in the course of a day's work. There was the busy day involving Specialist Five Ruckhaber, a hulk of a man and a good soldier. He was a hard-driving, hardworking, conscientious medic who possessed a delicate touch that belied his size. He also was a magnet ass. Flying missions with Ruckhaber always produced excitement. The mission on that day was a pickup in a large expanse of rice paddy. There were some wood lines but they were far off, and enemy fire didn't figure to be a problem. We had four wounded Vietnamese soldiers to evacuate, all with gunshot wounds. One soldier was reported to have a bad head wound and was in critical condition. We followed standard procedures, and everything went according to plan as I landed to identified smoke in the rice paddy. Ruck and the crew chief quickly disembarked to load the wounded while I talked to the American adviser on the tactical net. Then Ruckhaber yelled into the intercom that the men handling the litters had all hit the dirt. Automatic weapons opened up on us.

I shouted for him to get the wounded on board ASAP. Ruck said he was disconnecting. He was moving away from the ship beyond the reach of his intercom cord. I could see him and the crew chief going after the litters.

Ruck ran toward the Vietnamese troops, his hands and arms making threatening gestures. I couldn't hear him, but I knew he was cursing. The troops got the message, picked themselves up out of the rice paddy, and brought the litters to the helicopter with Ruckhaber right behind hurrying them along.

I got back on the net and asked the adviser for his position and how the enemy fire was affecting him. "Look to your ten o'clock position about twenty meters, next to the rice paddy dike," he answered. Sure enough, there he was waving to me as he lay in muddy water alongside the dike. He'd been there when I landed, almost invisible. I gathered that he was in that protected position waiting for me to take the wounded off his hands before going after the VC in the distant tree line. As I looked in his direction, I saw a burst of gunfire throw up little geysers of water on the other side of his dike. The VC were excellent gunners and displayed a high degree of accuracy at such extreme range.

Ruck came back on the intercom and said we'd be loaded "in a sec." When he gave me the word, I got out of there. I was disturbed that the adviser hadn't told me he was under fire when I made my approach for the pickup. Then I thought, what the hell, I'm out of there, high and dry. That poor bastard's still hugging that damn rice paddy dike for protection. I hope he and his Vietnamese counterpart can handle that force of VCs.

I called the rear: "How are they, Ruck? How's the one with the head wound?"

"He's doing better. I've changed his dressing. They should all make it, sir." It was a short flight to Can Tho, where we dropped off the wounded for transfer to the hospital.

Later that day we picked up a soldier, supposedly with malaria, near the Seven Mountains. This was one of those "flaky" missions we occasionally received. The soldier may have been ill, or feeling poorly, but he didn't have malaria. He was ambulatory and got on board under his own power. I suspect that his unit was using dustoff to get him on his way for R and R. It wouldn't have been the first time that happened.

I'd been under way for a few minutes and hadn't bothered to get off the tactical net, which suddenly came to life with an excited transmission. "Dustoff 88, are you still on this frequency? Dustoff 88, come in, please."

"This is Dustoff 88. I hear you. I'm still on your push. What can I do for you?"

"Dustoff 88, this is the RTO at Tri Ton. You departed our pad a few minutes ago. We have an emergency here. An officer has been shot in the chest. I think he's dying."

"This is Dustoff 88. I'm turning around right now. I'll be there as fast as this machine will go. In the meantime, do all you can for your wounded man."

The return to Tri Ton was flown with the airspeed needle nudging and occasionally pushing past the redline, which was 120 knots. Under the circumstances, it seemed woefully inadequate. Exceeding the redline meant that I was making between 121 and 125 knots. Big deal. That was the best a Huey could do.

As I approached the strip, I saw a parked helicopter next to some troops gathered around a litter on the ground. They signaled me to land there, so I set down close by. Ruck jumped out and rushed to the litter with the crew chief right behind him. Ruck checked the man, saw his shallow and labored breathing, and motioned the crew chief to grab the other end of the litter. They quickly had the wounded officer on board, and Ruck tapped my helmet and shouted, "Let's go."

I took off, gave Ruck a few minutes to tend to his patient, then asked, "What's the situation? How's he doing?"

"Just a minute, sir. I'll be with you as soon as I can." I let Ruck-haber do his thing. I shouldn't have been so impatient; he knew his business.

I headed the chopper for the 3d Surg and switched to its net to let the medics there know we had a real emergency coming in, a life-or-death situation. Ruck finally got on the intercom and said that things were not good. Our patient's wound was caused by a bullet that had penetrated his upper torso from one side to the other. He was in shock and had probably lost a lot of blood. His blood pressure was low and his pulse was weak and erratic. There wasn't a lot of blood on the man's body or clothing except where the projectile had entered and exited. Ruck thought the bullet had either severed one of his brachial arteries or torn one open.

When we were about ten minutes from the 3d Surg, I asked Ruck for the patient's progress. He said the man was going downhill and didn't know if he'd last until we got to the hospital.

I asked if he had administered epinephrine. Ruck answered that he was delaying that action but would do it in a few minutes.

There wasn't much we could do to help except get the wounded man to the hospital in time. I made up my mind to speed the process as much as possible. I was in contact with the 3d Surg and informed the hospital staff of the nature of the patient's wound and the probability of severe internal bleeding caused by injury to one or both of his brachial arteries. I told them the patient's blood type and that epinephrine had just been administered.

I was familiar with the physical layout of the 3d Surg, and the location of its helicopter pad and entrance to the hospital. The pad was more than a hundred meters from the hospital entrance. If I landed at the pad, the patient would have to be transferred from the chopper to a gurney, then rolled along a narrow concrete path up to a double-door entrance to a hallway going to the emergency room. I decided to eliminate the hundred-meter-plus ordeal. I told the 3d Surg RTO to have the double doors closed until instructed by me to open them. I was going to land beyond the pad nearer the hospital and get as close to the entrance as my main rotor would permit.

I didn't know if saving a few minutes would be critical to the patient's survival, but I was going to do everything possible to expedite his arrival and transfer to the emergency room. As I landed and hovered toward the hospital doors, I noticed commo wires stretched across my path but couldn't gauge their height. They could be a problem. As much as I thought I knew the hospital layout, this was one item I hadn't noticed. I continued moving forward and, without stopping for a measurement, descended to the ground and skidded under the wires right up to the doors. As soon as the chopper stopped, I told the RTO to open the doors. The staff flung them wide open, rushed out with a gurney, and took our patient. It was up to the surgical team to finish the job and save our soldier. We had arrived in time. He was still alive.

That was the day's last mission. I went to the officers' mess for dinner and finished up at the bar. I was all smiles that evening.

Still, something about the mission bothered me. Something was missing. Then I realized that I hadn't actually seen our patient. I had no idea how he looked, how old he was, or who he was.

Before turning in for the night, I went to the operations section and saw Ruckhaber talking to the RTO. I told him how pleased I was with his performance that afternoon and asked if he had any word about our patient. He said he had called the 3d Surg and was told that our man was out of surgery. He was also quick to point out that his original diagnosis of damage to the patient's brachial artery had been correct. Without our prompt response to the distress call from Tri Ton, the man would have bled to death.

I suggested that we go to the hospital and check on our patient's condition. "They'll let us in even if it is a little late. We can say we're there to pick up some supplies, and while we're there we can ask to see our man. They know us. They know we keep irregular hours."

As it turned out, I knew the nurse on duty. She told us that our man was out of danger but had been restless all evening. She was concerned about his weakened condition but admitted us into her ward for a minute to see him.

We didn't say a word to him, but he must have sensed our presence, because he opened his eyes to slightly more than a squint and happened to look in my direction. I gave him a thumbs-up sign and he gave me a slight smile, then closed his eyes again. Before leaving, I looked at his medical chart and got a glimpse of his name. I'm not certain, but it appeared to be Captain Crapeau. That was the last time I saw him. He was evacuated stateside the next morning.

Within the week, Ruck and I flew together again. It was the usual gamut of missions, but one of his patients died while he was working on him. We were on the night shift and I could not see what was going on in the rear, but I recall the labored way Ruck called on the intercom: "Mr. Novosel, I've lost my patient."

Later that night we picked up a pregnant woman who was shot during a night attack on her compound. En route to the hospital Ruck called out excitedly, "She's going into labor. She's having the baby right now."

"You're the medic, Ruck. Take charge of the situation."

About halfway back to the base, Ruck announced that he'd delivered a baby girl.

The Lord does indeed move in mysterious ways.

It would be wrong to leave the impression that our war in Vietnam was all combat. It was not the same as a John Wayne movie in which enemy forces throw everything at you. The war did not go on every hour of the day and every day of the week. The Duke had it all wrong. There was plenty of time for daydreaming, being bored, just plain screwing around, and more often than not being distressingly lonely when visions of home and family blotted out everything else.

There were, however, too many incidents and occasions that made life miserable for us, such as the time Punchy Hoen asked me to go with him to the PX to buy beer. He said it was being sold by the case. Punchy enjoyed his beer but I could either take it or leave it. If we both bought a case, he'd have two. Good idea, good plan.

When we arrived at the PX, there was a long line of soldiers and airmen waiting for their beer. The line moved slowly and we waited for what seemed like hours. We were behind an air force sergeant who finally was next in line to get his beer. Just then the sales clerk announced, "Sorry, no more. The beer's all gone." The sergeant threw his hat on the ground and nearly had a fit. "Goddamnit, I must have been in that line for hours. Now this shit happens. It ain't fair."

Punchy? He just sat down and cried.

I also had an exasperating experience when I'd accumulated more cash than I needed and wanted to send some home. I went to the post office to buy a money order and found a lot of others had the same idea. There was a long line ahead of me. I couldn't do anything but wait my turn. Counting out the cash and getting a money order was apparently a slow process. It seemed I'd never get to the postal clerk's window. At last I was next in line. The man ahead of me counted out his cash and picked up his money order. As I was nestling up to the window, the clerk looked at his watch and said, "That's all for now. I'm closed for lunch."

I'd spent at least an hour in that line for nothing. I couldn't stay and wait for the clerk to return because I had work to do. I returned to the base and relieved the RTO so he could get his lunch. There was no closing the window for us.

My anger over the incident mounted when I learned that the postal detachment received a unit citation for duty above and beyond and all the accompanying verbiage of the presentation. Those bastards didn't do anything more than put in their days from nine to five and the rest of us be damned. The 82d Medical Detachment (Helicopter Ambulance) worked its proverbial ass off and got crap. It was difficult for a combatant to see the merits of an award of any kind for a support unit that didn't do anything more than show up for work.

A case in point. These same jokers delivered my mail. Because of their incompetence, it was not unusual to receive a letter from home in which my wife had written that little John was much better and was up and about. Then I'd receive a letter (stamped days before the last one) telling me that little John had a fever with a temperature of 104 degrees. He'd been on antibiotics and Ethel was up at all hours to take care of him.

Periodic shortages are common in war, but in Vietnam it was difficult to accept, especially with the outrageous size of the support complex. The PX was out of soap, except for Lava, for a month. One or two daily showers were the norm when in base camp. But human skin can take only so much abuse, and it was tested to its limits with those Lava showers. We all were squeaky clean but about as red as boiled lobsters. I placed the blame on the paper pushers and their administrative empires, which were nests of mismanagement. They didn't spend nights in the field, sleep on the ground, or go a day without a shower. They didn't know how a steady diet of C rations left one in a debilitative state of constipation. I suppose that what I resented most about the administrative types was the power and control they exercised over me.

There was one compensating factor for those who spent time in the trenches. Action-filled days, saving lives, flying or fighting until reaching a state of near exhaustion, and cheating the grim reaper made one forget all aggravations.

We didn't have much time off, but when it came we enjoyed it to the hilt. There wasn't a party that the nurses of the 3d Surg planned that didn't include the dustoff pilots. Within the Binh Thuy complex—which included the hospital, the navy, the air force, and dustoff—there was a party at least once a week. The radar operators at Paddy Radar Control always invited the dustoffers to their beer and barbecue outings. The air force radar operators and dustoff developed a strong rapport; our pilots were often the only ones flying around the delta at night. We kept the operators awake and occupied. Tracking us and talking to us all night broke up an otherwise boring time.

The Seawolves at Binh Thuy also never failed to include the dustoff pilots in their parties. They produced the biggest blowouts, which were attended by the 3d Surg nurses, the dustoffers not flying, the Seals and the officers of FASU, the air force, and anyone else who might drop by. There was always plenty to eat and drink. Barbecues usually consisted of hamburgers and hot dogs, often steaks, and always a generous supply of beer, wine, and spirits. I never missed a party except when scheduled to fly. It was my way to let off steam.

Strange as it may seem, official duties occasionally gave me a chance to relax. The administrative apparatus that was my bane demanded my presence at staff meetings at Long Binh. After the meetings, I'd go into Saigon to shop and cap the day with a meal at one of the excellent French restaurants that still flourished in the city. It was a rare break in my routine, but I'll always remember the superb chateaubriand and fine wine.

Our navy friends often engaged in touch football or softball games after work. Pilots and crewmen of the 82d were invited even though our schedule prevented regular participation. One day I was going to my quarters after work while a football game was in progress. I didn't have anything else to do and the game beckoned, so I joined the players. That was a big mistake.

I caught the first pass thrown to me but in doing so injured a finger on my left hand, the one that handled the collective when flying. The finger throbbed with pain, but I thought it was merely jammed and would get better in a day or two. It didn't. The pain became more than I was willing to endure, so I saw Doc Spence, the navy flight surgeon, who said that my finger was broken and had to be immobilized. I reminded him that the hand was needed to control the collective and throttle. He said he'd leave the other fingers free so I could work the controls. He constructed a small splint, which did the job. Doc said I had to wear it for at least six weeks.

Barely a week later I had another rare day when I finished work early. I saw Con Jaburg and Buddy Barnes playing softball. They'd organized a team of navy officers and were playing against a team of enlisted men. Con saw me and yelled for me to join them—they were a man short. I showed him my splinted hand, and he said it didn't matter. He positioned me in right field where I would not get much action, because our opposition had all right-handed batters. He was right. Most of the balls hit to the outfield went to left and center. I had to go after only one ball.

I did okay until it was my turn to bat. Because of my splinted hand, I had to bat right-handed. I held the bat with my right hand and used my left hand, hampered by the splint, to grip the lower end of the bat with only my index finger and thumb. The broken middle finger stuck out at an awkward angle because of the splint. I managed to foul off a couple of pitches when Doc Spence saw me. He was furious. "Who the hell said you could play ball?"

Without batting an eye, I pointed to Con Jaburg. "He did."

Doc was not amused. He hustled me off to his clinic and removed my small splint. He replaced it with one at least twice as large. It immobilized the broken finger as before but continued beyond the hand and almost encased the forearm. I could still use the throttle and collective. Doc Spence smiled at his creation. "Now let's see you play ball."

I did not play again. Doc was one tough character. I flew with that extra-large splint for another month before my broken finger was healed.

Rumors are endemic to a combat environment, and the latest one signaled another reorganization. We figured in time it would pass and nothing would come of it. We were shocked when it did happen: Don Bissell was told he was being transferred to a company in I Corps. Don and I would be split up. Neither of us was pleased; we'd been a good team and worked well together. I was sorry to see him leave.

Don was replaced as commanding officer of the 82d by Maj. Cy Simmons. There was no formal change of command ceremony; we didn't have time for such activities.

The operation of the detachment continued as before. Most importantly, the change of commanders took place without turbulence. Cy Simmons quickly received the support of his officers and men, probably because of his unassuming, quiet relationship with his subordinates.

Cy was an exceptionally capable officer and aviator. He took his turn on the duty roster just as Bissell had. We flew together on a few of his early turns of duty, but after the orientation flights he took his assignments as any other aircraft commander did.

Our continued presence on the field of battle resulted in aircraft being wrecked and many of our people being wounded (although we didn't have anyone killed in action). The choppers took a lot of hits, evidenced by patches of sheet metal and fresh paint to cover the damage. If the hits were in a noncritical area and the sheet-metal people were busy, the damage would be covered by green "hundred-mile-an-hour" tape.

The dedication of our pilots and their desire to render prompt medical attention to the wounded demanded operations under all-out flight conditions. Continuous, optimal use of our equipment had a deleterious effect on power plants and airframes. As a result, many of our choppers were replaced long before the end of their programmed life cycle.

Mission orientation was a trademark of the aviators of the 82d, so it was not surprising that an element of derring-do developed in their flying. They had confidence in their ability to see the missions through, no matter what. I decided that nothing would be gained by suppressing such a positive attitude and even encouraged it.

Pickups at insecure sites were routinely carried out, often without the support of covering fire. Extractions under difficult conditions, such as from the tops of mountains strewn with boulders or surrounded by trees, never deterred our pilots. They maneuvered into tight areas as far as possible, going until their rotor blades chopped off tree limbs. While the wounded were loaded, they'd half hover the chopper, only the front of the skids contacting the ground in the midst of enemy fire kicking up dirt all around them. Even in the middle of the night in torrential rain, with thunder and lightning striking all around, their attitude was always, "Let's go, we'll give it a try." Invariably they'd pull it off.

But as well as we took care of others, we also believed in taking care of our own. If one of our dustoffs was downed by the enemy, or by accident, the others quickly responded and swooped down to rescue their friends.

On one flight the boss man himself was a victim of our mission-oriented attitude. Cy had taken his turn on the roster and was first up. It was a typical pitch-black night in the delta with intermittent rain scattered throughout the region. The pickup was in a contested area with a lot of firing going on. The navy's Black Ponies (OV-10s) were pounding the Viet Cong positions while enemy tracers penetrated the darkness trying to destroy the attacking airplanes. The Viet Cong .50-caliber antiaircraft weapons were no match for the attackers but still held everyone's attention.

Cy made identification of the evacuation site by light signals and was being guided to a landing by a small, handheld flashlight. Suddenly he was blinded by a flare that had been accidentally ignited directly in front of his helicopter. He immediately attempted to put the chopper on the ground. Unfortunately he had too much forward motion and as he shoved down on the collective a skid contacted an obstruction, which caused the craft to slew to one side and roll over. Miraculously no one in the ground party or the aircrew was killed or seriously injured. In fact, the only injuries were minor cuts, bruises, and abrasions sustained by Cy and his men. Their pride was hurt more than they were.

While making a periodic check on operations that night, I was monitoring Cy's mission and talking to him on the tactical frequency. According to our SOP, he made his call going in for the pickup. I rogered his transmission and reminded him to call again when airborne. Five minutes went by without a call. After ten minutes without word from Cy, I called the tactical operations center (TOC) at Can Tho for the latest on the situation in the battle area. I also alerted my copilot to get the medic and crew chief on board our chopper and be ready to fly.

"You want me to start the engine?" my copilot asked as he gathered his equipment.

"Of course," I replied. "I'll be with you as soon as I get the latest info from TOC."

It was not long before I learned that Cy's aircraft was down and the crew members were injured. That was all the information I needed. As I rushed for my aircraft, I could hear the chopper revving up as the copilot started the engine. I jumped on board and motioned for him to lift off and get going. I strapped myself in and fastened my knee board, on which I had jotted down all the tactical information.

I was familiar with the area where the firefight raged and took over from the copilot as soon as I hooked up. I told the RTO I was switching over to the tactical net. He had the frequency and could monitor the action on one of the spare radios. I contacted the unit at the pickup site and was surprised to hear Cy answer me on the net. He said that everyone was all right except for some scratches and bruises but the chopper was a total wreck. I saw the enemy tracers and firing passes of the Black Ponies lacing brightly across the black sky. I had my light on for Cy to direct me into his position. In a matter of seconds he guided me to a landing next to his wrecked chopper. His crew had stripped the helicopter of all radios, guns, ammunition, charts, and anything else that might be of value to the VC. It was all stacked by the side of the wreck ready for loading.

The Black Ponies kept up their aerial assault as Cy and his crew loaded the critical equipment. When everyone was aboard, we got out of there.

In a moment Cy got on the interphone and thanked me for the prompt response. I said the reason I got him out without delay was to make sure he filled out all the reports on the loss of his aircraft. If he hadn't been able to get back, I'd have been stuck with the task.

Cy knew I was scheduled for third up and ordinarily wouldn't have been in operations. It was only by chance that I had passed by and learned he was involved with a hot mission. I was there and available when his emergency developed and hurried to help him. I knew he would have done the same for me. You could take that to the bank.

14 October 1969: An Impossible Mission

I celebrated my forty-seventh birthday in September 1969. I had been in Vietnam for more than six months and was on the downhill part of my tour of combat. Every day was supposed to bring me closer to the end of my war and going home. But I didn't look at it that way. I was aware of each day but not as an entry into a ledger of combat accomplished and combat yet to be performed. I knew that the last day of a tour could be just as deadly as the first. I wasn't keeping score. I was busy with duty rosters, crew training, administrative chores, flying missions, and staying alive.

I took advantage of every opportunity to relax. When I wasn't on the schedule to fly, I attended every soiree to which I was invited. Other nights I'd be at the Fleet Air Support Unit officers' club, just as often in the company of my navy associates as with my dustoff friends. I suppose that all of us who experienced combat spent more time at the bar than we should have. But I was always fit for duty at the appointed time.

My glaucoma was kept in check with medication; other than that, I was healthy. I was surprised by the number of our people who suffered from bouts of diarrhea. Their problem could have been caused by eating in the establishments of Can Tho or their penchant for the local seafood, which I never touched. Otherwise, it was a mystery to me how they became ill while I didn't. I patronized the same restaurants and often bought bowls of chicken noodle soup from street vendors. Operating from open pushcarts, they carried a limited number of bowls, which were "cleaned" after each use by sloshing them in a container of supposedly hot water. The bowls were then restacked for use by other customers.

Some of the health problems were probably due to stress and fatigue. The flight schedule was relentless. Because it wasn't unusual for a first-up crew working a twelve-hour shift to still be flying after thirteen hours, timing and location of missions determined if and when they got something to eat or drink.

I remember one day when the missions never stopped coming. My crewmen had been flying without letup for hours and hadn't been able to relieve themselves except during stops for hot refueling. We had no time to eat and had used all our drinking water. Finally we received an evacuation mission at the navy's base at Sea Float, which was a collection of barges anchored in the middle of the Song Cua Lon, the southernmost river in the delta. The base was only twenty kilometers from the South China Sea.

We knew that the people at Sea Float always had sandwiches and plenty of cold drinks. As soon as I made contact, I told them we hadn't eaten all day and were out of drinking water. Their reply was not what I expected. They didn't have any food prepared and were out of sodas. They were also out of drinking water, because their water-purification system had broken down. The only thing available was cold beer. I ordered a can for each of the crew. Of course it was against regulations, but we needed something to drink. Regulations be damned.

The evacuation went as planned; the patients were placed on board while we drank our beer. We departed, relieved of our thirst, and returned to Binh Thuy. The patients were delivered to the hospital, and we returned to the base, logged in our thirteen hours, and were through for the day.

Training and upgrading the detachment's pilots continued to occupy my time. Warrant Officer Aberle was finally designated an aircraft commander (AC). His close friend Lt. Rich Pecararo, already an aircraft commander, volunteered to fly as his copilot on Aberle's first duty as AC. They were having a normal dustoff day. They were in and out of a couple of hot pickups, including the tops of the Three Sisters, where they were under fire but didn't take hits. Toward the end of the day, Aberle received an urgent mission. The pickup site was a small clearing in the Rach Gia area not far from the foot of the Three Sisters. It was situated on a small knoll surrounded by trees of indeterminate height. Entry into the site required a vertical descent. Landing and takeoff would be tight.

Aberle was flying and Rich monitored the gauges. The people at the pickup site said there hadn't been any enemy activity in the area for hours. The wounded soldiers were victims of VC booby traps. Aberle circled the site and maneuvered for the extraction. He made an excellent approach, descended into the area, and was almost on the ground when the situation went to hell. A trooper accidentally discharged a gas grenade. The aircraft was immediately enveloped in white wisps of tear gas whipped about by the rotors. It got both pilots and caused a strong stinging sensation as tears streamed from their eyes. It was no time to go blind. Aberle hadn't yet landed the chopper and in his excited state allowed it to drift until the main rotor contacted tree branches. Though still blinded, he knew enough to make what could be called a controlled crash. It was a jarring landing, but the aircraft was on the ground and the gas and its effects soon dissipated.

The pilots knew that the main rotor was damaged by the tree strike and the skids probably were overstressed by the hard ground contact. Otherwise the chopper appeared to be airworthy. The troops in the ground party were unaware of any damage to the Huey and hastily loaded the wounded. The medic and crew chief positioned their patients and signaled that they were ready for departure. Aberle applied power, and the chopper made a vertical ascent out of the area. Rich noted that the chopper had an unusual vibration. Aberle said he could feel it in the cyclic and they'd have to ground the bird as soon as they got back to Binh Thuy.

They returned to base, hovered to the ship's revetment, and shut down the engine. When the rotor stopped, they saw that both blade tips were badly damaged and the underside of each rotor was dented. Operations was told that the aircraft was grounded. It was time for first up on the night shift to take over, so Aberle completed his reports and called it a day. It was a fair introduction to what was in store for him as an AC and how cruel fate can be. They made all kinds of pickups, were fired on (as usual), and landed on mountaintops and in tight places. Then they almost crashed because of the actions of a soldier who should have been more attentive to his duties.

The next day Aberle was given a report on the condition of his helicopter. Both main rotor blades had to be replaced along with the skids and mounts, which were damaged by the hard landing. Pecararo heard the maintenance report and told Aberle not to feel too bad about the incident. "At least you won't have to pay for the repairs."

Aberle and Pecararo went on to complete their tours. I was sorry to see them leave when their time in country ended. Life was never dull when they were around.

Most of our missions were completed routinely. But there were the inevitable exceptions, such as the night that Buddy Barnes and I flew together. It was extremely stormy, and a strong wind was blowing in from the Gulf of Thailand. We received a mission about ten klicks north of Rach Gia that involved a rendezvous with an agent of one of our intelligence organizations. We were to land at the cement plant to pick up our contact, who then would guide us to the extraction site.

Buddy and I headed for Rach Gia with flight-following assistance from Paddy Radar Control. We soon discovered that we were fighting a forty-knot headwind. That's not much for a C-130, which indicates around three hundred knots at cruise speed, but for a UH-1, which flies at about a hundred knots in weather, that's a lot of drawback. The distance to the cement plant was about forty-five nautical miles, a relatively short flight, but with the gale blowing directly against us we couldn't do more than a mile a minute. It was solid instrument flying in heavy rain and turbulence. When I found myself fighting spatial disorientation, Buddy took over for a spell. He developed similar symptoms and I had to take back the controls. It helped that there wasn't much lightning with the heavy rain.

As I talked to the people at the cement plant, Buddy was at the controls trying to land. I saw that he was having difficulty with the strong crosswind, so I got on the controls and together we manhandled the chopper to a landing.

When our "secret agent" jumped on board, I asked what frequency he would be using so I could hear the transmissions. He said he had a special radio. "Your equipment is not compatible with the advanced gear our company uses," our unnamed and unknown passenger declared.

I didn't like his attitude of superiority and affectation of secrecy; he was probably just another CIA clown screwing up the war. But I had been given the mission by the chain of command, so I didn't have a choice except to continue.

"Well, what do we do now?" I asked.

The man gave me a heading to fly and said our destination was no more than five minutes away. I took off, turned to the given heading, and after five minutes established an orbit in the absence of any direction from the "boss." It was pitch black and raining heavily. I was flying on instruments and couldn't see anything below. I could tell that my passenger was engaged in animated conversation with someone on the ground. I was completely in the dark, figuratively and literally.

I had the crew chief tell the passenger that I wanted to talk to him on the intercom as soon as he was through jaw-jacking with his contact. I wanted to be let in on the action or whatever was going on. When he switched over to the ship's intercom, I asked, "What the hell is going on? I don't like working this way. I've got to know where I am, where I'm going, and what the hell I'm supposed to do."

"Cool it, dustoff," he said. "My mission's been scrubbed. The person I was supposed to pick up hasn't arrived as planned. His location is unknown. Take me back."

I cursed and did as ordered. The wind was as strong as ever on the trip back to the cement plant. Our man jumped off as soon as we were on the ground, didn't say a word, and disappeared into the night. We'd busted our butts in some of the worst weather I'd seen in a while and hadn't accomplished a thing. Then the ungrateful "I've got a secret" agent just took off without a hint of a thank you.

There was still the flight back to Binh Thuy. I took off and gave the controls to Buddy. The rain and turbulence had not abated, but the return flight was aided by a forty-knot tailwind. We made it back in about twenty minutes.

I wasn't happy about our totally screwed-up mission; the secret operations in Vietnam never impressed me. They usually were nothing more than murder or mayhem carried out by a bunch of sadistic goons and covert clowns. In fact, I'm not certain that our mission was supposed to evacuate any injured person. I'm almost convinced that dustoff was exploited by people engaged in clandestine operations. In this case, because the weather was so bad, the clowns couldn't get the job done using their assets. But this wasn't the only mission that infuriated me.

A day or two later I flew a mission in the Vi Thanh area with Ruckhaber as the medic. It was our first mission of the day. The pickup site was the hamlet of Ap Hoa Trung, about ten kilometers west-southwest of the city of Vi Thanh. The Army of the Republic of Vietnam (ARVN) was on a sweep through the village and was met by a force much stronger than expected.

The resistance was fierce, and the Viet Cong inflicted heavy casualties on the ARVN troops. Flying over the battle area, I saw many hooches burning in the village and the entire area covered by smoke and haze. I was delayed for a short time while the wounded were assembled for evacuation. I heard gunfire in the background each time the unit RTO transmitted instructions to me. Finally we landed to get the wounded. There were eight in serious condition and three ambulatory. I told Ruckhaber we'd take them all at once.

As they were being placed on board, I saw two ARVN soldiers bringing a winnowing basket up to the ship. Ruckhaber saw them at the same time and yelled into the intercom, "Look what those bastards are bringing us!" Two dead kids, each about three years old, were on the basket. Their plump little bodies were stitched with bullet holes, each shot at least a dozen times. What I saw was not the result of accidental hits. They'd been deliberately butchered. They apparently were victims of some ARVN's desire for revenge.

I knew that all wars brought forth the basest, vilest, cruelest instincts in some combatants, resulting in ignoble and heartless actions below the dignity of an animal. I didn't ever expect to witness such an act. The scene was so horrible, so inhumane, that I almost threw up. The realization that such an atrocity was perpetrated by allies shook me to the core. I almost decided to leave without taking on any wounded when I realized I couldn't retaliate against such horror by coming down to their level. I called Ruckhaber on the intercom. "Tell those bastards to get that basket and those mutilated bodies out of my sight. I won't be a party to such an atrocity."

"Yes, sir," Ruck replied. I saw him wave his big arms threateningly at the two troops to get out of the area with their abominable load. They got the message and left.

This evil act was brought on by the savages that war produces. Yet there wasn't anything we could do about it. This was an ARVN action, and any report would have to go through the highest channels. The Vietnamese would emphatically deny all allegations of wrongdoing, and eventually the report would be lost in the entangling red tape of the American and Vietnamese commands. Relations between the two would be strained temporarily because of the incident, and the only one to get blamed for anything would be the whistle blower. We took off with our wounded and continued with our duties. What a lousy war. I'll never forget what I saw.

Later we received a mission for an urgent pickup west of Ca Mau on the edge of the U Minh forest. We established communications and were able to identify the extraction site. I didn't know it then, but we were supporting a Marine Corps officer, Capt. Thomas V. Draude, and his Vietnamese counterpart. Tom Draude was the senior adviser to the 5th Battalion, Vietnamese Marine Corps.

When I arrived over the area, I saw Draude's troops maneuvering through a rectangular, swampy area with tree lines cutting across the ends of each long axis. Draude said that he and his men were being harassed by sniper fire and that thirteen Vietnamese Marines were casualties. "Dustoff, I'd appreciate it if you could get them off my hands in no more than two lifts." As I landed in the rice paddy, Draude continued, "We're being harassed by sniper fire from the distant tree line. I'm in the tree line to your left."

"Roger, this is Dustoff 88. Have all your wounded brought to the chopper. We'll try to get them out in one lift. No sense being exposed to snipers more than necessary."

I saw Draude's tree line but couldn't spot him in the vegetation. His troops emerged from cover and brought several litters to the aircraft. We had to double up the litter patients but got everyone aboard.

"This is Dustoff 88. I'm going to be quite slow getting out of here with this load. I'd appreciate some covering fire as I depart."

I pulled pitch and the aircraft slowly lifted off. I continued the takeoff and climbed out in an ascending arc in and out of trees to make the ship harder to hit. We got out of there safely, and Tom Draude continued his sweep through the area.

Sometime later I was pleasantly surprised when Draude wrote a letter to my commander, Cy Simmons, thanking our unit for its outstanding support. He was particularly generous in his praise of my crew for extracting all thirteen of his wounded at one time. I was greatly impressed that this busy man, with little in the way of creature comforts, took time to pen such a letter of praise for our work. We received many sincere thanks from the units we supported. Some of the overexuberant promised medals for our efforts—promises soon forgotten when the heat and danger of battle subsided. Getting a personal letter such as Draude's was better than all the promised medals.

During the last week of September, events taking place along the Vietnam-Cambodia border had a major impact on me, although I was totally unaware of these activities at the time. The Viet Cong were deployed on both sides of the border conducting operations, the nature of which was largely unknown to our forces. The Cai Co Canal, which defined the border in this sector, continued in a southeasterly direction following the outline of the Parrot's Beak, so called because this part of Cambodia thrusts into Vietnam much like the head of a bird. The operational area could be described as the underside of the parrot's throat.

Viet Cong forces had been increasing their activity along the border since the previous summer. Enemy elements on the South Vietnamese side involved units ranging in size from platoons to companies. They were observed constructing bunkers and other fortifications. The buildup continued until the VC force consisted of two battalions in South Vietnam. The size of the enemy force on the Cambodian side remained a mystery. Action was about to be initiated to eliminate the enemy presence on the Vietnamese side. It was time for Operation Python.

The operation, as chronicled by the official dustoff history, was directed by Company D, 5th Special Forces Group, headquartered at Can Tho. Detachment B-41, based at Moc Hoa, was in command of the attacking forces. The order of battle included three Vietnamese mobile strike force (MSF) companies, five U.S. Navy Tango boats, four river patrol boats (PBRs), and a Monitor. There was also a battery of U.S. Army 105mm howitzers, Vietnamese Air Force A-1Es, U.S. Air Force F-100s, and U.S. Army helicopter gunships. Jump-off for the operation was 0645 on October 2, 1969.

On the evening of October 1, while I was at dinner in the officers' mess, Con Jaburg sat down at my table. "I hear you're first up tomorrow morning," he said. "If you are, how about putting me down to fly with you?"

"Your intelligence staff has given you correct information as usual. I've already scheduled one of the new replacements from Long Binh as my copilot, but I'm sure he won't mind the change. I'm going to the club for a few drinks before turning in. I'll see you there after you finish your meal."

The aviator I'd scheduled as my copilot was WO Tyrone Chamberlain. He'd been sent by the 45th Medical Company in answer to my pleas for additional aviator help. Tyrone flew with the 45th Dustoff out of Long Binh, so he wasn't new to Vietnam. But he hadn't had his taste of combat flying in the delta. I told him there had been a change in plans, and he'd be scheduled to fly second up the next day.

I went to the officers' club for a few gin and tonics before going to my quarters. As I took a seat, the bartender, whose name was John, asked, "You want gin and tonic, no?"

"I want gin and tonic, yes. Can't stay too long tonight, John. First up tomorrow morning bright and early."

I was nursing my drink when Buddy Barnes came into the club. "Have you seen your boss, Jaburg?" I asked. "He was supposed to meet me here after dinner. We're flying first up tomorrow morning."

Buddy didn't know where his boss was. "He probably stopped at his office before coming here. I'm sure he'll be along soon."

I was on my second gin and tonic when Con sat down next to me. "Mike, there's been a change in my plans. I've got to be in Saigon tomorrow morning. Admiral Zumwalt has called a meeting. I don't know what's up, but this is one meeting I can't afford to miss. I'm sorry if I've screwed up your schedule."

"No problem, Con. I'll just go back to plan A and install the original schedule. I'll let my copilot know he's back on duty with me tomorrow. Enjoy your trip to Saigon, and stay out of those massage parlors. When I finish this drink, I'm out of here."

I stopped in the transient area, found Chamberlain, and told him about the change of plans. I reminded him that we had to be preflighted and ready to go by six in the morning. He said he'd be ready.

I returned to my quarters and decided to write to Ethel, to let her and the children know that all was well with me. (I didn't write home every night. With my schedule, that was almost impossible. But I tried to write to Ethel at least every other day.) In my letter, I mentioned that I was first up the next day. I finished the letter and hit the hay. Being first up would bring in the usual number of missions. We'd no doubt see the whole of the delta. I expected a busy day.

I was up before five. I showered, put on a clean uniform, and went to the officers' mess for a quick cup of navy coffee. Chamberlain was already there finishing breakfast. He said he'd preflight the aircraft if I wanted to get a bite. I took him up on the offer and had hot cakes, sausage, and more coffee. I didn't know it, but that was the last food I would have all day.

When I entered operations, Chamberlain and the rest of my crew were waiting for me. My medic was SP4 Herbert Heinold and my crew chief was SP4 Joseph Horvath, two exceptionally capable people with whom I'd flown many times. The RTO said the only mission pending was a routine one at Tra Vinh, a town about forty nautical miles southeast of Binh Thuy. It would have to wait until we received a higher-priority mission in the vicinity.

It wasn't long before we were alerted for a mission at Rach Gia. En route I was told of an additional urgent pickup at the Three Sisters. It was going to be one of those long days. We had missions without letup all morning and into the afternoon. Hot refueling was necessary between missions. It looked as if we'd never catch up.

Operation Python was launched at 0645. The three MSF companies moved out of their assembly areas toward their objectives some 1,500 to 2,000 meters away. A command and control (C&C) helicopter monitored the operation as it advanced. The company on the left flank reached an area dotted with countless hummocks (large earthen mounds six to ten feet high, overgrown with trees and vegetation) but didn't meet any resistance. At 0800 the company on the right flank reported unidentified movement in the objective area, but it hadn't received any fire. It also came upon hummocks in their sector. At 0810 the company advancing in the center came under withering fire from hummock positions on its flanks. The two flanking companies also took fire. In an instant nine soldiers of the MSF lead element lay dead, and the rest of its troops clutched at the ground trying to hide from the deadly enemy fire.

The 105mm artillery battery went into action to lay down supporting fire, but after three or four rounds the guns sank into the soft, muddy ground and were out of action. At 0820 air force tactical air support was requested with an operational immediate priority. For some strange reason, the request was disapproved. Another request for tac air went forward. This time the mission was approved, but the aerial support didn't arrive on the scene until 0950. Meanwhile, Delta Military Assistance Command sent army helicopter gunships to support the beleaguered troops. Vietnamese A-1Es came in also and attacked the Viet Cong with napalm. But the strikes didn't have much effect. There seemed to be no lessening of incoming fire.

The Viet Cong response to the MSF was well directed and amply supplied. The VC's equipment and ammunition, more than adequate for the occasion, consisted of Browning automatic rifles (BARs), rocket-propelled grenades (RPGs), AK-47s, Chicom (Chinese communist) rifles, mortars, machine guns, and a 12.5mm heavy machine gun configured for use as an antiaircraft weapon.

The terrain also favored the Viet Cong. The ubiquitous hummocks dotting the area offered the VC excellent firing positions and cover. They moved from hummock to hummock to keep the MSF under observation and fire. The hummocks also provided ample protection against aerial attack. A direct hit by a 500-pounder on one side of a hummock couldn't guarantee eliminating a soldier seeking refuge on the other side.

The area under attack contained simulated forts built by the Viet Cong for training purposes. The forts enabled the VC to study and determine the best method of assaulting such installations and simultaneously train their troops in the approved plan of attack. It was this training complex that Operation Python was designed to eliminate and the Viet Cong were determined to preserve.

Air Force F-100 fighter-bombers hammered away with powerful, accurate strikes on the VC positions with 500-pound bombs and 20mm cannons. Several F-100s were hit by antiaircraft fire, as were some of the army's gunships. One was forced down by hits to its transmission system but made it to a safe area south of the battle; the aircraft and crew were recovered later that day. All the F-100s made it back to the base. Weather temporarily deteriorated and low ceilings moved in over the battle area to prevent the strike aircraft from returning until two o'clock that afternoon.

The impact of the battle on the MSF troops was vividly described by the initial report of Sergeant First Class Hughes, the American adviser with the right flank. Early in the fighting he radioed that he had several wounded men on the ground but couldn't confirm the number. He couldn't give an accurate assessment of the situation because of the ferocity of the fighting and limited observation due to the high elephant grass. Adding to the confusion was the fact that his MSF platoon leader and first sergeant were among the first killed. As Sergeant Hughes took cover behind a hummock, he saw two of his men killed as they tried to drag their wounded comrades to safety.

When the F-100s returned, they conducted several especially strong air strikes, which enabled the MSF troops to withdraw from their exposed salient. Several of the F-100s were hit again by enemy fire, along with two AH-1 Cobras covering the withdrawal. Six hours had passed since the initial onslaught by the Viet Cong. As the majority of the MSF troops disengaged from the battle, they had to leave behind many of their wounded comrades who were surrounded by the Viet Cong. Their rescue appeared dim indeed.

The situation was obvious to the VC, who proceeded to lay down a vicious mortar barrage on the MSF troops remaining in the area. They had become separated from their units and American advisers in the initial onslaught and had expended all their ammunition. They'd thrown aside their useless weapons and lost all communication with the main body of troops. Their only chance to survive was to hug the ground, to find some depression where they might remain unseen, and hope that the tall elephant grass would prevent observation of their hopeless state. The surrounded troops were as good as lost.

Captain Cook, the senior U.S. Special Forces adviser in the battle area, was responsible for the initial request for tactical air support by the F-100s early in the battle and for the repeated request when the first one was denied. He saw the battle from its first shot until the disaster that now loomed. He knew there wasn't a shred of hope for the surrounded remnants of the MSF troops with the assets he controlled. He had contact with the C&C helicopter circling overhead at 2,000 feet and also Swamp Fox 15 in a small Cessna O-1 observation airplane above him at 2,500 feet. The C&C and Swamp Fox had observers with binoculars on board who spotted the surrounded troops on the ground. After talking to the men in the aircraft, Cook decided to call dustoff. It was after 1500 when he radioed his headquarters at Moc Hoa and sent a request through the operational net for an evacuation helicopter. The request made its way to the 82d Medical Detachment at Binh Thuy at 1600. Red tape and myriad support people were bound to get in the way, even in the modern age of radio.

Except for a lull in activities in the early afternoon, Chamberlain, Heinold, Horvath, and I had been continually on the go. We had worked hard especially during the last three missions, which were viciously contested by the Viet Cong. We were returning from our latest extraction and all was quiet. We thought we might have a respite from additional missions. But when we were within a few minutes of Binh Thuy, the RTO called, "Dustoff 88, I have a mission for you. Are you ready to copy? Over."

"Aw, shit, what have you got for us now?" I copied the transmission and checked the time. It was just after 1600. After decoding the message, I plotted the coordinates of the pickup site to be on the Cambodian border in the vicinity of the Parrot's Beak. "Damn, that's a good forty minutes' flying time from our position," I exclaimed. "Chamberlain, how long have we been flying today?"

He checked the aircraft logbook. "According to our entries, we've logged seven hours up to now."

"Well, we've got what looks like another long mission before we're through for the day. We're headed for the border, next to the Parrot's Beak. It'll take us a minimum of half an hour just to get there. The mission statement from the RTO indicated multiple casualties, number unknown, all urgent life or death. I thought that with the last bunch of missions around Ca Mau, we would be through for the day, but that's not going to happen. Heinold, Horvath—we've got a long flight to the pickup site. Get some rest."

I told the RTO that we had the mission and were on our way. The weather ahead was not the best; I saw a number of thunderstorms. We avoided the most dangerous-looking ones but still were bounced around by a couple of thunder busters. No sweat; the rainstorms washed off the windshields and got rid of all the insect smears. About midway to our destination, I informed base that I was switching to the tactical frequency and would most likely be out of radio range for the rest of the mission.

I finally made radio contact with the people directing the action. My contact's call sign was Concert Bravo. After I verified that the geographical coordinates were correct, I got down to the business at hand. "Concert Bravo, this is Dustoff 88. Let me have the tactical situation as best you can. We're still about ten minutes from your location. Also, I would like confirmation of the number and condition of the wounded."

"Roger, Dustoff 88. We have an unknown number of wounded soldiers on the ground. They're cut off from the main body of troops and are in a bad way. We don't know the extent of their injuries because we've lost contact with them. From all indications, they're out of ammunition and appear to have abandoned their weapons. Those we can observe are hugging the ground and moving only to find more secure positions. All are Vietnamese troops."

"Concert Bravo, the picture I get is not good and not exactly clear. Are there any Americans on the ground with them? I've got to have someone down there I can talk to; otherwise, I can't do my job. I've got to have more information."

"Dustoff 88, this is Concert Bravo. I'm the C&C helo circling at two thousand feet. I have observers with me who can see the troops on the ground. Swamp Fox 15 is in an O-1 Bird Dog five hundred feet above me. He too has an observer with him to help direct you."

"Concert Bravo, this is Dustoff. Roger your last transmission. What is the enemy situation? What weapons do they have? Who will be giving me covering fire?"

"Dustoff 88, the VC are laying down mortar fire on the friendlies and backing that up with automatic weapons. They also have RPGs. I'm sorry to say that at present there is no covering fire available. We had fighter-bombers and helicopter gunships with us earlier, but all are refueling and rearming at base. I have no idea when they'll return."

"This is Dustoff 88. What about the main body of troops? What's their location? Will they be able to give us support, some covering fire?"

"Negative, Dustoff. The main force broke off contact some time ago. They're at least two klicks away continuing their redeployment. There will be no covering fire till the F-100s or the gunships return. Either you wait for them or you go in on your own. However, I must remind you there isn't much daylight left this late in the afternoon. Extractions after dark will not be possible."

At that instant Swamp Fox 15 broke into the conversation between me and Concert Bravo. He said he'd been listening and was on the net with us.

"Roger, Swamp Fox, this is Dustoff 88. Do you have anything to add? Any suggestions that might help? I've got to make a decision soon. I'm only a couple of minutes from your location. As a matter of fact, I think I have you and the C&C in sight."

"Dustoff, this is Swamp Fox 15. I have nothing to add. You're definitely on your own if you try to get those troops out of there now. I'll do my best to give you any clues and cues that I might be able to pick up from my position."

"Roger, I've received your briefing. You haven't given me much to go on. I'll orbit the area now that I'm here. I want to get a feel for the situation before I decide on a course of action."

The information given me presented an impossible situation. I couldn't believe that my crew had been called upon to come so far to undo someone's grossly inadequate planning and military misadventure.

I hadn't said a word to the crew. I knew they'd heard the entire dialogue with the other two aircraft. I was interested in the picture below. There was an immense expanse of flat terrain dotted with hundreds of brush-covered hummocks stretching several kilometers west from a tree line and stream; it was the Vietnam-Cambodia border. This was the area identified in the mission request as coordinates Whiskey Tango 820 170, the pickup site. I noticed what appeared to be two fortifications in the midst of the numerous hummocks. One was triangular and the other square.

"Concert Bravo, this is Dustoff 88. What are the brush-covered mounds down there and what's the situation at those defensive structures, the square and triangular forts?"

"Dustoff, those are hummocks, eight to ten feet high. The VC troops are using them as firing and observation positions. The two forts are simulations of fortified hamlets found throughout the delta. The VC use them as training sites to teach their troops how to attack such installations."

From surveying the scene, I could tell that much labor had been expended in the construction of the hummocks, which covered several kilometers of level terrain. There were hundreds of them interspersed among parcels of land that once were farmed but showed no sign of recent cultivation. The plots, lying fallow, appeared as haphazard shapes scattered in indiscriminate fashion. It was impossible to say which came first, the hummocks or the areas meant for cultivation. It was all mysterious and somewhat foreboding.

Although the area was extensive, the battle was taking place at the eastern edge of this unusual territory adjacent to the Cambodian border. The two simulated fortifications were situated in the midst of the area under contention, and it was on this terrain that the surrounded MSF troops were seeking cover.

I took the crew's silence as a commitment to any decision I made. In truth there wasn't time to engage in the democratic process. Something had to be done right away. My thoughts were interrupted by a call from Concert Bravo.

"Dustoff 88, I have a wounded trooper located within the southern angle of the triangular fort. My observers have noted his movement into a shallow, furrowlike depression. Do you want to try to get him? The enemy mortars have been quiet in that sector for the past few minutes."

"Okay, Concert Bravo. We'll give it a try. It's getting late. If those troops aren't brought out soon, they'll be goners by morning."

I turned my attention to the crew. "Chamberlain, stay on the controls with me. We'll see what we can do. Heinold, Horvath, I don't know what to expect down there. This isn't your ordinary dustoff mission. We'll play it by ear. Above all, don't do anything stupid."

What we were about to do couldn't possibly be measured by any sanity scale, so my last statement to the crew was questionable.

I was flying from the left seat so, as was my habit, I rolled the helicopter in my direction and shoved the nose toward the ground. We started from about two thousand feet. It would be only a matter of seconds until we were over our pickup spot.

With the nose of the chopper pointed at the ground, I rolled first in one direction, then in another to make us more difficult to hit. My rapid descent was intended to prevent the enemy gunners from getting set for a shot. I saw my airspeed holding just above the redline, but my main concern during the dive was the rotor revolutions per minute (rpms). When in a dive, the rotor tends to increase its rpms and if not kept under control with the collective pitch lever would soon pass its maximum allowable limit. At the last instant I recovered from the dive with a strong flare and applied power to stop the descent. We finished at a hover within a few feet of the ground. We were inside the triangular fort where the wounded man was last seen.

"Dustoff, you're right over him!" said Concert Bravo excitedly. "You're hovering right over him!"

As Concert Bravo spoke, automatic weapons opened up. Heinold and Horvath reported fire from the hummocks to our rear and gun flashes everywhere.

"We're taking fire from around the clock," yelled Chamberlain.

I felt some of the rounds hit the ship. The pedals were sensitive enough to transmit the telltale vibrations associated with projectiles hitting metal in the tail section. Thankfully there weren't any mortar rounds impacting in our immediate area.

The wounded man below wouldn't show himself. More quickly than the telling takes, I moved off to the side but couldn't make out anyone below the aircraft. Unknown to Concert Bravo, the elephant grass in the area was so thick that our rotor wash folded it over the trooper. Hearing all those automatic weapons firing, our man apparently decided he was safer where he was than standing up to be rescued. And he was probably scared to death being underneath a huge machine that was beating the air and thrashing the grass all about him. I'm not surprised he didn't make a move.

The Viet Cong laid down a vicious barrage from all directions. I never heard so many automatic weapons before. I made a fast turn to the right and got out of there. As I crossed a nearby stream, the intensity of fire increased even though I would have thought that impossible. I remember telling Concert Bravo, "Hey, they're most unfriendly over here."

"That's right, Dustoff. That stream is the border. You flew into Cambodia with that right turn. That's where the main enemy force is. I suggest you avoid that area."

"I was right where I was supposed to be in that fort," I told Concert Bravo, "but the wounded man wouldn't show himself. The elephant grass is so high that my downwash folded it over him and none of us could see him. What do we do now? We picked up a lot of fire, and I know we took some hits."

"Dustoff, I suggest you try once more. Maybe this time he'll stand up as soon as you arrive. Maybe he'll understand you're there to help him. You know where to go."

I alerted my crew, gave them the same instructions as before, and headed for the ground. Everything was fine until I again came to a hover over the trooper. The VC opened up immediately, the volume of fire as heavy and intense as ever. I held my position and looked for the man, but I still couldn't see him because of the thick, folded grass.

In the second or so we were there, I swung the tail around to get a more complete view of the spot, but the wounded soldier refused to show himself. We had to get out of there. The Viet Cong had our range, and any minute they could throw mortars in our direction. This time I turned to the left to avoid the force in Cambodia.

The first time I left the pickup area, I climbed back to altitude to talk over the situation with Concert Bravo. This time I remained low but temporarily flew out of the battle area to consider my next move. It was apparent that what we were doing was not going to work.

"We haven't done a thing on those last two tries except waste time and take hits," I told my crew. "We've got to try a different tactic. We've got to make the wounded troops aware of our presence and make them see we're in the area to help them get out. We're going back in, and I'm going to fly in and around the locations where the wounded most likely are hiding. There'll be hummocks in the area, so we've got to be alert for enemy fire from them. Keep your eyes and ears open. We're not going to stop for any pickups. If the wounded see us and are willing to show themselves, we'll slide past them, and you—Heinold and Horvath—pull them aboard while we're still moving. We can't under any circumstances make standard dustoff pickups where we stop and load. There's just too much enemy firepower against us. Even this might not work, but we've got to give it a try."

Nobody dissented and again I took the crew's silence as agreement to my course of action. I didn't discuss any details of our plan with Concert Bravo. I just told him we were going to be moving about looking for the wounded. If he saw any in our path, he could report them to us.

Our absence from the scene of battle was only a minute or so while I explained the change in tactics to the crew. I maneuvered just south of the triangular fort even though the tactical situation there was not the most favorable. I believed that most of the wounded were in that area. I flew an extremely low and slow racetrack pattern that I figured covered enough ground to include all the surrounded troops. There was an uncommon element to our situation: We were moving among an unknown number of surrounded troops. That meant we too were surrounded while operating in that area. It was all insane. But then it was a crazy war.

The VC continued to hose down the area as we maneuvered through the hummocks, but our steady movement disrupted their aim. Their fire was not as effective as it had been during the first two attempted pickups, although at times it became intense and threatening.

I completed one circuit, without results. I made a slight adjustment and maneuvered through the area closer to the ground but in the same oval pattern. I was just off the ground, occasionally in elephant grass so high it was at eye level, but always moving forward, sometimes skidding across the grassy terrain. I was less of a target than before.

Sometime during the second circuit, a soldier stood up in the grass and waved his shirt as we neared his position. Either Heinold or Horvath, hanging from a litter strap, grabbed the trooper by the wrist and yanked him on board. He was our first success. The Viet Cong undoubtedly saw this and hopefully so did the rest of the MSF soldiers. I continued skidding across the grass in the racetrack pattern as the terrain and conditions permitted. I was elated when I saw another man repeat the actions of the first. He too was yanked on board as we moved past him. The enemy gunners responded with a particularly vicious barrage, and I could see that they were beginning to get the range. I applied maximum power and got out of there.

As I circled and returned to the oval pattern from another direction, Heinold told me that both rescued men had shrapnel wounds, which he was tending to. I cautioned Heinold and Horvath to be alert for others who might pop up out of the grass.

The Viet Cong were not letting us get by without reminding us of their presence. They kept up a constant barrage in our direction and dropped occasional mortar rounds near us. Staying low to the ground and always on the move made us a difficult target to acquire, but the VC didn't give up. More than once I had to fly out of the battle area because of the intensity of their fire. Some of the rounds found their mark, but fortunately nobody aboard our Huey was hit. I continued to maneuver and returned to the racetrack pattern from other directions as we searched for survivors.

Our plan was working. Two troopers stood up in the grass as we neared them. They were quickly yanked on board. Everyone we picked up was wounded, some seriously. If they hadn't been rescued that afternoon, they wouldn't have lasted through the night.

Heinold had his hands full. He told me we'd picked up ten wounded and he'd done all he could for them. I said we'd leave for the Special Forces compound at Moc Hoa, where the wounded would get more specialized care.

It was a short flight to the outpost, where we also picked up some much needed fuel. We didn't tarry long at the camp, taking on only half a tank. I wanted to remain light to retain maneuverability, knowing that if all went well we'd take on about ten more wounded.

While returning to the battle area, I contacted Concert Bravo. "This is Dustoff 88. Do you have any information on air force or army aerial fire support? I could sure use some help. The VC are improving their aim. They got us good a few times, and our ship took more hits. I had to get out of the area and return from another direction a couple of times because of the intensity of their fire."

"Dustoff 88, this is Concert Bravo. I saw all your maneuvering down there. I wish there was something definite to tell you, but I don't have anything on the arrival of either army or air force."

"Dustoff 88, this is Swamp Fox 15. I've observed three troops crawling slowly into your area of activity. They appear to be injured. When you return for more pickups, you can be on the alert for them."

"This is Dustoff. Thanks for the info, Swamp Fox. We'll be in our pattern in a minute. Keep me posted if you see any additional movement, friendly or otherwise."

During the previous series of extractions, I hadn't had much chance to discuss or critique our operations with Chamberlain, Heinold, or Horvath, but nobody objected to the procedures or suggested any changes. We'd had good results, so we continued as before. We'd survived the ordeal thus far; we hoped our luck would continue.

During the previous action, the medic and crew chief were on the intercom, not necessarily one at a time. One or the other, and sometimes both, would yell out when they'd spot the wounded waving rags or shirts. Then they'd loudly announce success when a trooper was pulled aboard: "I have him! Keep going! Don't slow down! Don't stop!"

Chamberlain was also busy. Every time a burst of fire came close and the ship was hit, he'd go through his spiel. He'd call out the emergency procedures, letting me know that the engine was still operating and the rotor still turning. He sounded like a tobacco auctioneer. Invariably we'd take more hits and he'd have to do it all over again.

As a recent flight school graduate, Chamberlain was still a victim of failure mania. It wasn't the intent of flight training to leave students in fear of things going wrong, but that often was the result. Regardless of the branch of service, the curriculum emphasized emergency procedures so much that students didn't know what it was like to fly without an emergency. They were regularly given engine failures, radio communications failures, hydraulic failures, flight instrument failures, landing gear failures, flap failures, and just about every malfunction except wings or rotors coming off.

Chamberlain's flight with me was his first real combat mission. We were exposed to a constant barrage of enemy fire while the aircraft took hit after hit. Suddenly exposed to honest-to-goodness, real danger, and having recently been in an environment that emphasized things failing, Chamberlain knew that something was bound to go wrong. (It had; but it was the mission, not the equipment.) My analysis of Chamberlain's training is not made in a pejorative sense, but he should have been told that once in a while the engine does not fail. In fact I commend Chamberlain for his zealous attention to his duties. I'll be the first to admit that I didn't once look at my instruments. I flew by instinct, by feel, by experience born of twenty-seven years in the cockpit of military aircraft. As far as I was concerned, the engine was not going to quit. *It dare not.* Chamberlain was a great help to me during that mission. Under the circumstances I wouldn't have wanted anyone else to be sitting next to me. He was there when I needed him.

While we set up our low-skimming racetrack pattern, I sensed that the VC were not pleased with our previous success and objected even more to our return. The enemy had been blasting the area for hours, and their fire should have slacked off. But the intensity had increased. It also appeared that the VC had repositioned themselves closer to us.

There was little delay before one of the wounded showed himself. He was immediately yanked aboard. As we skidded along the grass, more wounded now showed themselves without hesitation, and some even ran toward us to get on the chopper. I wasn't aware of the nature of their wounds until I saw one of the wounded stand up from his concealed position and run toward us holding his belly with both hands. He was partially eviscerated and was clutching at his abdomen holding what looked like a mess of sausages. Miraculously, he made it to the ship under his own power.

What stamina—what will to live—what a hell of a lot of dying it takes to kill a man.

Just as I got the word that the man with the belly wound was on board, I saw another trooper rise up from the grass and run toward our craft. He was not as fortunate. The Viet Cong gunners riddled him with a volley from their automatic weapons, and he collapsed in a heap into the grass. I didn't bother to check on him as the ship passed within ten to fifteen feet of his crumpled body. I knew he was dead. The same gunners opened up on us as we passed their line of fire. I felt the impacts as their rounds penetrated the chin bubble under my feet. I got out of there—fast.

I maneuvered for another entry into the racetrack pattern, avoiding the sector where we'd taken the latest rounds. The beleaguered troops who initially hadn't responded to our attempts at rescue finally got the message and were cooperating with our plan. They'd seen others stand up to be muscled on board the helicopter with the red crosses and saw it as their avenue to salvation. When we approached their concealed positions, they'd pop up at the last second and dash for the chopper. The Viet Cong weren't giving up and kept blazing away at our chopper as we skidded over the ground. The only reason they weren't more successful was our low profile and constant movement. The elephant grass was sometimes so high that it wasn't uncommon to see only the shoulders and a waving arm holding a rag or shirt.

The enemy troops stayed concealed but moved from hummock to hummock seeking better angles of fire at the moving chopper. Because they were not any taller than the troops we were rescuing, their ability to scan the area and fire effectively was hampered by the heavy grass. They continued to harass us with occasional mortar rounds, but that was more of a diversion than a deterrent. Still, the constant automatic weapons fire directed at the dustoff was disconcerting and caused me to exit the area when it was too close and too intense. The VC tactics continued to delay our efforts to gather the wounded, and I knew that time was of the essence. There was little daylight left.

"Heinold, how many have we got on board now?" I asked. "We're low on fuel."

"We have nine on board, sir."

"Roger. I'm going to fly one more circuit, then leave for Moc Hoa whether we get another person or not."

I estimated that with one more half tank of fuel, we could remain in the area until nightfall. I intended to start back as soon as I made the turn in the direction of the Special Forces outpost. Before making the turn, we came upon one more wounded. I couldn't see the soldier clearly, but it looked to me as if his face was covered with blood. He was grabbed by the hand and muscled aboard. I headed for Moc Hoa.

"Heinold, what's the condition of the men on board?"

"Sir, these people are in sorry shape. I hope they all make it. You know about the one with the belly wound. The one we just picked up took a round through the nose and mouth and looks a real mess. Another has lost a hand, and most of the rest have bullet and shrapnel wounds about their bodies. It's best we're taking them back now."

In a few minutes we were back on the ground at Moc Hoa. "Horvath, let's take on half a tank of fuel so we can get back to the pickup site and do some good for those poor bastards still there. It'll be dark soon and impossible for us to continue."

"Right, sir. I'll have us refueled while Heinold unloads the wounded."

"Chamberlain, you haven't said much except to keep me posted on the condition of the aircraft. Are you all right?" I asked.

"I'm okay, just tired and hungry. We haven't had a bite to eat since breakfast. That was about sunup and we're approaching sundown now. What a long day."

"Yeah," I answered. "They never did have a class in flight school about how to survive without eating, did they? I always said the whole flight program was impractical. It never zeroed in on the real world."

I turned to Horvath. "Aren't you finished refueling? I only want half a tank, remember?"

"Roger, sir, I'll be through in a minute. Everyone else is on board and ready to go."

I looked back and saw Horvath buttoning up the fuel tank. He got on board, and Heinold gave me the signal from the rear. "All on board. Ready to go, sir."

I took off and headed back to the battle area. In addition to racing death, we were racing the clock. My other concern was the lack of fire support for us. I got on the tactical net with the C&C.

"Concert Bravo, this is Dustoff 88. We've been here almost two hours and haven't received any air cover. What's the holdup? I'm on my way back to continue with the extractions. What have you got for us?"

"Dustoff 88, I'm sorry to tell you I still haven't received any information from the air force or the army. I have no idea what's keeping them."

I'd been expecting covering fire from somebody since I first arrived. I didn't care who furnished the fire support; I just wanted some help. I was angry. "Look here, Concert Bravo—and you too, Swamp Fox 15. We don't have any effective weapons with us. In your spare time, fire an occasional M79 grenade at the VC down here. Maybe that'll help keep their heads down," I said sarcastically.

"Aw, what the hell," I continued. "I'm still better off than those poor bastards I'm picking up. I'm sorry about getting on your asses for something that's not your fault. I guess I'm getting tired and losing my sense of humor. Get on your command net again and try to get me some help. The VC scored too often to suit me during that last series of extractions."

With that last transmission, I at least let off some steam and let them know how frustrating it was to be down in that hellhole all alone. I reentered the combat area, and immediately some of the wounded showed themselves. There were three of them standing almost in a line as if to buy tickets to get on a bus. They were hauled aboard, and suddenly I was feeling better. Then I received a pleasant surprise. Concert Bravo was calling on the net. "Dustoff 88, Dustoff 88. Come in. Over."

"Concert Bravo, this is Dustoff 88. What's the problem? What's up?"

"Dustoff 88, we have two F-100s coming. They're prepared to resume bombing."

"This is Dustoff 88. What the hell are they waiting for? It's getting late. Tell them to lay it on. If they can, have them hit the hummocks about a hundred meters north of my position. The Viet Cong in that sector are really making it rough for me."

There was a slight delay. I wondered why the F-100s weren't hitting the hummocks I'd pointed out. Meanwhile, we were sliding along the ground but not having much luck finding more wounded. We might have extracted all that we were going to get.

Concert Bravo called back. "Dustoff 88, the air force pilots said they can't attack the enemy positions while you're down there. You'll have to exit the area before they'll drop ordnance. Something about their SOP."

I was about to say where they could jam their SOP, but this was no time to get into a pissing contest. If I was going to get any more wounded out of there, I'd have to do as the air force directed. I climbed out of the site, and the fighter-bombers went into action, bombing and strafing the Viet Cong positions I had pointed out.

Watching the F-100s, I took note how religiously these air force pilots complied with their SOPs. My compliance was not as rigid. My actions went against every clause and sentence of the SOP directing aeromedical evacuations: There was no American on the ground, no communication with the unit, no smoke signals for identification, no security or covering fire, and no way to tell friend or foe. Dustoff pilots bent the rules once in a while to save a life, no matter whose.

As soon as the air force jets had unloaded on the Viet Cong, Concert Bravo called to clear me to reenter the battle area. It was almost dark when I told the crew we had to get as many of the remaining MSF soldiers as we could in the next few minutes. As I resumed going over my racetrack pattern, it appeared to me that the air strike shook some of the wounded troops out of their holes. As soon as I got into the circuit, one man sprouted out of the grass to get on board. On the next circuit two troops rose up almost in front of the chopper and were either yanked or jumped on board. Both were wounded but hadn't lost their agility or desire to get out of the hell they'd endured for the past ten hours. The Viet Cong again got the range, and the ship took several more rounds. It was time to leave and maneuver for another entry into the pattern.

The air strikes hadn't reduced the effectiveness of the enemy's fire. The VC had kept their heads down during the bombardment and knew when the danger was past. They were again as active as ever.

The Viet Cong observed my reentry and appeared more determined to get at me and my crew. On this our third series of extractions, the fire directed at us couldn't have been more intense. Time and again I had to leave the area in a hail of heavy fire. They had repositioned their weapons closer to my flight pattern and definitely made it more difficult for me to continue. I had to reenter the circuit after being shot out of the area three times during this series of pickups. We got another wounded soldier on board as I continued across the grassy area. On the next trip around, Heinold and Horvath hauled two more aboard. Just then I received a call from Concert Bravo. "Dustoff 88, two Cobra gunships have arrived. They're coming up on your rear."

In an instant I saw the army helicopters fly over my chopper at about two hundred feet. One of the pilots called: "Sorry to have taken so long to come to your assistance, Dustoff, but weather delayed us. We'll cover you until you're through."

"This is Dustoff 88. There's not much light left. We're not going to be in the area long. I've almost got a full load. I'll probably depart in a few minutes."

The Cobras flew in a tight circle over our ship as we skidded across the grass and got one more wounded trooper, then completed two more circuits.

"Looks as if we've got everyone we possibly can," I told the crew. "There's barely enough light to see the gunships overhead. I'm going to make one more circuit. If we don't see anyone, that's it for today. It's too dark to continue."

Just then Horvath yelled over the intercom. "A man off to our left is waving his shirt."

There was so little light that I could barely make out the form. He was about fifty meters from us and close to a hummock. "We'll go get him," I said to the crew, "but this will be our last one." As things turned out, it was almost a prophetic statement.

The person we were going after was standing in waist-high grass about ten meters in front of a hummock, one of many from which we'd received fire. Some of the wounded used these same hummocks as refuges. While moving along my racetrack pattern, I'd passed by hummocks on either side of my aircraft without taking fire. It was evident that the VC weren't at every one of them; they moved from one hummock to another seeking better firing positions. It was a fluid situation, but it favored the VC, because they were in control and could occupy any sector they wished.

I didn't like what I saw. It was too uncertain, but we couldn't abandon the soldier to the enemy. The firing had abated temporarily, maybe because of the diminished light or the presence of the Cobras, although neither had deterred the Viet Cong before. I was certain we'd draw fire as we approached our quarry. There were too many VC firing positions close by.

I alerted the crew about the procedure we'd use to get our man. "Heinold, Horvath, I'm going to hover backward until we're abeam of the individual. Whoever gets to him, haul his ass on board. Tell me when you have him, and I'll stop backing and immediately go into a takeoff mode. You have only a second to get him. Do you both understand?"

After I got two quick responses, I continued my instructions. "I want you both to lie flat on the deck as I'm backing up. That way if the Viet Cong open up, their bullets will have to pass through the entire tail cone and fuel cell before reaching the crew compartment. By then the projectiles should have lost most of their energy and you two should be all right. At least I hope so. If they open up on us before we reach our soldier, I'll abort the pickup and get the hell out of there. I realize it means abandoning him to the Viet Cong, but some things are not always possible. Chamberlain, I want you on the controls with me on this one. If either of us is hit, the other has to continue."

During the few seconds it took to brief the crew, the VC kept up their sporadic fire, which was more disruptive than effective. I maneuvered the chopper into position for the backward approach. For an instant I was at a stationary hover. The Viet Cong didn't open up, and I couldn't understand their lack of aggressiveness. We were such an inviting target.

Hovering a helicopter backward is not difficult; the only concern is that the area to the rear is clear of obstacles. Once I started, I kept the Huey moving rearward at a constant rate to come abreast of the waiting soldier. I slowed only when Heinold yelled into the intercom, "Horvath has him." Hearing that, I shoved the cyclic forward and was increasing collective for maximum takeoff power and a fast getaway. It was then that my world almost came crashing down around me.

As I applied power and rotated, a VC jumped up from his hiding place in the grass. He was at my ten o'clock position not more than thirty meters away when he methodically emptied his entire AK-47 ammo clip at me, point blank. I was his one and only target; he couldn't possibly miss from that short distance. Viet Cong gunners to our rear also opened up. The action, which seemed to take an eternity, lasted only a fraction of a second.

Armor protection for Huey pilots left much to be desired. The armored seats gave limited protection against fire from the rear and sides. The armor plate extended from the base of the seat up as high as the armpits of a normal-sized man and was effective only against small-arms fire. The frontal armor—the "chicken plate" that chopper pilots wore—protected the abdomen and chest area. Everything else was exposed to fire from the front. The quarter-inch-thick windshield was the only other barrier between the pilot and the projectiles, and it couldn't stop anything. A section of it blew away; then I felt a bullet glance off the rubber sole of my left boot. Three rounds impacted on the inside of my armored seat on each side of me, chest high, and fell harmlessly to the floor. (They were retrieved later.) It was as if the hand of God had intervened to save me.

The noise of the firing AK was deafening as it resonated with deep-toned, cannonlike sounds. Shrapnel from the AK's projectiles and the aircraft structure tore into my right leg above and below the knee. Simultaneously, my right hand was hit by shrapnel and caused me to jerk back on the cyclic. In that minisecond, my right leg reacted spasmodically to the shrapnel impact. It twitched backward, then strongly and uncontrollably forward, causing the nose of the helicopter to yaw violently to the right. The combination of blows to my right hand and leg, the spasmodic reaction of my limbs, and a bullet glancing off my left shoe resulted in the chopper jumping into the air in a nose-high, right-yaw attitude. We were temporarily out of control, but I had the presence of mind to bring in maximum power to keep the helicopter airborne in its unusual attitude while I exclaimed, "Aw, hell, I'm hit!"

I felt my copilot's grip on the controls as he overcame my involuntary reactions. Chamberlain brought the helicopter under control and kept it level. When I got over the initial shock of the hits to my leg and hand, I realized I hadn't suffered any disabling injuries. I got back on the controls with Chamberlain as we recovered from the unusual attitude and finally accelerated into forward flight. I felt the presence of Heinold about to get me out of my seat to check my wounds. I told him I was all right and didn't need assistance. Heinold persisted and was about to flip my seat back to get to me.

"I'm okay, Heinold. I'm not hurt."

"Are you sure you don't need any help?" he asked.

"I'll be all right. It's not serious." It was the shock of the moment and the uncertainty of my injuries that had caused me to say I'd been hit.

In those seconds of utter confusion while the helicopter was temporarily out of control, a drama was being played out in the rear of the aircraft. When I initiated the takeoff, Horvath was in the process of pulling the trooper onto the ship but hadn't yet brought him aboard. The loss of control caused the man to slip away from the chopper, but Horvath managed to retain his grasp of the man's wrist. Fortunately, as the trooper slipped from the deck of the chopper, his legs straddled its skids and prevented him from falling farther. By the time Horvath managed to pull him into the helicopter, we'd regained control about sixty feet in the air and were headed for Moc Hoa.

When Chamberlain saw the enemy rounds impacting around me and heard me say I'd been hit, he had immediately called Concert Bravo. "The aircraft commander's been hit. We're heading for Moc Hoa."

One of the Cobra pilots came on the net. "Sorry we didn't see the source of fire or we'd have blasted him. We'll cover you till you get to Moc Hoa. How serious is the AC?"

By now the radio traffic was getting out of hand. When I had alerted the crew to my wounds, I wanted Chamberlain to take control of the aircraft. I didn't know the extent of my injuries and may have been incapacitated. When I realized that my wounds were minor, I said as much to my crew, but by that time Chamberlain had made his transmission to the C&C. I came on the net before the nature of my condition was misinterpreted.

"Concert Bravo, this is Dustoff 88. I'm okay. They just grazed me; it's just a scratch. I'll see you back at Moc Hoa. Also, you Cobra jocks couldn't have seen the VC gunner. He was hiding in the elephant grass waiting for me. There was so little light when he fired at me that I couldn't make him out. All I saw were the muzzle flashes."

My transmission to the people in the area eliminated any anxiety that might have been generated by Chamberlain's original call. However, C&C had already sent the information to his base. The message soon reached Cy at the 82d, and he was about to launch a rescue mission on my behalf. He was eventually apprised of the true nature of my injuries before an unnecessary mission was launched. Otherwise, he probably would have been on his way to repay the favor I had done him a month or so earlier.

It was totally dark as Chamberlain flew on to Moc Hoa, so he turned on the navigation lights. That was normal procedure in the high-density area around Long Binh but not in the delta. In my tired state I hadn't noticed the lights or the fact that Chamberlain had leveled off at five hundred feet. He wasn't familiar with the area and headed in a direction he thought was for Moc Hoa but instead put us over Cambodia. The Viet Cong let him know about the error by sending up a volley of beautiful red tracers. Their aim was worse than poor, but I still told Chamberlain to turn off the lights and climb to a higher altitude. I had to have been tired, because I was usually aware of deviations from procedures.

I feared that my crew was also approaching a state of exhaustion. They hadn't eaten since breakfast, more than twelve hours earlier. For some reason I didn't have hunger pangs or a desire for food. I was probably running on nervous energy, and I suspected that the others were too. The last two and a half hours of flying had been traumatic and drained us of all normal feelings and reactions. The Viet Cong's constant, intense firing, the continual search for the wounded, and the success of rescuing so many lost souls from the grasp of the enemy were more than a person should experience.

Thoughts of the last few hours raced through my weary mind as I sat back to rest while Chamberlain flew.

After landing and engine shutdown, I didn't move out of my seat and just watched as the wounded were unloaded. There was no hurry anymore; we could relax and take a breather. Those who were hungry could get something to eat. After a while I felt an intense thirst and alighted from the helicopter. I asked one of the Green Berets for water. Concert Bravo landed a few minutes after we'd unloaded the wounded and came over to talk to me. He introduced himself as Capt. Harry L. Purdy. In the faint light of the landing pad, I couldn't make out his facial features, but he had a solid look about him that seemed standard with all Green Beret officers. He seemed to be quite tall, but from my five-foot-four disadvantage that assessment could have been wrong. He complimented me and the crew on a job well done and said he never believed that any of the surrounded troops would be recovered. "Your work and that of your crew was out of this world. When you landed in that triangular fort and the VC opened up from all sides, I thought you were goners. Then you went in again. I shouldn't have asked you to do that."

I replied that it was the second attempt inside the fort that convinced me that the extractions couldn't be accomplished by directions from the air. "The wounded troops had to be part of the evacuation process. They had to help me by showing themselves in that tall grass. It was up to them to try to make it within the confines of my racetrack pattern. It took the wounded soldiers a while to get the idea, but they caught on. That was the reason for our success, pure and simple."

Captain Purdy agreed. He said he had to make a report of the action to his headquarters, and we bid each other good night.

Heinold came up to me after the wounded were dispatched to the medical facility and asked to see my injuries. I showed him my right hand, which had stopped bleeding, and he looked at my right leg. There were dozens of small perforations from the shrapnel that had impacted above and below my knee. Most of the bleeding had stopped. I was lucky indeed to come out of the action with such minor wounds. Heinold recommended that I have the leg X-rayed when I returned to the base, and I agreed. He also reminded me that

I hadn't had my eyedrops; they should have been administered at six that evening, more than two hours before. I realized that I'd also forgotten to apply the drops at noon because of the press of missions. I'd forgotten one treatment and was more than two hours behind schedule with the latest. It was not the first time I forgot the eyedrops and probably wouldn't be the last.

I saw Horvath checking the hits on our helicopter's tail area and asked if there was any reason we couldn't make it back to Binh Thuy that night. He said he wanted to make a complete inspection of the aircraft before declaring it fit for flight.

"Okay, Horvath, but make it snappy. I don't want to remain here any longer than I have to. I'll have the copilot assist you."

I told Chamberlain to help Horvath because I wanted to return to the base that night. He cautioned me about the late hour, the distance to the base, and the fact that the helicopter had sustained considerable damage.

Chamberlain also mentioned that his airspeed indicator didn't work. I replied that the pitot tube probably had been shot away by the last burst of gunfire but it wasn't necessary to know how fast we were flying. The engine torque meter would give us all the information we needed. The only time I observed my airspeed was during emergencies or during dives into pickup areas.

I also told Chamberlain that the Moc Hoa Special Forces compound had a reputation for being hit by Viet Cong mortar attacks, which at times were heavy and inflicted considerable damage. "I've had enough of the Viet Cong for one day," I told him. "I'm not about to give them another chance at me if I can help it, okay?"

"Roger, that," he replied. Then he went off to help Horvath with the inspection.

Heinold was busy washing down the passenger compartment with a fire hose. Hauling the wounded troops had left the rear deck bloodied. If not washed within a reasonable amount of time, the aircraft developed a disagreeable odor. As the helicopter was cleaned and checked for damage, I had a chance to relax for the first time. I asked a Green Beret if there was coffee available. He said he'd get me some and in no time brought me a canteen cup full. The hot black coffee was just what I needed. I found a seat, savored the aroma, and slowly sipped the hot brew. It's amazing how little is required at times to make a person feel so contented, so pleased, so relaxed.

I sat back and watched my crew go through its paces. Heinold washed and tidied up the crew compartment while Chamberlain and Horvath climbed up and down the helicopter checking it out. As I finished my coffee, Horvath said that except for the bullet holes, the loss of the airspeed indicator, and the damaged windshield, the chopper was flyable. It was the verdict I'd expected all along. He added that the main rotor had taken three hits; I figured that was responsible for the unusual vibrations.

Chamberlain added that two of the ship's radios had been hit and were inoperable. "All we have left is our fox mike for communication purposes."

"Well, if you're both satisfied with your inspection, we'll move out," I said. "Tell Heinold to finish with his cleanup, and I'll tell the Special Forces people of our intentions. They can contact our operations and let them know we're on our way home."

After a couple of hours on the ground at Moc Hoa, we were rested and prepared for the flight back. We boarded our chopper, cranked it up, and took off. Except for the slight vibration, the ship reacted normally to control inputs. I felt the air coming through the gaping hole in my part of the shot-up windshield.

I noticed that my airspeed indicator read zero. "Well, Chamberlain, it seems that we're moving right along even though our two airspeed indicators aren't giving any readings. You can tell your friends you've learned to fly by the seat of your pants."

Chamberlain nodded. "I'm as pleased as you are to get out of Moc Hoa tonight. I don't ever remember having a day like today. Things at Long Binh were never this hectic. Is every day in the delta like this?"

"Not exactly," I answered.

The flight to Binh Thuy took about an hour. After parking the chopper in one of the revetments, I disembarked and had Chamberlain go through the shutdown procedure. Cy Simmons and a group of my friends, including some of the Seawolves, greeted us.

Cy shook my hand. "I was ready to go get you. One minute we had you shot up, and the next you're okay. What the hell went on?"

"It all happened so fast. I got zapped in the hand, took a bunch of shrapnel in the leg, and a bullet glanced off the sole of my shoe. I told the crew I was hit so Chamberlain could take control of the chopper. He, in his excited state, told the C&C, who didn't waste time and quickly relayed it all to his base. The report made it to Can Tho, and then you were brought on line. However, it wasn't long until you received the additional information that I was okay. That was it and here we are."

Con Jaburg was present. "It looks as if you're the new magnet ass around here now. That thing you flew back will have to be junked."

"It probably will, Con. Well, gang, I have a mess of paperwork ahead of me and my afteraction reports to fill out. After that I have to report to the 3d Surg to check the shrapnel in my leg. For your information, we logged eleven hours of flight time today, and I've been on duty more than eighteen hours. As soon as I complete my work, I'm hitting the sack. I'll see you all tomorrow."

Cy and the gang understood and departed. I finished my paperwork in about half an hour and reported to the hospital. The X ray showed more than thirty pieces of metal and plastic embedded immediately above and below the knee but no further injuries. The doctor swabbed the area with disinfectant, told me to let him know if any infection developed, and released me for duty.

On the way to my quarters, I was too tired to stop by operations, as was my custom. It was a little after midnight when I got home, poured myself three fingers of Chivas Regal, and downed it. I turned out the lights, hoping to get some badly needed sleep, but I was overcome by a postcombat high. I'd experienced this before. It slowly took over my whole being; it was a wonderful feeling. I seemed to float in a sea of euphoria as the pleasantness of the moment totally consumed my body and mind. I relived the flights in and out of the combat area, the enemy blasting away at us all the while, and the mad dashes away from their projectiles. Even the narrow escape from serious injury and death when the AK was emptied at me seemed to add to my euphoric state. I floated about in the midst of an ocean of recollection until I lost the sensation of time and finally dropped off to sleep.

It was almost noon when I awoke the next day. I showered, put on fresh clothes, and had some coffee at the officers' mess, then went to operations to check the duty roster. I had completely forgotten who was scheduled for first up that day. The way our tours of duty came around, I could have been scheduled for second or third up that night. As it turned out, I wasn't on the schedule. I was free for the entire day.

The RTO told me that Wayne Aoki was first up and had been busy since coming on duty. "Looks as if it's another full day. I sure had one yesterday," I commented. "Is Major Simmons around?"

The RTO said the major had gone to the PX and should be back soon. I didn't have anything to do, so I took over the RTO's duties while he went to lunch. Aoki had a couple of missions pending. He made his reports as he went in for the pickups and again when he made it back up to altitude. After his last report, I told Aoki that there weren't any other missions and he could return to the base and get some lunch if he wished. He rogered my transmission and said he expected to land in about ten minutes.

Aoki came into operations and greeted me in his usual droll manner. "I hear you damn near bought the farm yesterday. The VC almost shot your ass off. It would never have happened if I'd been with you. When you try to outwit an Oriental, you need the assistance of another Oriental. How many times have I told you that? You need the firm hand and advice of a son of Nippon."

"Look, Wayne, the only heritage of your Japanese ancestry you've retained is your attraction to sake. You can't even eat raw fish, and I know you don't care for rice. So how's it been going today?"

"I'm glad to see you're okay, Mike. You know you had us worried for a while yesterday. I would have stayed to see you when you returned, but I had to get some sleep because I was first up today. It's been busy all morning—a lot of missions but not too much enemy activity in the pickup areas. This is the first break we've had all morning. Want to join me in a little lunch?"

"Glad to, Wayne. I just got up and all I've had is some coffee. I'll have to wait for the RTO to return from his lunch. Then I'll join you in the mess."

"Okay, Mike. I'm starved. All that saving lives and cheating death has given me a big appetite. I screwed up and didn't have any breakfast. See you at lunch."

Aoki and I were close friends. He was from the big island of Hawaii and a graduate of the university system that his state saw fit to offer all its citizens. He was not the most gifted aviator I'd known, but he was dependable and I liked his attitude toward work. Aoki had an odd sense of humor, and I never knew when to take him seriously. For example, he proudly asserted that as a 100 percent pure Japanese he was also a Buddhist. I didn't know if he was pulling our Christian legs about his religion. It was often hard to tell.

Whether he was joking or not, I thought Aoki's pride in his background was admirable. I suppose that me being a first-generation American was another factor in my acceptance of Aoki as a friend. We shared a common background. His parents had arrived in Hawaii on a boat, the same way mine got to America. Consequently, we both were victims of discriminatory practices by the power structures of our respective communities. Such actions by elements of our society were shameful and cowardly and will probably never change. Discrimination and prejudice are as American as apple pie. Wayne Aoki was a good man.

When I arrived for lunch, Aoki and his copilot were almost done with theirs. I brought Aoki the latest mission. It was a pickup south of Ca Mau, a flight of about an hour. "Sorry, Wayne, but that's why you're getting flight and combat pay. The taxpayers appreciate getting their money's worth, you know."

"Save your bad jokes for someone who cares, Mike. I'll see you when I get back."

"That reminds me, Wayne, if you don't come back from this mission, can I have the bottles of Crown Royal you've got stashed in your room?"

"Don't hold your breath, Mike. I'll be back. I've placed a mark on my opened bottle and I'll have your ass if one drop is missing."

Such a tête-à-tête was standard fare for dustoff pilots. It eased tensions and let a little bit of humor trickle into an otherwise potentially disastrous situation.

Aoki went about his duties and I checked in with the boss, Cy Simmons. There were a few thoughts I wanted to share with him. I found him in his office. He moved his PX purchases off the only chair in the place except for his so I could sit down.

"Well, Mike, you sure had a tiger by the tail yesterday afternoon. How do you feel now that you've had a chance to get some rest?"

"Cy, as I began flying that mission yesterday, I didn't think it would be any better or worse than any others. But things got rougher and rougher and tougher and tougher. I saw men who were horribly wounded, men who desperately wanted to live. I've seen soldiers in worse shape, but their comrades were with them and did everything to help them. These poor souls were on their own. They didn't have anyone to ease their pain and suffering until I came along with my crew. That was hours after they'd been cut off and surrounded by the Viet Cong.

"I pity those poor bastards who got caught in that wringer and those who didn't make it," I continued. "My crew did some damn good work yesterday. Not one of them wavered performing his duties and never remotely suggested that we get the hell out of there. You know that Chamberlain flew his first mission with my crew. We borrowed him from the 45th a couple of days ago. As for Heinold and Horvath, I can't say enough about their performances. They really stuck their necks out. I couldn't have pulled off that mission without their absolute commitment to their duties. Cy, I think they deserve some reward, some recognition for their actions. They put out more than a normal dustoff day's effort."

"What do you think we should do, Mike? Remember, you led the mission all the way. Any recommendation for an award has to include you also."

"I know, Cy. I'm recommending the entire crew for the Silver Star. I'd hope the Special Forces people we supported would take the initiative in this matter. It would have greater impact if they did."

"Mike, let's be practical about the matter. The people we support are grateful for our efforts, but they have priorities of their own and just as many administrative responsibilities as we do. They don't have the time to initiate awards for people they don't know and are not likely to see again. If you want to recommend the crew for an award, you've got to do it yourself."

"I get the drift, Cy. I want every member of my crew to get the Silver Star for what they did in that hellhole on the Cambodian border."

"I think you're on the right track," Cy said. "I believe the Silver Star is appropriate in this instance. Get individual statements from each of your crew, including yourself, and submit your recommendations through channels. I'll pay a personal visit to the commander of the Special Forces unit at Moc Hoa and get supporting documentation from him and the C&C who was involved in the action. That way we'll close the loop with everybody involved and there shouldn't be a problem getting the award approved. It's too bad we can't get statements from the people you saved. I'm sure they'd be more than happy to help."

That subject being out of the way, Cy and I got down to the more pressing problems of the day. We discussed upcoming losses of aviators who were completing their tours and decided who'd be next to upgrade to aircraft commander. We also ironed out some administrative matters.

The nurses of the 3d Surg had a party scheduled that night, and the 82d's aviators were invited as usual. Cy and I planned to attend, so we left for our quarters to wash up. We stopped at operations and checked with the RTO, who said that everything was running smoothly. Aoki had been busy all day and was returning to base.

After a quick shower, I donned my "drinking shirt" and slacks and was ready to party. The soiree was in full swing when I arrived. Most of the dustoff pilots not on the schedule were there, and some who were dating nurses at the hospital had staked out their territories already. Pecararo and his sidekick, Aberle, were there. Pecararo was trying to put the make on one of the nurses but had competition from a doctor. The situation had all the possibilities of degenerating into a confrontation.

Most of the hospital folks had heard of my squeaker the night before, and many asked if I'd recovered from my brush with the grim reaper. I hadn't realized how quickly the staff learned about the mission and how close I came to being seriously injured. It was heartening to know that so many people, some unknown to me, were concerned about my safety and well-being. There was no doubt that their feelings toward me were indicative of their concerns for each and every dustoff pilot.

The party was a resounding success. Everyone had a fine time, and as usual a few had too much firewater and were out cold. Some dustoffers were successful in the pursuit of their prime objectives, but Pecararo was not as fortunate. He struck out, but so did the doctor who'd been interfering with his plan of attack. The objective of the two lotharios flew the coop when she saw trouble brewing between them. In a way, Pecararo won. The two came to blows after leaving the party, and Pecararo decked the doctor with one punch.

Parties were welcome breaks for those who saw the war on a daily basis. They offered a chance to let off steam. It was comforting to be near and talk to round-eyed women who carried with them the hint of Chanel or some other fragrance. Just to hear the higher pitch of a woman's voice was reassuring to anyone who'd spent hours listening to fox mike radio transmissions mixed with the resonance of automatic weapons.

I spent a relaxed evening and had a good time, then left at a reasonable hour. I knew there was a lot of work the next day. I wanted to assemble my crew members and tell them that I had recommended them for an award. After that would come the hard part. Each would have to write a statement describing what occurred during the mission. Most people can't write clearly and they hate the task; my men were no exception. But after a week of writing and rewriting, they produced statements that appeared to be composed by people who had studied the English language for a few years.

Cy Simmons made his flight to Moc Hoa and got corroborating statements from the Special Forces commander and Concert Bravo, Capt. Harry L. Purdy. His was particularly glowing in praise of the crew and the manner in which the mission had been executed. Photographs of the battle area were part of the recommendation.

All of the efforts to prepare the recommendation took time and were sandwiched into the daily work schedule. For example, it took about a month to receive Captain Purdy's statement. The photographs took another month, and we were near the Christmas holidays before the package was completed. By then Cy Simmons had been reassigned to company headquarters and replaced as commander by Capt. Ed Moate. I recall Ed's statement to me after forwarding the recommendation to higher headquarters. "The package looks good, Mike. But don't be surprised if the award is downgraded to a Distinguished Flying Cross."

"Yeah, I know, Ed. At least I've done my duty and carried out my responsibilities to my crew. We'll be thankful for whatever the big wheels decide to dole out."

The recommendation for awarding the Silver Stars was in the administrative pipeline. I had no idea how it would be received and forgot about it. There were more important matters to attend to. There were missions to fly, and it was time to make our monthly request to the company for additional aviators. I hoped for a reduction in enemy activities, which would make the holiday period enjoyable. There were rumors of a truce, but only time would tell.

15 A Father and Son Combat Team

It was December 1969 and we were anticipating the holiday season at Binh Thuy. Back home there was a family event of significant importance. In mid-December Mike Jr. completed the army flight training program, which he began when I left for my second tour in Vietnam, and received his wings and rank as a warrant officer. He also received orders to go to Vietnam.

Mike graduated from flight school and celebrated his twentieth birthday, a situation similar to mine when I finished flight training twenty-seven years earlier. With a son who was a full-fledged army aviator, I should have asked myself what I was doing in Vietnam. I was flying combat missions as a "peter pilot" when most military aviators my age were drawing retirement pay. The majority couldn't pass a flight physical after twenty-seven years of military aviation duty. Although I'd been grounded when diagnosed with glaucoma, I received a waiver to continue flying.

I received a wonderful letter from Ethel telling me about Mike's graduation. She went to Hunter Army Air Field to pin on his wings and sent a picture of the two of them after the graduation ceremony. She was as beautiful and trim as ever, but Mike appeared to have put on a little weight. I figured that flight school must have been getting easier. I had been almost skin and bones by the time I graduated.

I was proud to have my son follow in my footsteps. I showed the picture to Ed Moate, Con Jaburg, and Buddy Barnes. They were delighted about the news that my son had received his wings but were noncommittal about his coming to Vietnam. I hadn't told anyone within my circle of friends that I had a son in flight training. Ethel's letter didn't indicate when Mike would report for duty in the war zone, but I figured he'd have a month or so at home before coming over and would write and tell me the date soon enough. The news about Mike remained the topic of conversation around the base.

Many holiday activities were scheduled in the Can Tho–Binh Thuy complex. Parties were planned by Paddy Radar Control, the 3d Surg, the Seawolves, the civilians of Lear Seigler Inc. (LSI), and IV Corps headquarters. The latter two were at Can Tho. Attendance at all festivities depended on the tactical situation, but for a change even the Viet Cong seemed to be in a cooperative mood. Maybe they also needed a breather, because they drastically reduced their activities during the holidays. For a while, first up day and night were able to handle all evacuations without help from second up. Nobody had to log flight time in double digits for a day's duty.

One of the best soirees was the one at Don Parcell's place in Can Tho. He and his LSI crew put on a terrific party. There was ample food and wine, plus women to add to the spirit of the occasion. More formal festivities at IV Corps provided an excellent opportunity to mix with the people in our chain of command.

The wildest party was at the navy officers' club on New Year's Eve. Everyone in the Binh Thuy–Can Tho area was there. They came from the air force, the hospital, the Seawolves, Can Tho, and the dustoffers. I left the party at 3:00 A.M., and when I returned at noon the next day some diehards were still sitting around drinking. Perhaps they had left earlier and returned after getting their second wind. Soon, others who had rested after the previous night's festivities returned, and the partying resumed. The barbecue fires were rekindled, steaks were brought from the mess, and holiday gift packages fresh from the States were opened and shared. It was as if the New Year's Eve party had never stopped.

The first-up crew was called out early New Year's Day. Because I was second up, I didn't participate in the renewed activities, although the need for second up didn't materialize. Not joining in the drinking was probably the best thing I could have done. As I sat there sipping coffee and watching the revelers, I noticed Con and Buddy at one of the tables with John Rodebaugh, a new dustoff pilot. They were a sad sight. It was only a matter of time before they'd succumb to the effects of their bacchanalian activities. I would have been with them but for the grace of the flight schedule. Eventually the partying ran its course and the tactical situation returned to missions as usual.

Many of the old heads completed their tours and were gone. Bissell and Simmons were transferred. I received a Christmas card from Aoki, who had finished his tour and was on leave on the big island of Hawaii. I missed the old gang, but their replacements filled the gaps well and were into the swing of things, including partying. Our latest additions were 1st Lt. Stu Robinson, WO Bob Singleton, and Rodebaugh, all fresh out of flight school.

Rodebaugh arrived as a first lieutenant, but within a week he was promoted to captain and took over Aoki's slot in operations. Following personnel practices of the times, he made captain after only two years of commissioned service. He had been in schools learning to be an officer and aviator. At the 82d he had his first opportunity to perform the duties of a commissioned officer.

The arrival of the replacement aviators increased my duties as training officer. I gave them orientation flights and training flights, taught them how to fly dustoff, and introduced them to combat. Their flying under instrument conditions left much to be desired, but in time they learned to handle their aircraft in the worst weather. We brought them along slowly but methodically.

Postmission training sessions gave me time to check our pilots to see how well they operated. On a few occasions I used the sessions to upgrade a person to aircraft commander. Rex Smith was our latest.

"That was all right, Rex," I told him after he completed a training session. "Congratulations. You're an aircraft commander now."

"You mean you were giving me an AC check ride?" he inquired. "If I'd known that, I'd have busted it sure as hell."

Rex was a young string bean of a man who worked well with the other pilots. He always showed a positive attitude and accepted constructive criticism as it was intended. I knew he'd make an excellent aircraft commander, and he didn't let me down.

Except for Capt. Ed Moate, the commander, and myself, the unit's aviators were in their early twenties. Although they required considerable supervision, their dedication to the dustoff mission equaled that of their predecessors. However, one slipped up badly. He was one of the "older" ACs, older in the sense that he had less than six weeks remaining in Vietnam. He came to me early one afternoon when he was scheduled first up night. He said he was going into Can Tho on personal business.

"Don't forget, you're first up tonight. Don't be late getting back," I said.

"I know. I'll be back in plenty of time."

As it turned out, flesh was weaker than the spirit and he became involved with a local beauty. When he didn't show up for work, second up took over. Our Romeo didn't return until 8:00 P.M., apologizing for being late, and indicated he was ready to take over as first up. In his condition he wouldn't have been safe riding a carnival merry-go-round.

I was mad. I told him that until his tour of duty in Vietnam was over, he was a "prisoner of war" and was not to leave the compound without my permission or the commander's. "If you want to take the matter up with the CO, go ahead," I shouted.

He said he'd go along with what I offered (a wise choice). He knew if he contested my method of aviator control, Ed Moate would come down on him harder.

Moate was new to his position as commanding officer; the 82d was his first command. But he quickly showed his pilots that he could be as tough as the next man. He took his turn on the duty roster, the same as the others. Once when he was flying second up, his flight path crossed that of first up, Mike Adams. Moate was cruising at two thousand feet when he saw Adams hedgehopping over the rice paddies, buzzing the farmers working their fields. Combat was dangerous enough without adding the unnecessary risk of low-leveling at full speed and missing people and obstacles by a few feet, sometimes inches.

When Adams returned to the base, Moate called him aside and told him that his aircraft commander orders were revoked. He was to fly as copilot until further notice. The action was a severe blow to Adams's ego, but he knew better than to argue. He'd screwed up and violated unit SOP just for the sake of showing off.

On another occasion when Ed and I were in operations lounging around, an urgent life-or-death mission was given to me. My medic had gone to the 3d Surg to pick up medical supplies and hadn't returned. Ed didn't hesitate. "Let's go, Mike. I'll be your medic on this mission." That was the way Ed worked. He didn't feel it beneath his dignity to work at a level other than commander.

Ed Moate's attitude was indicative of the way medical people worked in Vietnam. When Colonel Stanley, the brigade surgeon, arranged to fly with me as the medic, I told him he could be out for the entire day because the shift was 12 hours. He said he understood. He knew that our pilots often flew 140 hours a month and our medics and crew chiefs as much as 160 hours—even more on occasion. "I just thought I'd give one of them a rest," he said. "Besides, it would be nice to know if I still can function as a medical technician with the bare essentials your crewmen have."

As it turned out, we were gone for most of the day, and the colonel got his wish. The brigade surgeon worked like a real trouper. When our shift was supposed to be over, we were still on a mission. By the time we returned to base and parked the chopper, we'd been on duty for more than thirteen hours. Colonel Stanley complimented the crew on its work, and I acknowledged his contribution to our efforts. If he had any fear of flying combat missions, it disappeared on the first pickup. He did extremely well.

When not flying, I attended to my administrative chores, filling out the too numerous and idiotic reports invented by a hierarchy that had nothing better to do. One day I had finished my paperwork and was monitoring the RTO and his mission board when the phone rang. The RTO answered, looked in my direction, and said, "It's for you, sir."

The call was from a captain with the aviator assignments section in Saigon. "Your son has arrived in country and wants to be in your outfit," the captain told me. "I wanted to check with you before I made that assignment. Will it be all right to send him down to the 82d?"

Without giving the matter much thought, I said, "Certainly, send him right down." I hadn't seen Mike for almost a year, when I was returning to Vietnam and he was going into flight training. It would be good to see him again. But the situation raised problems not encountered by any combatants I'd known. We would be the only father and son pilots ever assigned to the same unit and flying together in combat.

Because I'd be one of his supervisors, there'd be the possibility for preferential treatment or, more accurately, perceived preferential treatment. We were a small detachment with twelve pilots, and Mike and I would represent one sixth of the unit's aviators. I'd have to be careful. There couldn't be any indication, not the slightest hint, of favoritism in assignments or placement on the duty roster.

Then there was my social life. I was the partying type, and that would have to change. After all, Mike and I were writing home to the same person—I to my wife and he to his mother. I had my work cut out. But even with all the problems that could arise, I was happy to know he was going to join the outfit. He'd be a part of the finest dustoff detachment in Vietnam.

I told Ed Moate about Mike's upcoming arrival. He congratulated me and said he was surprised that the command allowed us to be together. I voiced my concern that some of the pilots might have misgivings about Mike's presence because of my position in the 82d.

Ed put that thought aside. "Mike, I've known you for a long time. I'm absolutely sure you'll handle this matter with fairness and impartiality."

I hadn't told anyone else about the arrival of my son, but it was not long before everyone knew. I received all sorts of comments and advice; most of my friends thought it was great that he was joining me. The consensus was that if he had to be an aviator in Vietnam, he couldn't have a better assignment than with the 82d working with his dad. But there were also the pessimists who visualized us being shot down and killed in the same aircraft. Then there were the "legal minds" who claimed it was against regulations to have a father and son in combat together.

Jaburg was all smiles when I told him about Mike's assignment. "When does he arrive in Binh Thuy?" he asked.

"I forgot to ask the assignment officer, Con," I replied. "Most likely in a couple of days. The 45th Company will probably fly him down here. We should be getting a call to let us know he's on the way."

I knew from experience with the replacement depot that Mike wouldn't get a chance to call me. He probably was a prisoner of the same second lieutenant who wouldn't let me use the phone.

On January 6, I was flying second up and was on a couple of missions while first up was operating in another sector. I was airborne when the RTO raised me on the fox mike to tell me that the 45th was flying my son to Binh Thuy that morning.

My missions kept me busy for more than two hours before I could return to the base. I landed, shut down in the revetment, looked around, and saw a group of our troops off to the side. As I alighted from the chopper, I saw Mike come out of the crowd to greet me.

"Hi, Dad. I'm here," he said.

"Around here I'm not your dad. But I'm glad to see you and have you with me in the 82d. Let's go to my quarters, where we can talk."

My quarters were in a long, two-story building in a central location in the Binh Thuy complex. Each officer had a private room, somewhat small but adequate. My room was next to the detachment commander's. Mike hadn't been assigned quarters, but I knew he'd be on the second floor. Most of the quarters weren't air-conditioned, but mine was, thanks to Don Parcell and his friends. The weather in the delta was always warm and humid. It took little exertion to be covered with perspiration.

I turned on the air conditioner when we entered my quarters, then sat on the bed while Mike took the only chair in the place. It was good to see him again. He was wearing a new two-piece Nomex flight suit, the first I'd seen. We'd heard about the new fire-retardant material used in the suits but hadn't received any. Mike said that each aviator was issued three sets before leaving for Vietnam and everyone in the Saigon area was wearing them. That last bit of information didn't surprise me at all. The rear-echelon troops were always the first to get equipment meant for survival in combat.

"How's your mother doing, Mike? Has she been able to get to the store and do her shopping? I know how much she loves to get out to buy things whether she needs them or not. Shopping has always been one of the pleasures in her life."

"She's okay and so are Patty, Jean, and John, who as usual still gets colds. Mom took him to see the doctor, and he told her to have

John's tonsils removed. She's going to have that done as soon as you get home, so you know what you can expect."

"What did your mother have to say about your coming to Vietnam? Did you tell her you were going to request assignment to the 82d Dustoff?"

"She didn't like the idea. But I told her you'd be home soon and there was no sense in delaying my arrival in country. I'd still have to come here and put in my year of combat. She accepted that but told me to be real careful. I had to laugh when she said that. She has no idea I'm with you."

"Maybe she meant for you to listen to those who know more than you about flying and to learn from them. You'll have your first flight with me either tomorrow or the day after. All new arrivals get their orientations and training flights with me."

"Well, I'm anxious to get some flying time, Dad. I haven't flown since graduation."

"Flying time is one thing that's not lacking around here. All of us have flown our asses off since coming to the delta. I've repeatedly asked for augmentation of aviator strength, but all I get is a few people for a few days from the 45th. I go through the same drill every month with Roler and Temperelli. I've already flown well over a thousand hours in the last nine months, and there isn't an aviator in the 82d who won't have more than a thousand combat hours upon completion of his tour. It won't be long before you'll be looking forward to some time off. That will be your primary concern, not the flying."

"Look, Dad, I'm ready to do whatever is necessary. I won't rock the boat or do anything stupid. How about my quarters? Where do I put my bags and personal things, and where do I draw my combat equipment?"

"Rex Smith and Stu Robinson have taken down some walls and made sort of a suite out of three rooms upstairs. They have an extra bed up there. Put your things in that area and tell the officer in charge of billeting that I put you there. The only combat gear you get here is your chicken plate and an M16 rifle. You'll keep the chicken plate in your locker, but the rifle must be checked out of the arms room before each mission and turned in immediately after return to base. It's a lot of unnecessary red tape dreamed up by the administrative geniuses and the high brass. I never take my rifle with me. I can't use it and fly the helicopter at the same time, so I leave it in the arms room. I've never signed it out; they can keep the damn thing. That way I don't have to clean it, and I never worry about losing it. If I were you, I'd do the same."

"I've already met Rex Smith," Mike said. "He told me that you made him an aircraft commander a while back. He said he was surprised the way you did it."

"Yeah, Rex is a good pilot—very sensible and dependable. You'll probably fly with him a lot. Mike, there's one very important thing you have to understand. I can't give you any special consideration in assignment of missions or position on the duty roster. You'll take your turn like all the rest. This is a small outfit, and anything out of the ordinary would be noticed. I hope you understand. I must make certain there's absolutely no display of favoritism. If I gave anyone special treatment, it would have an adverse effect on morale and we can't have that. The CO and I agree with that policy. He'll treat you right if you cooperate with him. Just do your duty and you'll be okay."

"All right, Dad. I understand. I'm still not over jet lag. I'd like to get some shut-eye. Guess I'll take my bags upstairs and rest a bit."

"Okay, Mike. Glad you're here. I know you're tired. Why don't you rest here where it's air-conditioned? I'll dash off a short letter to your mother tonight and let her know you arrived safely. Maybe we can get an orientation flight tomorrow."

So ended our first meeting in Vietnam. It was hard to believe that Mike was an army aviator and we'd be flying together, maybe even draw fire from the Viet Cong. Being the only father and son pilots in the same unit in combat was a signal honor. An unusual set of circumstances had to fall into place for this to happen: There had to be a war; both father and son had to decide on careers as military pilots; they had to survive the most demanding and intensive course of instruction conceived by man; the father had to stay healthy and pass about twenty annual flight physicals (in my case twenty-eight); and both had to agree to serve together, because regulations allowed either one to defer the assignment as long as the other was in combat.

I was proud of my son and highly honored that he followed in my footsteps. Con Jaburg put it right. When Mike arrived in the 82d, Con said, "I'd give anything to have my son join me as a pilot in my outfit and fly with me in combat."

I was second up on the day shift when Mike was scheduled to fly with me. We were ready to go by six in the morning. As was my habit, I had Mike perform the preflight while I drank my coffee in the officers' mess. Mike got the same treatment meted out to all new aviators.

As soon as we received a mission, Mike and I were airborne. Orientations in the 82d were conducted while regular missions were in progress. I pointed out prominent landmarks, noted clues to locations in various sectors, and stressed the importance of knowing one's position at all times.

During Mike's orientation, he was shown the immense size of the evacuation territory, close to thirteen thousand square miles. In due time he'd become so familiar with the delta that he wouldn't have to check his charts to set a heading to the next pickup. There was a lot for a new pilot to learn and not enough time to be taught as thoroughly as I preferred.

As soon as our missions were completed, and none were pending, I headed for the special rice paddy I used for training. Among other things, I wanted all 82d aircraft commanders to be proficient in autorotations. If their helicopters lost power, they had to be able to autorotate to preselected spots and land safely. Rich Pecararo coined the phrase, "You can't make aircraft commander unless you can hit the spot." He generalized the criteria, but it was true that autorotations were a crucial part of an aircraft commander's training.

Autorotation is a helicopter's ace in the hole when engine power is lost. It is similar to the ability of a fixed-wing aircraft to glide. A helicopter in autorotation loses altitude faster and more dramatically than a gliding, fixed-wing aircraft. But a person is safer in a helicopter without power than in an airplane in the same condition. The airplane must maintain airspeed all the way to the ground, and the speed causes damage, injury, and often death. A helicopter's descent and minimal forward speed in autorotation can be dramatically reduced before ground contact. Properly performed, an autorotation can be completed with a featherlike landing.

When Mike and I arrived over the training area, I explained that the objective of the session was to illustrate different methods of autorotation. I demonstrated an autorotation from two thousand feet and landed next to a small shrub. Then I showed him a high-speed, low-level engine failure from about fifty feet and landed next to the same shrub. Then I let Mike try an autorotation from altitude. When he landed satisfactorily in the middle of the rice paddy, I said, "Okay, but you didn't land next to the shrub."

"I didn't know you wanted me to do that. Besides, you can't be sure you can do it at will."

"You want to bet?" I asked.

For a first attempt at autorotation, Mike did well. He landed in the middle of the big paddy, which was the safest thing to do. I had pulled his chain when I asked if he wanted to bet. "Tell you what, we'll hover to the shrub and have the crew chief tie a rag to it. I'll autorotate from two thousand feet and set down by the shrub close enough for me to touch the rag. If I miss, I owe you a beer. If I don't, you owe me. Okay?"

"You're on. I don't think you can do it. Even if you do, it'll be just plain luck."

I climbed to two thousand feet, cut the power, autorotated, landed next to the shrub, and easily reached the rag. "That's a beer you owe me. Want to try it again?"

"Sure, I know damn well you can't do that two times in a row."

"I'll give you a chance to get even this time. As soon as I get to two thousand feet, I'll let you cut the power when you wish."

As I knew he would, Mike cut the power while I headed away from the bush. He wanted to make it tough for me. But there was no problem, because I was not about to place myself out of range of the target. As I autorotated, I turned 180 degrees and sighted the bush; there was no way I'd miss. I ended the autorotation next to the bush, reached out, and touched the rag. "That's two beers, Mike. Want to try again?"

"Yeah, you've been lucky so far. I know you can't do it three times in a row. You're bound to miss on this one."

I didn't miss that time or that afternoon. I stopped taking Mike's money after he owed me a six-pack. He got the same treatment that all new guys got on their introduction to spot autorotations.

Contrary to the official position of flight schools, the rice paddies allowed experienced aviators considerable latitude performing autorotations. The water and the muddy bottom were not the dangerous elements portrayed in school, and the pilots could still make autorotative landings according to the book.

To prove that the helicopter wouldn't roll over in a rice paddy if autorotated with too much speed, I demonstrated autorotations with touchdowns at different speeds up to forty knots. The latter was something to witness: At forty knots the skids sent out two trailing rooster tails as they cut through the water. My intent wasn't to make light of the instruction the aviators received in their formal training but to expand their knowledge of the helicopter's capabilities in autorotative conditions. The procedures in school were excellent, but the canned scenarios were not always present in Vietnam. Mike and I continued our training for a couple of hours, then headed for the base.

We'd completed our first flight together in Vietnam. Fortunately, there was little in the way of enemy activity while we went about our duties. We made four separate extractions that day without being fired upon. Mike and I took turns flying, and I saw that he was as proficient an aviator as any we'd received from the training command.

New aviators were easy to spot. They'd move the cyclic around as if they were stirring grits to keep them from sticking to the bottom of the pot. This was a carryover from their training. Some instructors used the technique of constant movement of the cyclic while teaching their students to hover. The theory was that constant movement canceled out errors as they occurred. Because it worked when learning to hover, the students reasoned that it must be all right when flying. In some part of the training process, that "stirring" should have been stopped but never was.

I got on Mike's case as soon as I saw him stirring the pot. "What the hell are you doing with that cyclic?"

"Nothing. What's wrong? I'm heading in the direction you told me and I'm holding my altitude."

"It's all that unnecessary cyclic movement. You're wiping out the cockpit. You don't see me doing that when I'm at the controls." With that I took the controls and held the cyclic firmly and without movement. "See what I mean? You don't have to move the cyclic unless you want the bird to do something. Make every control input count. Every little movement has a meaning all its own."

The cyclic problem was the only time I corrected Mike's flying. We flew another training mission together, then I placed him on the duty roster as Rex Smith's copilot. Mike's baptism under fire came the following week when his aircraft took several hits. That was the rite of passage into the community of combat aviators. He became a 100 percent real live dustoff pilot.

Mike had no problem flying missions with Rex Smith; they made a good team. He learned his role in the unit with minimum effort and got along well with everyone. This diminished the pressure on our working relationship. It was evident to the 82d aviators that there were no special deals. I shouldn't have had reservations about that. I never asked my aviators to do anything I wouldn't be willing to do, and they knew it.

I set the pace for the detachment. I knew they felt the heavy pressure of the flight schedule; but as long as the old man worked without claiming fatigue, they couldn't in good conscience complain. We all worked hard and took our turns on the duty roster, because there wasn't any other way to accomplish the mission.

During one of my turns as first up, I received a mission that involved a young captain, Roger Deal, whom I'd evacuated twice before. His wounds on those occasions had occurred while he was acting as an adviser to a Vietnamese army unit. In both instances his injuries were not serious, and he returned to duty after a short recuperation.

On this mission I was called to evacuate three Vietnamese soldiers from a field site that turned out to be an open rice paddy. Communication with the unit on the ground and confirmation of smoke and color had been completed, so I went in for the pickup. Nothing seemed amiss; the area was quiet. There was a tree line not far from the site, but the American directing me was standing on a rice paddy dike indicating where he wanted me to set down. Because he was fully exposed, it appeared that enemy activity was at a minimum in the sector. How wrong we were.

As I set down, I recognized the American. It was Roger Deal. At that instant a Viet Cong mortar round exploded in the water about six feet to the side of Roger. The detonation knocked him off the dike; I knew he'd been hit. Other rounds were going off around the site, and I yelled for the medic and crew chief to get the wounded aboard, including the captain if he was still alive. In a matter of seconds, the three Vietnamese were loaded, and my crewmen picked up the luckless American. I was pleasantly surprised to see that he was able to stagger toward the ship with the assistance of my crewmen. He was dripping wet from his bath in the paddy. I'm sure he hadn't anticipated being wounded and airlifted out of there. He had several shrapnel wounds and would be out of action for a while.

Roger was lucky to be alive. If that mortar round had hit anywhere except in the water, he'd have been completely blown away. As it was, the water allowed the mortar round to penetrate deeply into the mud before it exploded. That kept shrapnel from going laterally, as it would have on solid ground. Roger led a charmed life.

We delivered Roger to the 3d Surg, where he at least could sleep in a clean bed for a change. I visited him at the hospital before he was discharged. About a month later, he came to the 82d to visit me and tell me he was leaving for home.

"I don't know how it happened that each time I was wounded during my tour, you were there to pick me up," Roger said. "I want to thank you for all you've done for me and my troops. Here's a small token of my appreciation for your work. I hope you like it."

Roger handed me a Chicom rifle, a war trophy that he wanted me to have. He had cleaned it and varnished the stock during his convalescence. I thanked him and told him I appreciated his gift. I haven't seen him since but wish him the best.

A few weeks after Mike arrived, John Ryan, an Associated Press (AP) correspondent, came to our base to do a story about Mike and me. Somehow he'd heard that a father and son were assigned to the same unit and flying together in combat. Ryan arrived the day I was first up and would have to fly with me if he wanted my slant on the story. That didn't deter him one bit. He was ready to go and jumped on board. My copilot for the flight was Stu Robinson.

We had the usual heavy workload during the day. In addition to the dustoff missions, I was giving Stu a check ride to upgrade him to aircraft commander. We took fire on a couple of pickups but weren't hit. We had been airborne about ten hours when we received what was to be our last mission of the day.

The pickup site was a small hamlet about fifteen minutes' flying time from Binh Thuy. It even had a small pad on which to land the helicopter. We hadn't received any reports of enemy activity in the area, so Stu continued with a normal approach into the pickup site. We were about fifty meters from touchdown and coming in nice and easy when all hell broke loose. Streams of tracers streaked through the air ahead of us as fire came from a wooded area to our right. The first stream of tracers was followed by a second heavy volley. The tracers appeared to wave at and around us as the Viet Cong tried to get the range while adjusting their fire on our moving helicopter. The first volley was well off the mark, but the second was more accurate and we took a few hits.

"I've got the aircraft," I yelled to Stu, who was concentrating on his approach. He was shocked when he realized what was happening. I immediately turned left to distance us from the enemy and climbed rapidly to get to a safer altitude. I put the evacuation on hold for the moment. No one on board was hit.

I noticed Ryan putting on his flak vest. It wasn't totally effective against the ammunition used by the VC, but it was better than nothing. Ryan had taken the vest off earlier when he found it heavy and uncomfortable. I called on the intercom, "I thought you knew better, John." He gave me an embarrassed grin and didn't answer.

I wanted to make that extraction if possible before going off duty. I knew that Mike and Rex were first up on the night shift. If we didn't make the pickup, they'd have to, and it was more dangerous at night. I flew to the general area of the VC emplacement, orbited the position, then told Horvath, the crew chief, to unload his M79 grenade launcher on the enemy. I descended to five hundred feet and circled the Viet Cong while Horvath sent round after round on them.

"I'm out of ammo, sir," Horvath called.

"Get the medic's M16 and use that," I ordered.

Horvath was firing away at the Viet Cong when I remembered that a war correspondent was on board. I wondered what was going through his mind. What was his impression of my order to fire on the enemy? After all, I was the aircraft commander of a helicopter ambulance that boldly displayed red crosses on its nose and both sides. This was the sort of incident that could generate repercussions up the chain of command all the way to the White House if it was picked up by the wire services.

I called Ryan on the intercom. "John, if I don't get that wounded soldier before I'm relieved by the night shift, first up will have to make the evacuation. With the Viet Cong force in the area, it will be a lot more dangerous at night. First up tonight is Rex Smith, and his copilot is my son. Under the circumstances, I want you to know that all the firing you just witnessed is off the record. Do you understand?"

"I understand, Mike," Ryan answered without hesitation.

As it turned out, the people at the extraction site returned to their fortified village and delayed the evacuation until the VC force was dispersed. My plan couldn't be carried out and there were no other missions, so we returned to the base. Rex Smith and Mike made the extraction around ten o'clock that night without incident.

Although Ryan had witnessed a juicy tidbit that I'm certain would have heated up the wires all the way to the Pentagon, the halls of Congress, and the White House, he did not report the incident. He did write an excellent story about Mike and me being in Vietnam and flying together. His piece made every major newspaper in the country, and we received numerous letters and clips of the articles from total strangers. All the letters were complimentary; they were morale boosters. I never had a chance to thank John for not reporting the incident, and I'm sorry I haven't seen him since.

About a month after Mike joined the 82d, the 57th Medical Detachment was transferred to Binh Thuy. It doubled the dustoff force in the delta. At long last, the augmentation I'd requested was a reality.

The 57th was supposed to ease the pressure on the 82d, but at first it had little effect. There were problems in the initial phases of the relocation. For example, the detachments had their own communications specialists and related equipment. We decided that both outfits would operate better under the direction of a single RTO. Some crowding would be inevitable, but we could learn to live and work together.

I flew with the pilots of the 57th a lot. It was my job to check out each of its aircraft commanders in the area of operations, and I used the same methods of instruction as I did with the ACs of the 82d. Some thought I was too demanding, but I won them over in the long run.

The 57th's commander, Capt. Tom Jacoby, and I worked closely together to ensure that his people were totally qualified. He welcomed the strict attention to detailed knowledge of the delta they were required to master. One of his aircraft commanders was a young warrant officer, Bill Shirah. He was nicknamed Wally because of the similarity of his last name to that of a famous astronaut.

Wally was from Destin, Florida. His presence at Binh Thuy gave us four dustoff pilots from the Fort Walton Beach–Destin area. There was Kline, a graduate of Choctawhatchee High; Wally, from Destin; and Mike and I from Fort Walton Beach. We had many bull sessions about the goings-on in our hometowns in Florida's panhandle.

A situation developed as a result of a mission that involved Wally's crew and mine. I was to extract four seriously wounded ARVN troops whose unit was still in contact with the Viet Cong entrenched in a tree line. The American adviser assured me that his troops would lay down heavy covering fire while I made the pickup.

"Make sure they keep up a constant barrage on that tree line while I'm being loaded," I told the adviser.

"Roger, Dustoff, I understand. The fire will be maintained hot and heavy."

With that assurance, I initiated a fast, extremely low approach. Because of the open paddies covering the tactical area, I could see the pickup site and keep the tree line under observation during my incoming dash for the extraction. I saw the identifying smoke directly off my nose and glanced at the airspeed, which was better than a hundred knots. A fast, decelerative flare was next. I raised the nose and lowered the collective as I came up to the friendly lines and simultaneously flared and flipped the tail in the direction of the tree line. I slammed the skids of the chopper on the ground facing away from the VC. Suddenly I heard the distinctive sharp reports of automatic weapons and felt hits to the tail of the bird. I heard the ARVN troops returning fire, but their M16s didn't measure up to the sound and volume of the enemy's weapons.

Before the medic and crew chief left the aircraft, and before the ARVN wounded were brought to the helicopter, an even heavier volume of automatic weapons fire blasted our ship. This time the crew chief yelled that the fuel cell had been hit and JP-4 was streaming into the crew compartment. The American adviser came on the net yelling for me to get out of there, that the VC had me zeroed in.

I glanced to my rear and saw the medic and crew chief on board, so I pulled pitch. "We're getting the hell out of here. How are those leaks in the rear?" I asked.

"Me and the medic are doused with JP-4," the crew chief answered. "We'd better land as soon as possible. I can see fuel streaming from the rear of the ship and from underneath. We're losing fuel fast."

"No sweat," I replied as we gained altitude. "I see Soc Trang up ahead. We'll be on the ground soon."

I called the tower, declared an emergency, and asked for a fire truck to stand by just in case. I came straight in and landed in a clear area off to the side of the ramp. The fire truck was right there. I didn't wait for the engine cooldown procedure. I shut off the fuel as soon as I touched down and we exited the ship. My crewmen, soaked with JP-4, immediately removed their flight gear. I told them to find a shower and wash off quickly, because the fuel could cause great discomfort and burn the skin. I hadn't had time or altitude to notify our RTO, who no doubt wondered what happened when I didn't call back up. The tower sent a message notifying our base that we needed transport back to Binh Thuy, and in about two hours a dustoff came to get us. It was Wally Shirah. He had a big grin on his face.

On the twenty-minute flight back to base, Wally, still grinning, signaled for me to hook up to the intercom. "Looks like you damn near had your ass shot off, sir," he said.

"Ah, hell, Wally, they just got off a few lucky shots. Besides, the ARVN troops weren't ready with their wounded when we set down. If they'd been prepared, we'd have picked them up."

"From what I saw of your ship, if you'd waited one more second the Viet Cong would have nailed you but good, sir."

Maybe Wally gave me the "sir" treatment in deference to my age, but more likely it was because of orders from Tom Jacoby.

"As it turned out, I got your mission and got the four wounded ARVNs out of there with no trouble at all," Wally continued. "I just dazzled them with my footwork. Yep, I had to do the old man's dirty work. Us guys from Destin always were the ones who ran interference for the Fort Walton running backs. Nothing's changed. If Choctawhatchee High had a winning football team, you can bet the guys from Destin were responsible."

Wally was feeling his oats. He'd been able to complete a mission that I couldn't. I just laughed and let him have his say. After all, what he said about the mission was true. What he said about the football team was a bunch of bull. The guys from Destin could barely read let alone remember numbered plays. Wally's folks back home knew me, and I'm sure they were as pleased at his success as I was. Wally didn't delay writing home to relate what happened, and I was glad to contribute to his good fortune.

As the days went by, Wally smiled whenever our paths crossed. "Let me know if you need any help with your evacuations," he said. "Glad to be of assistance anytime."

"Wally, you'll be the first to be called if I can't handle the situation."

We continued ribbing each other for a good while. It was something we could share in our bull sessions at the bar or at parties and barbecues.

Meanwhile, there was work to be done and missions to fly. Mike and I saw each other daily at the flight line, in the officers' mess or the club, or when we flew together. When off duty we also made the party circuit. Eventually Mike met most of the nurses and in due time was dating one.

February arrived and I had about six weeks left in Vietnam. But in the early part of the month, a seven-day period produced an unbelievable series of events affecting my son and me. It started on a day when Rex Smith and Mike were first up, and my crew and I were their backup. They had an active day, but I wasn't called to give assistance until midafternoon. They were working in support of an ARVN sweep in the vicinity of Tra Vinh, about forty-five miles southeast of Binh Thuy. It was a major operation and produced a lot of casualties.

Meanwhile, my crew and I flew missions in the lower delta, some as far south as Ca Mau and others at Kien Long, Vi Thanh, and Phung Hiep. The latter was called "The Wagon Wheel," because it was at the center of eight canals radiating from the town. We delivered a load of wounded ARVN troops from there to the hospital at Can Tho.

Rex Smith and Mike were still occupied supporting the operation in the Tra Vinh area, and it looked as though they'd be there the rest of the day. My crew and I were lounging around in operations when a mission came in for an extraction near Tieu Can, about ten miles from where Rex and Mike were working. They'd been informed of the mission but said they were tied up with their ARVN operation and couldn't leave. We took it.

In about half an hour, we arrived on the scene to get the wounded soldier who was reported to be in serious condition, a matter of life or death. When we got him on board, the medic said he had several shrapnel wounds in his legs and thighs but they were not life threatening. As I took off from the extraction site, I looked toward where Rex and Mike were busy. I saw three columns of smoke in the distance. It looked as though the ARVN had a lot on their hands. Based on experience, I visualized ARVN armored personnel carriers being blasted and burning. I continued my climbing turn toward Binh Thuy when I heard Rex on the unit frequency calling out that his ship had taken several hits and was going down. I immediately called to let him know I was close by and coming to help.

"Rex, this is Dustoff 88. I'm in your area, probably less than ten miles from your position. Try your best to make it to a secure location."

"Dustoff 88, roger your transmission. We're leaking a lot of fuel; we've taken hits in the fuel cell and the transmission section. It looks as if we'll be able to make it to a small fortified village I've spotted a few miles from the battle area. Don't know my exact location. Everyone is okay, just in case you want to know."

"I'm on a northeasterly heading. I can see Tra Vinh at my one o'clock position, Rex. Give me additional directions as soon as you spot me."

"Dustoff 88, we've been working the rice paddy area southwest of Tra Vinh near the burning APCs. I'm on a westerly heading going away from the battle area. It looks like I'll have to set it down in the next minute or so. I'm losing my hydraulics. I'll be down next to a village four to five miles due west of the smoke and fire."

"Roger, I have the general area in sight. I'll be over your location in two to three minutes. As soon as I have you spotted, I'll drop down to get you and the crew. Rex, what's the tactical situation in the area?"

"Okay, 88, we've made it—we're down safe. For your information, some troops are coming forward from the village. They look like local militia. I've shut down the engine, but I'll stay on the radio to guide you in. By the way, I have a helicopter coming in from the south. Looks like it's about two thousand feet up. Should be your bird."

"Right, it's me. I don't see any other aircraft flying around here. I've turned on my searchlight and landing light. Let me know if you've spotted them."

"Roger, I have you in sight. You're coming right at us. You're about a mile out."

"Rex, I have your ship spotted. I'll be coming in making a tactical approach, just in case. Have all your weapons, ammo, radios, charts, and SOIs [signal operating instructions] with you and ready to go. Don't worry about the aircraft. There's plenty of time for it to be hauled out by a Chinook later this afternoon."

"Roger, 88. We'll be ready with all the equipment when you set down."

As I neared the village, I saw the downed aircraft and its crew standing to one side. I came right over the top of the pickup site, made a tactical approach, flared, and set down. Rex, Mike, and the medic and crew chief tossed all critical equipment and gear on board and jumped in. We were out of there.

I called the RTO as soon as I climbed to altitude and told him that the downed crew was picked up and also that my evacuation was completed. We'd be back at the base in about half an hour. The RTO rogered my transmission, and I proceeded to give him the geographical coordinates of the village where the downed chopper could be retrieved by a Chinook. The local militia would handle security for it.

I looked back and saw that everyone was all right, then asked Rex what had happened.

"As we were coming in for a pickup, the Viet Cong hit the area with mortars and heavy automatic weapons. The troops in the evacuation area scattered, and before we could set down we took quite a few hits in the tail, the fuel cell, and the transmission section. It happened in that instant when I turned the rear of the aircraft toward the enemy position and just before I would have set down. I decided to abort the pickup. But before I could move out, another heavy burst hit the ship—probably the main rotor and the fuel cell. I could smell JP-4 all around. We finally got out of there and made it to the village where you picked us up. The controls were getting real heavy as I set it down—the hydraulics were just about gone."

"You did all right, Rex," I said, then I turned to Mike. "You told me that your mother said for you to be careful while you're here. What's the matter, don't you listen to her anymore?"

"I was real careful. Rex was doing the flying on that pickup. We didn't take any hits when I was at the controls."

"You're getting to talk more and more like Wally Shirah," I said. "You luck out on one mission and think you have all the answers. Better watch your ass, Mike. The Viet Cong don't care who's doing the flying when they're doing the firing." I didn't tell him, but I was relieved that they had set their chopper down without additional damage.

When we returned to the base, I learned that another crew, one from the 57th, had been dispatched to complete the mission started by Rex and Mike. I told Rex that his crew was relieved and had the rest of the day off. They were to meet me at the club; they owed me a drink for taking time out of my busy schedule to pick them up.

Mike asked if I was going to mention the incident in my letters home. I told him I didn't think that would be wise and said for him not to say anything about the matter either. After all, being shot down was nothing unusual in the dustoff trade. Our aircraft took hits every day.

"Make sure you bring Rex to the club," I told Mike. "This is a special occasion. I'll bet it's the first time a pilot shot down in combat was rescued by his father, also a pilot."

When I came into the club, Ed Moate, Con Jaburg, Buddy Barnes, and a collection of dustoffers and Seawolves were there. Mike and Rex came as promised, and we all had a big time toasting the rare occasion.

"What the hell were you and your son doing?" said Con. "Trying to set some kind of a record? You don't have to do that. Your being here together in combat is record enough."

There were a lot of happy pilots drinking, joking, and backslapping—all in all a fine finish to an eventful day. We left the club in high spirits.

It's uncanny how combat flying can become routine. We flew missions day in and day out, took our hits, and were thankful that no one was injured. The mind must be extremely resilient to become accustomed to and routinely accept experiences that are frightening the first time they are encountered. Thought processes can become warped to the extent that expectations become distorted. For example, we'd almost be disappointed when an anticipated enemy response didn't materialize, when the Viet Cong held their fire and we knew they had us boresighted. It was as if we didn't count, as if they didn't consider us worth the ammunition. Strange thoughts indeed, but then the whole Vietnam situation was strange.

Exposure to dustoff duty left its mark on anyone engaged in that work. The most hardened person was mellowed by the scenes of misery and pain, the traumatic amputations, chest wounds and their distinct rasping sound, bodies torn apart by land mines, and blood coloring and covering all. That was my world, my mission, as I rushed to aid the wounded and evacuate those poor, wretched souls. Most didn't know why they were asked to do the fighting. Their lot was to serve, to obey orders; they didn't have other options. I looked upon those sorely wounded bits of humanity with great compassion. They never seemed to be able to cry out or shed tears of pain. I too felt the sting of the enemy; I knew the feeling. I saw so much suffering that I had to close my mind to the reality of the battles. I forced myself to think of them as numbers or phrases. In the words of the press releases, they became the "approximately fifty casualties in a victorious

battle with the Viet Cong" or "the heavy casualties recently sustained."

It was evident that the many months I spent in Vietnam weighed
heavily on me. I'd seen more wounded and injured people than one
can imagine, but all the horror of my war would end soon. I was
about to finish my tour of duty; if I survived, I'd be home in about
a month. The idea that my son would be left behind consumed my
thoughts and heightened my anxiety. I had to cast aside my worries
about him and realize where my ultimate responsibilities rested. I
was needed at home. I could choose to extend my tour, but that
wouldn't be fair to my wife and family, or to Mike. He'd made his
choice of careers, and it was up to him to succeed or fail. He didn't
need me around. He was well trained and could take care of himself. After all, I was his trainer and mentor. I was proud to have taught
him and his contemporaries the art of survival in a flying assignment
that each day faced the greatest risks in all of Vietnam.

Before long, I was first up again, with Bob Aberle as my copilot.
I was giving him a periodic check ride on another hot and heavy
day; we'd been airborne since reporting for duty early that morning. We flew down to the Ca Mau peninsula twice before noon and
made another evacuation from a naval vessel in the Gulf of Siam.
It seemed as if every mission we received was as far from Binh Thuy
as possible.

We did a lot of flying due to the length of the missions. As we were
returning a seriously wounded ARVN trooper to the hospital at Can
Tho, the RTO called and asked if we could handle another mission
at Bac Lieu. I replied in the negative. Our wounded soldier required
immediate medical attention. The RTO rogered my transmission
and said he'd send second up.

Aberle reminded me that Rex and Mike were second up that day.
I knew that and mentioned it was only six days ago that I had picked
them up after they were shot down. "I hope they watch themselves,"
I said jokingly. "I can't be rescuing them every day."

After we dropped off the wounded at the hospital, we returned
to Binh Thuy to refuel and get some food. It was almost two o'clock
in the afternoon and we hadn't eaten since breakfast. But before we
completed refueling, the RTO called and said he had another ur-

gent mission for us. This one was in the area around Phung Hiep, the Wagon Wheel, about fifteen minutes away. I said we'd be airborne as soon as we were fueled.

"Looks as if lunch will have to wait," I told Aberle.

"Roger. For your information, we missed lunch more than two hours ago. Let's hope we get back in time for dinner. You want me to fly? You flew the last mission."

"Of course. It's your turn, and this one could be hot. It may give me a chance to see how you get the job done when the pickup is less than ideal. Let's get going."

Aberle took off, climbed out, and set a course for the evacuation area while I told the RTO we were on our way. I switched the fox mike to the tactical frequency to call the unit needing assistance. I had difficulty making contact; all I heard on the net was some shrill talk in Vietnamese. Shortly thereafter I made contact with the American adviser. It seemed that he'd been occupied with preparations for the extraction.

"This is Dustoff 88. We're inbound and should be over your position in another ten minutes. Let us know when you're ready to proceed with the evacuation. In the meantime, I'd like to know the tactical situation and the soldier's condition."

"Roger, Dustoff. I'm told there are two soldiers to be evacuated, both with gunshot wounds. As yet I haven't been able to locate them and bring them to me. The situation down here is somewhat screwed up. The company is spread out more than I'd like. I can't even find out where contact was made with the Viet Cong."

"This is Dustoff. Roger your last transmission. We're still inbound. Be ready to pop smoke for identification when I ask for it."

"Bob, this one looks bad. These guys don't have their shit together. You'd better be real careful."

"Okay, Mike. I sure hope they get things sorted out down there before we arrive. We're only a couple of minutes out."

I checked my 1-over-50 chart. The unit's reported position was near a canal that came out of the Wagon Wheel in a southwesterly direction. The canal joined a stream, which made snakelike S turns farther to the southwest. Heavy woods and brush covered both banks of the stream and extended more than a kilometer down the waterway. I was certain that was where the Viet Cong main force was concentrated. I showed the tactical chart to Aberle and told him my ideas regarding the probable VC deployment. If the friendly forces were in their reported positions, they were near the confluence of the canal and the stream. That meant the VC could be as close as a hundred meters. This was a real bucket of worms. I didn't like the setup one bit.

When we came upon the pickup site, I saw that the tactical chart accurately displayed the layout below. I called the ground commander to let him know we were ready for the evacuation.

"This is Dustoff 88. If you're prepared for the evacuation, pop your smoke."

"Roger, Dustoff. Circle the area for a minute or so. We've located the two wounded. Their people are having a hard time bringing them up to my location. The rice paddies in the area are flooded and the water is often waist-deep, which makes movement difficult. I'll delay popping smoke until we're all set."

"This is Dustoff 88. It looks to me like you're close to the tree line along the canal and the stream to your west. Isn't there enemy activity in that area?"

"I read you, Dustoff. That's where the initial contact was made, but I think the Viet Cong unit was too small to stay around. It looks as if they've left. We haven't had any action from that area since the initial burst of fire wounded our two troops."

"Bob, you heard what the man just said. I sure hope he's got his facts right. I'd be real careful when it comes to the actual pickup. Don't take his information as gospel, and make sure to flip your tail in the direction of the trees before you set down."

"I read you loud and clear, Mike. Have no fear, I intend to have my ass end pointed right at the VC. Still, I wish the friendlies were better organized. Hey, it looks like they've already popped smoke down there. I see green smoke. Better check it out."

"Okay, Bob. Be ready. I'll give them a call."

"This is Dustoff 88. Did you just pop smoke?"

"Roger, Dustoff. Green smoke is out. You can come in anytime now. I think the enemy has blown the area."

I told the RTO we were going in for the pickup and would call again when we were airborne.

Aberle did just as I thought he would. The area was wide-open rice paddies. Its uniformity was broken only by the canals that radiated from the Wagon Wheel, the occasional wood line, and the stream. He set himself up for a high-speed, low-level approach from west to east over the open paddies. Under the circumstances it was the best course of action. He shouldn't meet enemy opposition if he came in fast and hugged the surface. I'd have done the same.

As Aberle came in, I noticed that our airspeed was about a hundred knots. Up ahead we could see the trees where wisps of green still came out of the smoke grenade indicating the pickup site. As Aberle came up to the smoke, he raised the nose of the helicopter to slow his airspeed, then flared and flipped the tail in the direction of the enemy. At the same time I heard several automatic weapons open up on us, and I'm sure Aberle did too. I don't know if it disturbed his concentration, but I'm certain he saw the water being kicked up ahead of us by the incoming rounds. Long bursts of automatic weapons fire followed from the tree line. The ARVNs answered with heavy covering fire. I'd expected that something like this would happen when Aberle and I entered the pickup site.

But neither of us knew about an old tree stump hidden by brush growing in the rice paddy dike. When Aberle flipped the tail of the chopper in the direction of the trees, the tail rotor blades hit the stump and sent one of the blades sailing off into the distance. The unbalanced forces acting on the rest of the tail rotor assembly wrenched it completely out of its mounting in the vertical fin. I felt the impact and knew what to expect.

The tail rotor was gone, and our options were definitely limited. Aberle yelled that he didn't have any directional control. I felt the aircraft begin to turn to the left. Torque would soon have us spinning uncontrollably. I waited for Aberle to take remedial action and saw he was confused and undecided about what to do next. He tried to sort things out, but events occurred too fast for him to handle the problem. He didn't have my advantage of just sitting and watching the sequence unfold. But I was as much to blame for our sad situation as he.

With two pilots on board, one of us should have spotted the stump. But this was combat, and I'd been overly concerned with the enemy fire coming from the tree line. I'm sure that Aberle had been equally watchful. We'd been on duty since five that morning and it was at least two-thirty in the afternoon. We were airborne most of the day and hadn't eaten since breakfast, which was before daybreak. The mind, the body, the total man can endure just so much abuse before there's a deterioration of efficiency. I knew all that but wouldn't admit it. At his young age Aberle couldn't accept such an analysis. Besides, we had no choice but to keep to the mission schedule.

I knew what would happen if corrective action was not applied soon. Aberle worked the pedals, without result. He looked at me inquiringly but didn't say a word. He wanted me to say something, to give an order, a command, anything. I really wanted him to sort it out and do the only thing left for us. Our helicopter was sorely damaged; it was about to go completely out of control. As the chopper's turn to the left accelerated, I grabbed the controls and told Aberle, "I have it."

I chopped the throttle and jammed the collective downward. The aircraft splashed into the water and stopped its leftward turn. We were down, out of action, and had a wrecked helicopter on our hands. I just sat there as the ship settled farther into the ooze of the rice paddy. I watched as the water eventually lapped over the deck beneath my feet. The telling of the events leading up to the ignominious, purposeful crash takes far more time than the second or two that actually transpired.

I looked over at Aberle. "We just lost our entire tail rotor assembly. That's why you lost directional control of the ship. When you flipped the tail around, we hit something that destroyed our tail rotor. All we can do now is sit here till we're picked up. The ground commander will get a message to our operations soon, I hope." I turned to see how the rest of the crew had fared. "It looks as though everybody's okay in the back."

Fortunately for our crew, the ARVN forced the Viet Cong to abandon their position in the tree line. If they'd held on, I'm sure they would have been laying it on us hot and heavy. While we waited for our inevitable rescue, I pondered our miserable situation. I should have spotted the obstruction that brought us to grief. I'd always been alert to such situations before. Was I really so inattentive to such a hazard, or was I so fatigued that my brain ignored what my eyes saw?

I thought back to my last month of operational flying and realized that in the past thirty days I'd been grounded twice for the standard three-day period because I'd flown more than 140 hours. But that had happened to me quite often during my tour of duty. It was common practice for aviators of the 82d to go through that drill. I knew that Aberle was grounded in similar fashion from time to time, but he was a young man, only a year or two older than my son. I didn't want to admit it, but the flight schedule and my age appeared to be part of the problem. On night missions I had to wear reading glasses to plot the pickup coordinates on my tactical charts. I thought about the small party that the detachment had for me on my last birthday. I'd reached the ripe old age of forty-seven. "Hell, that was five months ago," I mumbled to myself.

A few days earlier I had logged my thirteen-hundredth hour of combat flying in the previous eleven months. I was more than twice as old as the average dustoff pilot, but I was flying more than anyone else. Then there was the nightlife, the parties, and the barbecues. I never missed those opportunities to unwind. I wined and dined with the best of the lot, but I'm not sure it brought the intended benefits. When I wasn't flying, I was in operations taking care of the web of minor details in the administrative process. I didn't even take time for an R and R. There was work to be done. It's a wonder that things hadn't caught up with me much sooner.

Confession is supposed to be good for the soul, but this bit of self-analysis didn't make me feel one bit better. Besides, all the blame that I laid on myself couldn't get our wrecked helicopter airborne again. In a bit of rationalization, I thought I could have been wide awake and Aberle still would have hit the stump. Maybe so.

Meanwhile, the RTO had noted that we were late reporting back up and decided to contact Rex Smith. He and Mike were returning from their extraction in the Bac Lieu sector and were given the coordinates of our pickup site and the tactical frequency. Rex was to check on us and find out why we hadn't called back up. He was about five minutes from our location when he received the RTO's request, and by the time he copied all the details he was almost on top of us.

Aberle spotted a chopper coming our way at about two thousand feet, but it seemed to be passing us by. Our radios had become in-

operable when we crashed into the rice paddy, so we couldn't call
out on the emergency frequency. But Rex and Mike must have spotted us, because they started a slow, descending orbit. Aberle yelled
that he could see the red cross on the aircraft; we knew that it was
one of our detachment choppers, but I had no idea who it might be.

Rex was in communication with the American adviser. He didn't
have to ask if we needed assistance; the crashed condition of the helicopter was evident.

Aberle went to the adviser's position and, listening to the radio
transmissions, learned that Rex and Mike were in the chopper coming to the rescue. He hurried back to my position. "It's Rex and your
son," he yelled. "They're coming to pick us up."

"Aw, shit. That's all I need to really screw up my day. I'll never hear
the last of this. They're not going to let me forget it, especially since
I made both of them buy me drinks for picking them up last week.
What a revolting development."

The adviser assured Rex and Mike that we were not injured and
there were two wounded soldiers to be lifted out with us. I watched
as Rex circled the area at low altitude and wondered why he didn't
set down. Why was he continuing to recon the area? I was surprised
when he finally made his approach and landed about a hundred meters from the crash site.

The adviser signaled us that they were ready to evacuate my crew
and the two "gunshot wounds." I'd have to negotiate the entire distance through the water and dirty rice paddy, which I didn't like a
bit. I gathered my bundle of tactical charts and stepped out of the
Huey into the rice paddy. I was in water above my waist and had to
hold the charts over my head to keep them dry.

I started for the other helicopter. The muddy bottom made the
going difficult, and I moved forward slowly, being extra careful with
my footing. I didn't want to lose my balance or slip and fall. The rest
of my crew did much better. After all, they were taller and weren't
carrying a load of charts. When they reached the rescue chopper, I
still had about thirty meters to go. Even the two wounded men were
carried to the chopper before I got there. To say that the situation
made me angry was an understatement.

The going got easier as I neared the helicopter because of shallower water, but even before I got to it I was livid. I handed my charts to someone on the Huey and finally got on board myself. I was covered with crap from the rice paddy and brought with me an odor more offensive than a broken-down garbage truck.

I grabbed the intercom. "Damnit, Rex," I hollered, "why in the world did you land so far away from us? Why'd you make us go through all that filth to get to your chopper? I didn't do that to you and Mike last week."

"I saw your chopper sitting in the rice paddy with its deck in the water," Rex answered, "and I decided to look for a better place to set down where I knew the water would not be so deep. I didn't want to take a chance of damaging my chopper and ending up like you."

"You could have hovered with your skids in the water near us. Then we wouldn't have had to grope through this damn crap that's all over us."

I wasn't getting any sympathetic reactions from Rex, so I lit into my son. "Mike, what the hell were you doing—just sitting there?" I figured he could have suggested landing closer to the wreckage.

"Hell, I thought Rex was doing the right thing," Mike answered. "We weren't that far away from you. The others in your crew didn't seem to mind. They were happy to see us and had no problem getting aboard. You're the only one bitching about having to walk through a little bit of muddy water."

That reply really got to me. My own son talking back to me. "That's a hell of a way to treat your father," I yelled.

Mike didn't bat an eye. "Don't forget, around here you're not my dad."

My own words were tossed right back in my face. I was crushed and defeated. I just fumed and sat back as Rex and Mike got us out of there and returned to Binh Thuy. I stopped off at operations to make certain that the Chinook outfit had been alerted to extract our downed craft. After I entered, everyone except the RTO hurriedly left. For some strange reason, I wasn't greeted with any enthusiasm. I really needed to take a shower.

I didn't bother to take off my shoes and clothes; I just jumped into the shower. Only after I was sure my clothes were thoroughly de-contaminated did I get undressed. After lingering under the re-freshing spray at least half an hour, I felt much better.

I donned fresh clothing and returned to operations to see if my damaged chopper had been retrieved. I learned that a Chinook was on station and in the process of extracting it. Within the hour the wreckage was deposited in one of our revetments. The damage couldn't be repaired at our level of maintenance. The chopper would be junked or returned to the States.

Rex and Mike took over my duties as first up and ended the day on schedule. By the time they finished work, I had cooled off. Rex and Mike were right about seeking a better place to set their heli-copter down for our extraction. My anger was due mostly to my dis-pleasure about not seeing the stump that damaged the chopper.

I finished dinner and was at the club when Rex and Mike entered. Mike reminded me that I owed them a drink, and I told John the bartender to give them whatever they desired.

The three of us were at the bar when Con Jaburg came in. "Yeah, the old man must be losing his touch," said Con. "He gets a simple evacuation mission, hardly any Viet Cong in the area, hears a little firing, and wrecks his chopper. Then he has his boy haul his ass out of the mud."

We all laughed at Con's antics as he continued. "I told you, Mike, you didn't need to set any records. You've already done that. So what do you do? You crash your chopper so your son can rescue you a week after you rescued him." Con was laying it all out as he saw it—a sce-nario that a Hollywood scriptwriter would likely reject as overly fic-tionalized. Yet it was all true. Mike and I had both been forced down as a result of combat action within a seven-day period and we had rescued each other. Unbelievable.

"If I were you, old man," Con added, "I'd take it a little easier. You have less than a month left in this godforsaken land. You're work-ing too hard and you're taking too many chances. You don't have to set the example for your young studs anymore. Take some time off and rest a bit. Go home in one piece, not in a body bag."

"You're a fine one to talk about taking chances, Con. Every time you fly with me, we get the shit shot out of us. You're a damn magnet ass. You know I'm not going to stop flying. I'll be taking my turn on the roster like I always do. If I did stop, who'd fly with you? All the guys know how you attract enemy fire."

Ed Moate came in and was listening to the conversation. He'd been to Long Binh attending a meeting with the 45th Company commander and just heard about my aircraft being downed.

"You know, Mike," said Moate, "Con makes sense. You've been doing a lot lately. You could ease off a bit. You've done your share. I don't mean for you to take yourself off the duty roster, but don't do any more than you have to. Do you realize that today's aircraft was your second contribution to the junk pile in the past three months? It looks to me like the Viet Cong have your range. I'd be careful."

I knew they were all concerned about me. Our aircraft were taking too many hits lately. The final month in a combat tour was known to produce unusual results, and I was certain that that was the basis of their fears for me.

"Look, I'm well aware of my DEROS [date of return from overseas]," I said. I knew from experience that short-timers can get their ass caught in a wringer. But on my previous tour I had eased up toward the end of my last month of flying, and I'd most likely do it again.

"Have no fear," I assured them. "The old man will be riding the Freedom Bird back to the land of the big PX and the realm of the round eyes. But I won't miss my turn on the roster until I leave. When I'm not flying, I'll be busy preparing for my departure and my next assignment in the States."

I didn't know it, but I had only three weeks left in country. In the meantime, I made certain I didn't miss any parties or other excuses to do a little celebrating. The 3d Surg staff invited me to a party that turned out to be in my honor. They gave me a plaque in appreciation of my work with them.

Orders for my next assignment arrived, along with a personal letter from my next commander, Maj. Jerry Plummer. I'd been assigned to the Golden Knights, the army's parachute demonstration team at Fort Bragg in North Carolina. I was to be the team's aviation officer, with responsibility for its aircraft, crews, and maintenance people. I looked forward to the assignment; it promised to be interesting.

I met my turns on the duty roster and even managed to get one more day's flying with Con Jaburg. Nothing had changed; he was still a magnet ass. We took several hits before the day was over. My helicopter hadn't been hit once in the previous week.

The navy scheduled a big party a few days before I left. It seemed that everyone from the local area was there: the folks from Paddy Control, most of the Seawolves, the 3d Surg doctors and nurses, and of course all the dustoffers.

Two of the nurses took me aside and asked how many jungle boots I had. I told them I had three pairs and asked why they wanted to know. They said they had difficulty finding shoes that fit; most were too large. My boots looked as if they fit a smaller foot, and they could use a pair of boots my size. That was a hell of a way to win a popularity contest with a couple of nurses, but I assured them I'd leave a pair for each of them.

On the day of the party I had an unexpected visitor. Major Ed Preston had been recently assigned to the 45th Company and took the time to visit me at Binh Thuy. Ed and I served together during our first tour in Vietnam. We were both at Tan Son Nhut in 1966 and took part in numerous battles north of Saigon. Ed hadn't known about the party and planned to return to Long Binh. I convinced him to delay his return until the next day. He agreed and had a great time.

Ed knew I'd be going home soon and reminded me that he occupied a trailer at the 45th. He said he had a good selection of whiskey and I should stay there when it was time for me to process out of the country. I asked if his air conditioner was operational, and he assured me it was. I said I'd take him up on his offer.

I continued to meet my flight schedule and even got in one last flight with Mike. On my last day of combat flying, I was under fire on only one mission. I happily reported that although I saw tracers go by my aircraft, I was successful taking evasive action and wasn't hit. I completed my work, set down in the ship's revetment, and secured the aircraft. Much to my surprise, the crew chief pointed out a clean bullet hole in one of the tail rotor blades. My helicopter had been hit and I didn't know it. The Viet Cong would not let me go away without a present.

Two days later I received a call from Colonel Roler, of the 45th. He said I was scheduled to leave on the Freedom Bird in five days and to get up to Long Binh for out-processing. I needed another day at Binh Thuy before departing and had friends to see before leaving. I told him I'd be there in time for processing.

"Good," replied Roler. "Your buddy Ed Preston says he has your Chivas standing by. We'll be expecting you. Meanwhile, no more flying. That's an order. See you."

I went to Moate's office and told him about the call. Moate said he'd been expecting it. We talked about our time together and how the 82d was doing. He expressed his appreciation for all I'd done controlling the young studs in the outfit. "I don't know how you managed it, but you kept them centered on the mission. I hope I get that kind of cooperation after you're gone."

"Look, Ed, they're eager to do what's right. They enjoy flying their missions. Just don't expect too much of a military attitude from them, and, above all, take your turn on the duty roster. The only edge I have is that they look upon me as they would their father. That's the reason they don't talk back when I get on their ass and chew them out for something they've done wrong. You're just going to have to give them a little more slack than I did. Remember that and everything will be okay."

The next day I gathered all my worldly goods together except the jungle boots I'd promised the nurses. My personal gear was easily packed in two pieces of luggage. My toilet articles were in a ditty bag, and my war souvenir, the Chicom rifle, was in a leatherette case. The rest of my gear and clothes went into a wooden crate, which constituted my hold baggage. It would follow me to the States by surface transport.

Moate told me to make myself available for a detachment formation on the flight line at 5:00 P.M. When I arrived, I saw that all members of the unit who were not flying were there. After listening to laudatory remarks about my work with the 82d, I was presented a plaque that contained my stats for the past year and the usual phrase: "For Outstanding Service and Dedication." The bottom line contained my score: 1,407 hours of combat flying time, 1,783 missions flown, and 3,588 wounded evacuated. Added to the figures of the first tour, they totaled 2,038 hours, 2,543 missions, and 5,589 wounded. I had often complained about the heavy administrative burden imposed upon those who have to do the fighting and the dying. Maintaining records such as those emblazoned on my plaque happened to be one of those burdens. Were they necessary to the conduct of the war? I suppose we could have accomplished our mission without them.

The numbers were impressive. Not many combatants ran up such a score in one year and such a total in two. As admirable a record as the figures implied, they would always be barren numbers. They could never show how much misery I had seen, how many cries of pain I heard, and how many deaths I witnessed. They could never address man's inhumanity to man. They can't describe the overpowering loneliness experienced during the moments of reflection upon home and family. The figures didn't—couldn't—list the times I cursed the war and all its misery.

I thanked the detachment and Ed Moate for taking time to honor me. I appreciated having so many of my crewmates on hand for the occasion. I stuttered and stammered as I admonished them all to continue their good work. I was not at all comfortable with the moment. It was hard to leave so many close friends who had risked their lives with me. Now I was going home. I was a survivor. Mike would fly me to Long Binh the next day for my appointment with the Freedom Bird. I didn't look forward to the heart-wrenching moment when we would part.

Early the next morning I gathered my luggage and war souvenir and placed them in Moate's jeep for the short run to the flight line. Mike and his crew chief were there preflighting the helicopter. When a combat tour was over, it was our practice to attach smoke grenades to the skids and ignite them during a low-level pass over the runway while the detachment cheered and waved good-bye. We'd continue that tradition.

Everything that had to be said was said the previous day, so there was no reason to delay. I shook hands with my navy friends, Con and Buddy, then Ed Moate, the dustoff pilots, and all the medics and crew chiefs. I gave them a salute and jumped on board the waiting helicopter. I was a passenger on this trip and took the copilot's seat. Mike had already started the engine and in another minute was hovering to the runway. I watched him do it all and just sat back and relaxed. He took off, climbed, and circled for the pass over the runway. I saw everyone lined up below as Mike placed the helicopter into a shallow dive. The crew chief set off the smoke grenades on command, and we skimmed over the runway, red smoke spewing along and behind the skids. I waved to my friends, who waved back. That was it. We were on our way to Long Binh.

In about forty-five minutes we were at the 45th, where Preston met us with a jeep. Before leaving I told Mike that after I stowed my bags at Ed's, I'd see him in operations. Mike was busy tying down the rotor while his crew chief refueled for the return to Binh Thuy. Mike just nodded his head. He wasn't in the mood for much conversation.

Ed showed me to a bedroom and, true to his word, there was a bottle of Chivas on the table. "That's yours, Mike, and if you need more let me know."

"Ed, I think one bottle will be more than sufficient. Thanks. Let's get over to operations. I want to say good-bye to my son."

Colonel Roler was at operations when I arrived and greeted me warmly. We'd known each other since our previous tour. He asked if Ed had taken care of my billeting, and I replied that he had. I stepped outside and saw Mike walking toward me.

"Well, Dad, there's no sense delaying my return to Binh Thuy. You know they're expecting me back soon. When you see Mother, tell her I'm doing okay. I'll see you in about nine months. So long."

Mike shook my hand, turned around, and headed for his ship. Neither one of us wanted to prolong the painful moment.

I saw the crew chief untying the main rotor. In less than a minute Mike had the engine winding up. He picked the Huey up to a hover and prepared for takeoff. Then he was airborne; he climbed out and turned on course for the delta. I watched until his aircraft was out of sight.

I felt drained and must have showed my emotions when I returned to operations, because Ed said, "Let's go to the bar, Mike. You look like you need a good drink."

The next two days were a drag. I didn't have any duties, and all I did was visit the operations section and talk to the 45th aviators as they went about their duties. The fast-paced activity I was used to at Binh Thuy was missing. At least after dinner the action picked up. It seems they had time for a nightly poker game.

I didn't care for cards and spent the evenings leisurely having a few drinks at the bar, mostly with Ed. I hardly touched the Chivas he had set aside for me.

The day of my flight out, I changed into a fresh uniform and Ed drove me to the terminal at Bien Hoa. I checked in, was assigned a seat, and in an hour was on my way home.

I thought that the flight to Travis would never end. Counting the time for refueling, it took almost twenty-four hours. When I got to the terminal, I rushed to a phone to contact Delta for a flight to Jacksonville, Florida. When soldiers left for Vietnam, the trip was arranged by the government. When they returned home, they were on their own. That's not a problem for an experienced traveler, but there were some who had never made a reservation or purchased a ticket and others who didn't know which large city was closest to their homes. Some soldiers had no money. These are details that those running a war don't know or care about. I assisted one such confused soldier and got him on his way, but I didn't have the time to help others. I had a plane to catch.

My flight was on time, but there was the inevitable delay in Atlanta, a two-hour stopover before continuing on to Jacksonville. I was home in time for dinner after thirty-six hours en route. I didn't know how tired I was. After dinner I stretched out on the couch to relax and immediately fell asleep. Yep, I was home.

16 The Medal of Honor

I arrived at Fort Bragg in early April 1970. It was here that I had returned to active military duty in late summer 1964. My assignment then was with the Green Berets. The place hadn't changed.

I signed in with the Golden Knights and met the commanding officer, Maj. Jerry Plummer, and his staff. I was impressed with the physical fitness of the people in the outfit. A steady job of jumping out of airplanes apparently requires strong bodies, and these soldiers were in excellent shape.

Major Plummer outlined my duties as the aviation officer and introduced me to the organization's pilots. One was John Gresset, the officer I was replacing. There were only two other pilots—Dick Del Conte and Paul Rose, both chief warrant officers.

The Knights had two airplanes supporting their mission, a C-47 Gooney Bird and a U-1 Otter. Plummer said that two more aircraft were to be assigned along with additional pilots and maintenance crewmen. In due time I'd have a sizable aviation section consisting of four aircraft, six pilots, and an appropriate number of maintenance people.

My assignment included a good bit of travel and temporary duty, especially during the summer months. We would be part of the air show crowd where we appeared with the air force Thunderbirds and the navy Blue Angels. I got to know them all as our paths crisscrossed the country, from rural towns to the largest metropolitan areas.

Civilian pilots were also regular participants in the air show schedule. Beverly "Bevo" Howard was one. He was an old acquaintance who displayed his many aerobatic talents with a Jungmeister biplane.

The air show business was not the safest of professions. I was present when Bevo was killed during one of his performances and witnessed other accidents resulting in the deaths of a Thunderbird pilot and two Blue Angels. During my time with the Golden Knights, we were fortunate not to have any casualties.

I enjoyed the assignment, especially the tours throughout the Midwest. We visited many small towns and operated our Gooney Bird out of their short strips, which seldom were more than three thousand feet long. They were also narrow: One in the Finger Lakes area of New York had a runway only forty feet wide.

The crowds made our visits special. They always seemed glad to see us and marveled at the ability of the Knights to maneuver and soar back and forth across the sky as they plummeted earthward. The skill and apparent fearless displays of our parachutists were greeted with enthusiasm. Even towns of only about five thousand people could generate crowds three to four times that to see the Knights. Cities such as Chicago, Cleveland, and Milwaukee produced more than a quarter million spectators.

Mike was still in Vietnam and no doubt seeing his share of combat. Ethel and I made certain that he received continual reports about the family. He didn't write often. I suppose he didn't want to say too much about his missions for fear it would upset his mother.

I had not yet moved the family to Fort Bragg. I was living in the visiting officers' quarters when I received a letter from Mike—one so special that it was hard for me to believe. Apparently the recommendation for award of the Silver Star had come to the attention of Gen. Creighton W. Abrams, commander of U.S. forces in Vietnam. According to Mike, the general signed an order awarding me the Distinguished Service Cross and recommended me for the Medal of Honor.

It was difficult to grasp the immensity of the situation. I knew that it couldn't be some fiction that Mike had made up. It was true, but I still couldn't believe it. This was a historic first: There never had been an occasion during any war that a soldier could write to his father, a fellow combatant, and tell him that the theater commander had recommended him for the Medal of Honor.

I called Ethel, who was packing and getting ready for the move to Fort Bragg, to tell her about Mike's letter. Initially she was as excited as I was, but then she brought us both back to reality. "Remember the time you said the units you were supporting were recommending you for an award, but nothing came of it? Don't be surprised if it doesn't happen again."

"You're probably right," I said. "But it was nice to hear that the American commander in Vietnam thinks I should be rewarded. We'll see what develops. I'm not going to hold my breath."

Soon after we settled in at Fort Bragg, I was on the road again. The demonstration schedule of the Knights picked up. I found myself on temporary duty twenty to thirty days at a time. Then during the summer of 1970, I was notified by XVIII Airborne Corps to be available for an awards ceremony: Lieutenant General John Tolson was to present me the Distinguished Service Cross. There was something to Mike's letter after all.

The ceremony was conducted on Fort Bragg's main parade field. Other awards for heroism were presented to soldiers who had returned from Vietnam. Mine was the last presented and was the second-highest award for heroism. I remember that General Tolson remarked as he pinned the medal on my chest, "They should have given you the Medal of Honor for what you did." I thanked the general for his kind remarks. He and I would have many occasions to see each other in the years to come.

The schedule with the Golden Knights remained heavy especially in summer, when there were demonstrations every week. The Knights had an annual commitment to participate at the Chicago Air and Water Show, which was followed by another major event at Billy Mitchell Airport in Milwaukee. We were there in late summer when the weather was cool. It was a beautiful time of the year in the Midwest.

The Chicago show was a real challenge. The sponsors, the Chicago Park District, planned for the Knights to jump into the city upon arrival. A lot of phone calls were made coordinating with the Federal Aeronautics Authority (FAA), air controllers in the area, and tower operators at Meigs Field, our destination in Chicago.

It took about five and a half hours to get to Chicago from Bragg. The FAA gave us a five-minute window over Meigs Field at thirteen thousand feet for the parachute team to jump into the airport. If we weren't there within the allotted five minutes, the jump would be canceled and the parachutists would arrive in the normal fashion, sitting in the aircraft. Meeting strict flight schedules was not new. If all went as planned and the weather cooperated, the Knights would be on the ground waiting for the Gooney Bird to land.

I am proud to report that I met that tight schedule. After the jump, the entire Golden Knights team lined up while a bevy of bathing beauties in bikinis presented each of us with a bottle of champagne. This was followed by three days of flight demonstrations, banquets, and parties that lasted long past midnight. I kept my equilibrium during the banquets and other social activities. It was rough duty, but someone had to do it.

The festivities at Milwaukee were just as involved and featured an outdoor barbecue and corn roast hosted by the Air Force Reserve at Billy Mitchell Field. There were kegs of beer, plenty to eat, and all the roasted corn one could want. The sweet corn was roasted still in the husks, and its fragrant aroma whetted the appetite.

After I'd been with the team for about a year, I got bold and took part in a few jumps even though I wasn't jump qualified. But my jumping came to an abrupt halt when I developed a streamer. By the time I shook it loose and the chute blossomed, I landed in the boondocks far away from the target area, and I sprained my ankle. When I came home limping, Ethel wormed the truth out of me and let loose with a blitzing lecture that I didn't expect from someone usually so reserved. I never jumped again.

My ankle hurt, but it didn't stop me from flying. In early June 1971 we were at Columbus, Ohio, for two days. On the first day of the air show, we were at the usual demonstration altitude of thirteen thousand feet flying our pattern over the target area. About half of the Knights had jumped and completed their specialties. As we prepared for another group to leave the aircraft, I saw an airliner coming in our direction. I expected him to turn away, but he continued on course. I maintained my orbit to allow our people to jump. The airliner and I were both being directed by the same controller and were on the same radio frequency. The airliner passed over us with a clearance of about three hundred feet. One of us was not paying attention to the assigned altitude. I glanced at my altimeter, which indicated thirteen thousand feet. Unless it was in error, I was exactly where I was supposed to be.

The airline pilot reported to the controller that I was at his altitude. The controller replied that I was assigned an orbit over the jump site at thirteen thousand feet and I'd reported being there. He reminded the airliner that he'd been assigned an altitude of fifteen thousand feet. The controller asked me to confirm my altitude, which I did. He cleared us to jump.

The airline pilot insisted that I had encroached upon his airspace. The controller handed him off to someone else, and I didn't hear him again. I dismissed the incident. We completed the tour and returned to Fort Bragg.

After a few days' rest at home, I flew the jumpers to Camp Mackall, the Knights' training site not far from Fort Bragg. We spent the day there as the jumpers worked on their specialties. When we returned to base, I found a note in my office telling me to check with Capt. Sonny Hill, the team's operations officer. I figured he wanted to talk about an upcoming demonstration, but all he had for me was a phone number to call as soon as I returned. "All I know is that it's important," Sonny ventured.

"Well, this looks like a Washington, D.C., prefix," I said. "Could be the Pentagon. What the hell do they want with me?" I recalled the encounter with the airliner over Columbus, Ohio. "I'll bet the captain flying the airliner that came close to us last week filed a flight violation against me. He was wrong, but now the bastard's trying to get me in trouble. I ought to be filing a violation against him. This number is probably FAA headquarters."

I dialed the number, hoping it would be busy. I wasn't in a mood to argue about a flight violation of which I wasn't guilty. No such luck. A lady answered and in my aggravated state I didn't catch the office designation.

"Just a minute, Mr. Novosel. Major Torretto will be with you shortly."

Who was Major Torretto, and what did he want with me? At least it wasn't the FAA, unless they decided to take action through military channels. After a short delay a man came on the line. "Is this CWO Michael J. Novosel of the Army Parachute Team at Fort Bragg?"

"Yes, sir."

"Good. This is Major Torretto from the Pentagon speaking. I've got some important news for you. Are you sitting down?"

I wondered why anyone at the Department of the Army was contacting me as I answered, "Yes, sir."

"Excellent, because the news I have for you is that President Nixon would like you to be at the White House on June 15. You are to be at a ceremony where the president of the United States will present you with the Medal of Honor. My congratulations."

"Well, I'll be damned. I thought you were with the FAA."

"No, Mr. Novosel. I'm not with the FAA. What I said is official, but you must not make any disclosure of the information I have given you. No press release of any kind, do you understand? That's the prerogative of the White House and its staff."

"I understand, Major. There won't be any leaks from this end, I assure you. But I've got to let my commander know about this, unless he's already been notified."

"Certainly, your boss may be notified. However, he also may not release any information relative to the award. Special instructions will be forwarded to you. The awards section at Fort Bragg will take care of travel arrangements for you and your family. From now until you arrive in the capital, all further communications concerning this matter will be relayed to you through the Fort Bragg awards section. Again, my congratulations to you, sir."

I was speechless. I hung up and just stood there, trying to think of something to say to Sonny Hill and the others in the office. They couldn't have learned anything of substance from my end of the conversation. I'd been more of a listener than a talker. Finally I blurted out, "Someone at the Pentagon says I'm to receive the Medal of Honor, but no one around here can tell the media about it." The people in the room seemed just as shocked as I was. They looked at one another and at me as if to say, what the hell did he say? What's he been smoking? I left without another word and went home.

As soon as I entered the house, I told Ethel the news. She smiled. "I think that's wonderful. You deserve it, as hard as you've been working."

"I don't think you understand what I'm saying. The president of the United States is going to present me with the Medal of Honor. We've been invited to the White House. By the way, you can't talk about it to anyone, especially your family."

Now it was Ethel's turn to be shocked. "You mean the whole family will be there in the White House? That means I've got to buy new outfits for myself and the children. We've got to look right."

"Do what you have to do," I said. "I have a hunch we'll be leaving in a few days. The ceremony is scheduled for the fifteenth of this month. They told me I'll be getting detailed instructions shortly, and after that we'll be coordinating with the folks at the awards section on post."

Mike was back from Vietnam by then and assigned to Fort Bragg with its dustoff unit. I realized with all that was going on, he'd probably not been told the news. He'd be as excited as his mother and I about the award. I had to alert him, because he would be going to Washington with us and would have to tell his commander.

I was busy the next day, mostly with the Fort Bragg awards people. Security considerations were extremely thorough. I had to give the names of my wife's parents and her date and place of birth. According to the protocol established for such occasions, my side of the family would be invited to the ceremony but Ethel's wouldn't. My brother Frank, a businessman living in Anchorage, Alaska, was invited. I had to answer questions about him and his background.

My mother couldn't make the trip to Washington by herself; she was eighty-three years old. My niece was available to be her escort, and that required more answers to security questions. I didn't have any idea how complicated it was to be presented the Medal of Honor by the president. The movie and news clips of the ceremony that I'd seen had made it all seem so easy and matter-of-fact.

Method did emerge out of the madness, and things began to approach normalcy. Ethel and I and the children were assigned an escort officer, who had two officers to assist him with the rest of the family. The pressure and anticipation of the event put me so on edge that I couldn't get a good night's sleep. The flight surgeon prescribed some medication that did the trick and I settled down.

Ethel and I and the children flew to Washington on Piedmont Airlines on June 14, the day before the ceremony. We stayed at the Madison. I was on hand to greet my mother and niece, then my brother Frank. I hadn't seen him in years, so it gave us a chance to get reacquainted.

My mother couldn't get over the fact that she would meet the president and kept asking me what I had done to bring about such an honor. Our entire family went out on the town that evening; Ethel, Mike, Pat, Jean, John, my mother, Frank, my niece, and I and the three escort officers made up the group. We had an excellent dinner, complete with champagne. The government picked up the bill, including the gratuity. We had a fine time, although we were responsible for a sizable increase in the national debt.

The next morning we boarded limousines that took us to the White House. After passing a string ensemble playing classical music, we were directed to the ornate East Room, where I met five other soldiers who were also to receive the Medal of Honor. Our positions in the huge chamber were outlined for us by names taped to the floor. We didn't have to wait long. The White House schedule demanded rigid timing.

The president entered, followed by the highest brass from the Pentagon, and the ceremony started. Mr. Nixon stepped onto a platform to address the awardees and witnesses to the presentation. On the platform at the president's right was the secretary of the army, Stanley R. Resor. Two aides were behind the president: the army chief of staff, Gen. William C. Westmoreland, and the assistant commandant of the Marine Corps, Gen. Raymond G. Davis. There were two additional aides to the far left and to the rear of the president.

On each side of the platform were two stands that held the Medals of Honor. The awardees and their families were grouped in a huge semicircle opposite the presidential entourage. The president spoke extemporaneously. His remarks were not lengthy but they were eloquent. He and the two aides then moved forward to make the first presentation, which was to Maj. Kern W. Dunagan. The president stood facing the major while an aide read a brief citation. After the Medal of Honor was draped around his neck, Major Dunagan saluted and shook Mr. Nixon's hand. The president was introduced to each member of Kern's party and spent about five minutes speaking with the group.

President Nixon then came to my family group and took his position directly in front of me. If I had been required to make a state-

ment at that instant, I wouldn't have been able to do so. I was pet-
rified, not because the president was standing in front of me but
because I found it unbelievable that I was about to receive my country's highest award for bravery. The president held my Medal of
Honor in his hands as he waited for the aide to finish reading the
citation. It was an awesome moment, full of emotion. When the aide
finished, President Nixon took one step forward and draped the
Medal of Honor around my neck. I saluted and shook his hand as
he said, "Congratulations, Mr. Novosel. I and the nation are proud
of you."

"Thank you, Mr. President."

"Is your son back from Vietnam now?" the president asked.

At that moment I realized how well briefed he was for the occasion. He knew that Mike had served with me and had remained in
Vietnam after I returned.

"Yes, sir, he's right there." I pointed to Mike, who was standing
next to my mother.

"Good, I'm glad to hear he has returned home safely. I'm sure that
you and Mrs. Novosel are quite relieved."

At that I introduced the president to Ethel.

"You are a remarkable woman," he said. "I don't know how you
were able to cope with both your husband and son being together
in combat. I admire your tenacity and your faith."

President Nixon next met with John, who was eight years old.
Then he was introduced to Patty and Jean. He said something or
asked a question of each member of the family. Finally he was introduced to Mike.

"How tough was it to work with your father and to fly with him in
combat?"

Mike answered that it was easier to fly with me in combat than it
was to work for me. The president replied, "I'm sure he was as tough
as the situation demanded."

Then Mr. Nixon came to my mother. "I'm certain I know this lady.
You must be very proud of your son, Mrs. Novosel. My congratulations to you."

We all were struck by the significance of the event. The leader of
the greatest nation on the face of the earth took time out of his busy

schedule to present awards to six soldiers who were fortunate enough to survive the horrors and perils of battle. I'll never forget it.

After the ceremony, the awardees and their families were introduced to Mrs. Nixon, who led the group into another room for coffee and assorted sweet rolls. President Nixon excused himself; he said he was running behind schedule. Mrs. Nixon was most gracious and made it a point to talk to each member of all the families.

The coffee with the first lady included meeting Mr. Resor, General Westmoreland, and General Davis. It was during this session that I noticed that General Davis was a recipient of the Medal of Honor. He became one of my many friends in the Medal of Honor Society, a special and select group. After the coffee, all the recipients received a detailed tour of the White House. That night we made a triumphal tour of the town—dinner first, then a few clubs. We would be going home the next day.

Our flight to Fayetteville departed at noon. Ethel, in her efficient way, had everything prepared. I was back at work early the next morning.

I left the Golden Knights in September 1972 to attend the University of Southern California. I took a course in safety engineering and was assigned to the U.S. Army Aviation School and Center at Fort Rucker in Alabama. Most army aviators took flight training at the aviation school, but because of my air force experience I had been placed on active duty without army flight training. This was my first assignment at Fort Rucker.

I was assigned to the Warrant Officer Career College as an author and lecturer and placed in charge of the international relations desk. It was an enjoyable and rewarding tour, even though my flying was held to the bare regulatory minimum. I held the position until the summer of 1976, when I was alerted for an overseas tour.

17 Korea, Fort Rucker, and Switches Off

I opted for a one-year assignment in Korea with a return to Fort Rucker. Mike, Patty, and Jean were married by the time I left, so Ethel had only John to care for. She arranged to stay with her parents while I was gone. It was a perfect chance for John to get to know his grandparents, and they were delighted to have their daughter and grandson coming for an extended visit.

I had no idea what kind of assignment I'd be given in Korea until I received a call from Ron Perry. He was a captain when we were assigned to Special Forces in 1964. Ron was now a colonel working with the UH-60 Blackhawk program.

"Mike, I hear you're headed for a year's tour in Korea. I've got a friend over there who could use an experienced aviation safety officer. Are you interested?"

"Ron, I'm not familiar with the army's aviation setup in Korea. Who's the friend and why would he want me?"

"The commander of the 2d Infantry Division is Major General Morris J. Brady. He's had some bad experiences with his aviation units. He lost five aircraft and had three fatalities recently."

"Ron, that's not bad luck, that's a disaster. What's he been doing to correct the situation, and why do you think I could help him?"

"I know him and I know you. You're unforgiving bastards who have reputations for kicking ass when necessary. You both get things done." He asked me again if I was interested.

"Maybe. How does he feel about me being his aviation safety officer?"

"Mike, he's asked me for help, and I think you can do the job for him. If you agree, I'll let him know you'll take the assignment."

"I guess it's better than going there unassigned. What the hell, I'll go. Is there anything special I've got to do once I get to Korea?"

"When you get to Seoul, call the general's office and one of his helicopters will take you to the division. That's all there is to it. I know you'll do a good job for him."

"Ron, I'll know when I return from Korea whether or not to thank you."

I stuck with my custom when going overseas and went first class to the West Coast. Then I reported to Travis Air Force Base. The place hadn't changed since I last saw it, but my treatment was something else. I was traveling in uniform, and when the operations sergeant noticed that I was a recipient of the Medal of Honor, he personally escorted me to the VIP lounge. I was the only one there until a colonel showed up and glanced in my direction. He didn't say anything but was probably wondering what a warrant officer was doing in the VIP lounge. I didn't say a word as I sat in an easy chair and read a magazine. The colonel studied me but turned away whenever I looked up. The bird was addled, but I figured if he couldn't recognize the distinctive ribbon of the Medal of Honor, he could just continue wondering.

The colonel looked shocked when the sergeant returned to tell me my flight was ready, then volunteered to take my carry-on luggage. I thanked him for his courtesy but declined the offer. I had only a small bag and an attaché case.

Again I was on a long, boring, uneventful flight, this time to Seoul. When I arrived, the air force people directed me to the VIP lounge. The place had a phone, so I called the number Perry had given me. The general's aide answered and said to sit tight, he'd send an aircraft for me. An hour and a half later, a Huey landed. It was my ride.

My arrival and assignment to the 2d Division was the subject of a lot of speculation among its aviators. Most thought I wouldn't accept the assignment. I wasn't aware that chief warrant officers fourth class didn't serve in the austere environment of an infantry division. It was alleged to be beneath their dignity to accept such a position, one in which they would be expected to go into the field on maneuvers, live and sleep in tents, and eat out of mess kits. They didn't get up early for physical training (PT), then go on a three-mile run.

I had unknowingly broken a sacrosanct warrant officers' tradition in Korea by taking a position so far north of Yongsan and Eighth Army headquarters. My unwitting acceptance of the assignment with the division, and being a recipient of the Medal of Honor, opened the floodgates for CW4 transfers throughout Korea to areas previously deemed undesirable. The brass reasoned that if I would do it, why couldn't the others. By my injudicious actions I had garnered the enmity of every CW4 aviator in Korea and every senior warrant aviator going there. But I'd given my word. I'd be with the 2d Infantry Division for the next year.

I was assigned to the 6th Aviation Battalion, where my quarters were rundown and left much to be desired. But I did have a private room and a shower with hot and cold running water. The majority of the division's aviators didn't enjoy these luxuries. I understood why some of the fainthearted senior aviators objected to such conditions.

I reported for duty on my third day in country by coming out for PT at 5:45 A.M. and going on my first three-mile run. The troops were surprised to see me join them at such an early hour. They were more surprised to see the "old man" keep up with them during the entire run. They didn't know that I ran at least four miles a day before coming to Korea. I was going to have a lot of fun jerking these troops around.

I investigated the accidents that plagued the division. The crash that had resulted in the loss of three lives involved another organization's aircraft but occurred while working with the division. But the other four losses were division responsibilities.

Two Hueys were destroyed after delivering troops on a ridgeline. The ridge was used to train aircrew insertion procedures onto otherwise inaccessible areas. The officer leading the flight caused the accident when he let his helicopter drift into a chopper next to his. He was warned repeatedly that he was not holding his position and drifting but ignored the warnings. Collisions were inevitable, but by some miracle nobody was killed.

Another accident involved a Cobra pilot hotdogging with a non-aviator friend. He misjudged his rate of closure on a strafing run and flew into the ground. Again it was a miracle that nobody was killed.

The fourth helicopter lost was another Huey. The fiasco, plucked right out of a Laurel and Hardy comedy special, had required a considerable lack of common sense to bring it about. A battalion aviator operating in the area saw his transmission oil pressure warning light come on. The operators' manual called for an immediate landing, so the pilot chose the nearest uncultivated area, a dry streambed. He reasoned that by landing there, he would not damage crops under cultivation. The latest procedures outlined by the army's Flight Safety Center emphasized that an aircraft making a precautionary landing would not be flown again until qualified maintenance people corrected the deficiency or authorized flight to a repair facility.

The helicopter was inspected by maintenance technicians, who found a sizable leak in the transmission oil system; its fluid was gone. On-site repairs were not possible, and flight to a maintenance facility was out of the question. It was too late in the day to airlift the stricken chopper by a CH-47 (Chinook), so arrangements were made to have it brought out the next morning. But the weather deteriorated, and the Chinook could not fly to the extraction site as planned.

The emergency landing had occurred at the onset of the Korean rainy season. The rain started with a drizzle and intensified to become a real gully washer. As the day wore on, water started to trickle through and around the gravel in the streambed. Soon there was a flow of water passing the Huey as it sat in the middle of the streambed.

The maintenance officer cautioned the officer in charge that something had to be done to get the helicopter onto high ground. He pointed out an elevated, flat ledge about fifty meters to the side of the stream. The aviation officer reminded the maintenance officer that the latest regulatory procedures prohibited flying the downed UH-1 until it was repaired. They could do nothing but wait for the weather to clear and the Chinook to arrive.

The battalion aviation personnel waited around as the rain continued. The flow of water in the stream increased. When it was about a foot deep, the maintenance officer again insisted that something be done to move the helicopter to a safer location. He said he knew about the latest regulations pertinent to the situation; but if the aircraft was not moved, the increasing flow of water would make any corrective action impossible. He added that he could fill the transmission with enough fluid for the helicopter to make the fifty-meter hovering flight to safe terrain.

Still the aviation officer wouldn't permit the move. "It'll be all right where it is," he said. The rain came down steadily, and the water lapped at the underside of the helicopter's fuselage.

The maintenance officer made one last effort to get the officer in charge to change his mind. "Sir, I can make my way to the ship before the water gets much higher. There's enough residual oil in that transmission system for me to start the engine and hover it to that high spot. It'll only take a few seconds once I start the engine."

The officer in charge was adamant and wouldn't give permission for the flight, even though the UH-1 would hardly be flying. The flow of water kept increasing until it reached the flight deck. Someone yelled that he saw the helicopter move. All eyes focused on the rushing water and the luckless chopper. They saw it move about a foot or so, then stop. Another surge of water followed and moved the helicopter. It stopped for a second but then slowly drifted along with the rushing water. The battalion soldiers walked along the bank of the stream, keeping pace with the moving chopper, which picked up speed as it was washed farther downstream. Finally it came to a depression in the streambed and appeared to drop a foot or so. It stopped, then was turned sideways by the rush of water.

The helicopter stood motionless in the water for a few seconds, then began a gradual tilt. The increasing volume of water slowly forced it onto its side. As the stream became deeper, the Huey turned round and round and over and over as it floundered along. The aviators and soldiers of the 6th Aviation Battalion witnessed the destruction of an army helicopter according to regulations.

The aviation battalion commander and I knew we had a job on our hands. We had to turn around this flight safety record. After a week of studying the problem, we presented our program to General Brady. He bought our proposed solutions.

Our methods did the trick. The rash of accidents stopped, and flying hours and training increased. The best news we gave the general came toward the end of our tours. We told him that a whole year had gone by without an aircraft accident.

My year in Korea was up, and I returned to Fort Rucker. When I got back, I received a call from an old friend, Col. Chuck Wingate. He'd taken over the Directorate of Evaluation and Standardization (DES) and asked me to be his safety officer. The position offered many challenges and was one in which I could make a lasting contribution. I took the job.

Fort Rucker received a new command team in 1982, Maj. Gen. Bobby Maddox and Brig. Gen. Charles Teeter. I'd been with DES for more than five years (1977 to 1982) when the command put me in charge of officer development of warrant officer candidates. I became the aviation center senior tactical advising and counseling officer, the senior TAC for more than seven hundred candidates.

My tenure with the candidate program kept me in excellent physical shape. Three or four of my TAC officers and I made daily runs during lunch hour. The summer temperatures in lower Alabama were often in the nineties and even the low hundreds, but we were acclimated to the conditions and were able to tolerate the heat and humidity.

In March 1984 General Maddox led the quarterly three-mile fun run and set an easy pace. After we finished he asked, "How was the run, Mike?"

"Not bad, General, but I noticed that even though you set an easy pace, some troops fell out and didn't complete the run. At their age they should be able to do better."

"I'm glad to hear you say that. I'd like you to take the air assault course. How about it? I'll have my aide take care of the details. We can get you into the next class."

"General, do you realize I'll soon be sixty-two years old? I'll be eligible for social security."

"I know, Mike. That's one reason I want you to take the course. I'm having trouble getting my young officers and noncommissioned officers to volunteer for it. I want to shame them into taking it. I know you can do it. Before you retire I want to pin the air assault badge on your uniform."

"Well, General, I've flown many rappeling missions since coming to the army. I've never known what it's like to be hanging from the end of a rope. I think it's insane, but you can tell your aide to sign me up."

That was it. I became a dope on a rope.

The course lasted ten days. I found the physical training within my capabilities and the rappeling not difficult. We finished with a seven-mile road march wearing a steel helmet and carrying a thirty-five-pound rucksack and an M16 rifle. The march had to be completed in two hours; I finished in an hour and forty-five minutes. The next day the general pinned the air assault badge on me. Things still happened fast in the army.

Some weeks later, DA informed me that my retirement was scheduled for November 30, 1984. The Fort Rucker command set up a task force for the retirement ceremony, and protocol sent out hundreds of invitations to friends, relatives, distinguished guests, and the media. Finally, the orchestrated ritual was at hand.

On the way to the reviewing stand, General Maddox and I passed scores of onlookers and were greeted by many old friends, including fourteen fellow recipients of the Medal of Honor. Fort Rucker had never before hosted such an honored group.

I saw my family—my wife, our four children, their spouses, and two of our four grandchildren. Mike was sitting next to his mother. I couldn't help but think of the times we'd flown together in Vietnam and when he came to my rescue after I crashed.

The public address system came alive as we took our places on the reviewing stand. "Ladies and gentlemen, your host for the retirement ceremony is Major General Bobby Maddox, and the reviewing officer is CW4 Michael J. Novosel."

As I looked over the troops, the inevitable question occurred to me: Did I really deserve this honor? I was a soldier, an army aviator who did what he was paid to do. When given a mission, I pursued it to its ultimate conclusion. I believed that was the way it was supposed to be, that all soldiers viewed their responsibilities in a like manner.

I savored the time and efforts of the command. It was a wondrous display of military pomp and ceremony: two brigades of troops on line, each displaying its flag, backed by eight battalions and their companies, their pennants also fluttering in the breeze.

At the head of this extended display stood the honor guard with the flag of the United States of America flanked by the U.S. Army flag topped with battle streamers marking a long, glorious military history. Each fluttering streamer saluted countless acts of uncommon valor and ultimate sacrifice. Was it presumptuous of me to think that my record as an army aviator was worthy of inclusion in that heroic history?

I took in the pageantry as the announcement came: "Ladies and gentlemen, please stand for the rendering of honors and the playing of 'Retreat.'" We stood at attention as the giant parade flag was lowered ever so slowly and retrieved by the flag detail as the last notes were sounded by the bugler. This was my final retreat as a soldier.

General Maddox, commander of troops Col. Jay Kitterman, and I proceeded to "troop the line." We stepped out smartly. These three old soldiers marched past each unit and received the salute of each commander. Maddox and I returned to the reviewing stand.

I gave the order, "Present the command." All unit flags and guidons were centered in front of the troops and marched in line to a position before the reviewing stand. On command, the troops snapped to attention for the national anthem.

Then the general and I left the reviewing stand and took positions in front of the color guard while a lengthy citation for award of the Distinguished Service Medal was read. General Maddox was all smiles as he pinned on the medal and congratulated me. We returned to the stand, where he addressed the assemblage.

"Mike, Mrs. Novosel, the Novosel family, Medal of Honor recipients, mayors, general officers, distinguished guests, ladies, and gentlemen. This is a very special day. The last combat pilot of World War II still on active military flying duty is retiring."

The general spoke at length about my military career. I felt he was overly generous with his laudatory remarks. I was getting uneasy with all the praise, but the general finally concluded: "So, Mike, we wish you the very best in your years of retirement. It's not possible to thank you enough for all you've done. But I declare that the street behind us, known as Headquarters Street, from this day forward will be called Novosel Street. The engineers at this very moment are making the change. This is a small measure for the endeavors and sacrifices of you and your family. Thank you, Mike."

It was difficult to assimilate all that was going on. Renaming the main street of Fort Rucker to honor one man was unprecedented. I had just been given the army's highest award for service, and now this.

I had to gather my wits; I was expected to make my departing remarks. I stepped up to the microphone and again looked at the display of flags, pennants, and streamers before me. I steadied myself and began.

"General Maddox, fellow Medal of Honor recipients, general officers, distinguished guests, ladies and gentlemen, and fellow soldiers. I wish to thank you for this tribute and this superb turnout.

"I speak to you with mixed emotions. I am leaving the life that I love, and the service that has honored me and my family so often. It has been a long and enjoyable relationship. My childhood dreams of becoming an Army Air Corps pilot were realized in the early days of World War II. Many years and flying hours have gone by since then. In all those years, there have been many challenges and rewards. I was given the opportunity to command, and know well its responsibilities.

"I have faced many perils, seen many battles, and witnessed the aftermath of war. I heard the cries of the wounded and endured the loss of friends. Yet I have survived and don't know why. I do know, however, that someone has been watching over me and guided my hand in battle. Why He ever took the time to do so I will never know. I know enough to thank God for the many blessings bestowed on our family and the good health granted me so that I could serve my country for so long.

"Those years in the army were especially rewarding. I cannot recall working with or for a single superior I did not admire and could not loyally support. I only hope that those who worked with and for me can say the same of me.

"It was my privilege to serve in Vietnam. I am proud of that service. It was there that army aviators produced a record of achievement unequaled in any war. It was not in the character of those young men to say, 'It can't be done.' Instead, their answer was, 'Can do.'

"Those soldiers have given you today's army aviation. Serve it well.

"Now, as the shadows grow long and the hour late, I know that I have been around somewhat longer than the law allows. It's time for me to depart. But before my service book is closed, I hope someone slips in a page that says he was a good soldier.

"Good-bye, good luck, and God bless you all."